HEALTHY SENSE OF SELF

Antoinetta Vogels

HealthySenseOfSelf Publications
227 Bellevue Way NE #502
Bellevue, WA 98004

To find out more about HealthySenseOfSelf, visit www.healthysenseofself.com,
You can also email us at contact@healthysenseofself.com, or call (425) 298-7649.

Disclaimer/Notice

THE ENTIRE CONTENTS OF THIS BOOK ARE PRESENTED FOR INFORMATIONAL and educational purposes only. Nothing in this book is intended or presented to cure, prevent, treat, or diagnose any physical, mental, emotional, spiritual, psychological, psychiatric, or medical disease or condition of any kind. If you have a problem or challenge of any kind, you are hereby directed to consult a competent, relevant, licensed practitioner.

The use of this material is no substitute for, nor is intended in any way to be used in connection with health, psychological, psychiatric, medical, legal, or other professional services. The author of this book is not a trained or licensed psychologist, psychiatrist, or professional health care practitioner of any kind, and does not represent herself or any of this book's content to be in the practice of those.

Everything presented in this book is speculation and anecdotal, and has not been tested or verified (yet) by scientific research.

You are hereby notified that, by reading any of this book's content, you agree that you alone are completely liable for any and all direct or indirect effects or results of that reading. By reading any of this book's content, you agree to hold harmless and indemnify everyone associated with this book, for any use, misuse, or non-use you make of anything included here.

Dedication

To our mothers and fathers, who could not help but pass along
the suffering they inherited from their parents

To parents like me who break the vicious cycle

To our children, who still have to deal with a lot of processing,
but who now are able to develop a healthier Sense of Self

To our children's children in turn, whose suffering and
wars may hereby be prevented

You only have one life to live; make sure it is yours!
~ Antoinetta Vogels

Table of Contents

"If a positive model of desire is established early, then the baby will grow up with natural desires that match its true needs. A psychologically healthy person, in fact, can be defined as someone whose desires actually produce happiness. But if the baby is imprinted with the opposite notion, that its desires are shameful and are only grudgingly met, then desire won't develop in a healthy way. In later years, the adult will keep searching for fulfillment in externals, needing more and more power, money, or sex to fill a void that was created in his or her sense of self as a baby; the person's very sense of being is judged to be wrong."

Deepak Chopra—The Way of the Wizard, *page 134*

Preface

THE START OF MY INNER QUEST

The development of the Sense of Self Method began nearly 30 years ago merely as my personal quest, as a new mother, to end insomnia. Now, this book represents part of a growing business, research, and educational project. Publishing this Method is the realization of my vision to contribute to a better life for each individual on a personal level, and on a bigger scale for the world at large.

It is 1985, and my daughter is three months old; it is time to return to work. I have a job as a bassoonist in the Amsterdam Philharmonic Orchestra, and the six weeks of maternity leave have come to an end. Why am I suddenly unable to drift off into a well-deserved and refreshing sleep, just when I need it most? Being a new mother is quite a challenge by itself, especially when your child is born prematurely. She was as tiny as a Barbie doll, my first-born. Combining the care of my baby with being in shape for my job required a clear mind and a well-rested body, but no . . . I can't sleep!

"No doubt I'm having trouble adjusting to my new situation. I trust it will gradually solve itself," I reassured myself. But it didn't. One night I would sleep reasonably well and the next two nights there would be little or no sleep at all. Not that I actually worried about something while lying in bed; no, my mind was totally blank. Nothing stirred. I had no idea what was going on.

In the months that followed the onset of this insomnia, I tried to cope in many ways. "Have a glass of hot milk before you go to bed," was my mother's advice. "A glass of red wine," a well-meaning friend suggested. "Stop doing anything an hour before you go to bed and do relaxation exercises," was someone else's advice. "No coffee for you!" I was ordered by many people. "No garlic and no peppers," was the remedy from a Tibetan healer, along with his prescription of a great number of bitter brown pills that made no difference. My doctor provided me with sleep medications, and yes, they did put me to sleep. But the moment I stopped taking them, it was over. I did not sleep anymore. As medical causes for my constant insomnia were ruled out, I despaired: "What else is left for me now but a lifetime of medication?"

I refused to start on that journey. I figured that sleeping is a natural process and if my sleep was being thwarted, there *had* to be a reason. I was determined to discover that reason. So I turned inward in my quest for the cause and the cure of what kept me awake at night and that was so damaging to my quality of life. It affected my ability to mother my child, maintain my health and resume my career, not to mention what it was doing to our family life.

In hindsight, I can say that I had more problems than just insomnia. They included an extreme temper. If things did not go the way I wanted, I would burst out in anger and blame everyone and the world for it. Even my best friend expressed her concern about my temper. My co-musicians complained that they felt I lacked team spirit. I had frequent colds on crucial performance days and a sore throat whenever I made a commitment to sing. "Your timing is off in ensemble-playing," my colleagues pointed out candidly.

I tried changing things *outside* myself: practicing like crazy, taking more lessons, getting help at home. Not a thing I tried had the desired result; as looking *outside* of me didn't really help with the problems, gradually I began to observe what was going on *inside* of me. I started to observe my thoughts and behavior. I delved deeper into all the things I was worrying about instead of pushing them away. "What are my motives for what I do or for what I try to avoid?" I wondered. I wondered what the underlying reason was for my explosions of rage, which seemed so out of proportion to what actually took place on those moments.

A Mini-Disc recorder became my confidante. I began to record my thoughts and feelings, and sometimes I listened to what I had said. For 25 years, I talked to and studied myself, trying to make sense of what motivated me and I noticed that often I seemed to work against, instead of in favor of, my personal goals and ambitions. I discovered my choices were based on subconscious, not conscious, motives. Decades later, an understanding emerged about what was really going on in my mind that previously had been totally outside the spotlight of my awareness. I was shocked time and again to find what I started to call my Hidden Agenda.

I discovered that I had motives that I had never considered. Some of the emotions I experienced on a daily basis were reactions to things I had no conscious awareness of. To my surprise, I realized I had many fears. So I followed the trail back to the roots of my fears and I learned what kept me imprisoned and *why certain motives were still as active in me as when I was a child or an adolescent.* I had yet to understand the reasons for my fears or for my insomnia. All I was able to create was a map, and as we all know, "The map is not the territory."[1] However, this map has proved very useful to me in changing the territory of my life, both internally and externally.

Many years later, I was able to describe the nature of many of my problems; I had to conclude that they stemmed from an unhealthy relationship with my mother. Unknowingly, an enmeshment had formed between the woman who had raised me and me. This state of enmeshment prevented me from developing any sense of being an independent and autonomous person. It kept me spellbound to try to live up to her conditions.

As a child I had subconsciously learned that trying to behave in ways that would please her was the only way to get my needs met of being seen, heard, and taken into account by her. Over time, I had internalized my mother's conditions to how I should and should not be to ensure her approval. Fulfilling these conditions became my only life's goal—even after I was an adult myself and my mother had passed away. A great fear would arise whenever I was about to fail, or when I was thwarted in my attempt to live up to the required standards of behavior, be it by circumstances outside, or inside, myself.

As my situation became clearer, I came up with ways to change the effect of my childhood experiences. I more or less reconditioned myself. It took all my time and energy, and for many years this activity filled my waking hours, as if it were my day job.

Paradoxically, the nights also brought me valuable insights. Desperate and determined like a deer trying to free itself from the claws of a mountain lion to survive, I held on to my scripted reconditioning texts. Finally, I was sleeping better, and many of my other problems diminished as well. Ultimately, they vanished, and my quality of life and that of my loved ones improved drastically. As I came to understand my own inner workings, I suspected I was not unique. I would be surprised if others did not have similar problems and similar inner workings. That is when I figured that my solutions might help others and I decided to write them down.

---

[1] Quote attributed to Alfred Korzybski, founder of the field of study of General Semantics.

Thus, I share my "Method" about the origin and nature of my own inner workings, with the hope and conviction that others might benefit, that my insights might hasten the arrival of a better quality of life for some of my readers.

SOMETHING WAS MISSING: MY SENSE OF SELF

In my search for the truth that would enable me to break free from my predicament, the discovery I made was quite unexpected, and one that I dreaded to even say aloud. It was the hardest truth I ever had to face, and even now when I think about how the ways of the world seem to trample people's holiest places, it chills my heart. The role and function of a mother is revered, and therefore I had great difficulty finding support among my family (father, brother, and sister) and even among friends, in contemplating the possibility that there might be any fault in the relationship between my mother and me. Even the Bible protects her: "*Honor your father and your mother,*" one of the commandments states. But how can we respectfully find a solution if things do not follow the commonly accepted picture of all-encompassing love?

Can we even allow ourselves to look at the (our) mother and find that she is just a person who has her own demons to fight? Should we not admit that, unless the mother is able and willing to get a clear sense of her shortcomings, she will not be able to attend to the needs of her child in a sufficient or optimal way. What I found was that I had never felt acknowledged and respected as a (valued) unique human being but that I had been treated as a pawn in her own game of life, which had thwarted in me the development of a healthy Sense of Self.

I then started to see how this lack of Sense of Self was then reinforced during other critical moments in my life, when I made poor decisions and choices, as they were not based on a healthy Sense of my Self. I began to see that something was fundamentally missing in me, a notion that wasn't at all unfamiliar to me.

I became aware that the overall goal of my life had been so far, to try to find what was missing, get hold of that unknown factor and incorporate it into my life. I studied the behavior and inner workings of others by asking them to describe what their Self felt like, how they would recognize their Self, and how they were sure their incentives stemmed from that source called Self. I learned that many other people had a completely different inner makeup and were less anxious and frantic than I was, so I compared what they *had* with what I was *missing*. This is when I discovered the importance of a healthy Sense of Self for the ability to lead a happy and productive life.

Instead of having an inner "home base" for my "me-ness," I depended on getting approval, mainly from my mother but also my father. Sometimes it wasn't my mother but a replacement for them, like an other "authority figure," who triggered in me the same need to feel accepted. Sometimes it just was, what I call, "virtual parental approval," as I had internalized most of their opinions and judgments, having been focused on them throughout my life.

Let us call that our VIPV, our Virtual, Internalized Parental Voice. Note that I used to take that VIPV for my own voice, as I had no idea that my care-giver's influence was so big that it dominated my mind. To get that approval generated in me a sense of safety and only when having lived up to these (internalized) parental expectations I was able to relax for a short moment.

For a brief while I would be OK, until the next urge to prove that I was able to fulfill those conditions kicked in again. My whole life was about this compulsion to do things to get approval so that I sensed that I was acknowledged as a worthy person. That notion generated the much-desired state of "Feel-good-about-Self" (FgaS) that I took for a sort of Self-realization. That fleeting feeling was the closest I could ever get to a sense/conviction/knowing that I truly existed as myself. I became more and more aware of the fact that this "Feel-good-about-Self-" state was a poor substitute for the real thing: a Healthy Sense of Self (HySoS). I diagnosed myself as having a lack of Sense of Self (lack of SoS) and as being dependent on a "Substitute Sense of Self (SSoS)" for my Self-experience.

PUTTING MY INSIGHTS TO USE

It was a pretty bleak picture, but at least I had the picture. I now understood I had to come up with my "real" Sense of Self. What I had to do was to find out what a Healthy SoS really meant. What was it that I had to implement within myself in order to restore my own truncated, thwarted SoS?

Out of my inner nothingness of the lack of a Sense of Self (SoS), I embarked on the journey of seeking to generate some kind of inner core of me-ness that would be independent from the approval by others and independent from the approval of my own VIPV (Virtual, Internalized Parental Voice). Studying the options of how to heal myself took place while I was battling my addiction to, what I would later call, a Substitute Sense of Self (SSoS) with its many symptoms of fear, anxiety, panic, rage, and shame. On top of that, I suffered from additional fears, anxiety, and depression as the responses from, what had been functioning as my survival system to its planned elimination. The SoS Method refers to this strategy as to the Early Childhood Survival Strategy (ECSS).

My life was quite an emotional jungle. My journey was mainly about finding my way through this entanglement by constantly scrutinizing and interpreting my symptoms—at whatever moments I could get out of the whirlpool of being absorbed by them. This task took over my life and by and by led me to follow a different path. This book is the result of that process.

Since then, my quality of life has gone way up. I am happier, healthier, more playful, and more successful. Occasionally I fall back, as I still need to refresh my reconditioning every so often. Through that, I can reach again, on the deepest level, the certainty that my *being* and my *doing* are separate. In order to *be* I do not have to *do*; in order to *do* I first have to *be*; *then* I have the choice of doing or not doing. My Being is no longer correlated with, or dependent on my Doing.

I can say wholeheartedly that every day, getting into the right mind-set and experiencing my Restored Sense of Self™ comes more easily. It needs to be said: My method of restoring one's Sense of Self is not a quick fix. However, everything is better than skipping your own life altogether—and honestly, it is mighty interesting as well!

I feel moved to share my story and my findings in the hope and expectation that you will find value in it. This sharing has required devoting myself nearly full-time for several years to developing the materials you are seeing. What motivated me to put in so much effort?

I have learned in the course of my healing process that we can break the vicious cycle, which perpetuates an unhealthy SoS from one generation to the next, by making our own SoS healthier. Once we will have taken care of our own SoS, we will be able to effectively facilitate a healthy SoS in our children. Then everyone's quality of life will improve considerably. There will be less violence, less war, less human suffering. I take pride in reporting about my life's journey so others can learn from my experiences and thus make this world a better place.

Sharing my findings with you, with the world, also fulfills a vow I made as a four-year-old girl looking at the ruins of World War II.

MY VOW AS A LITTLE GIRL

I was born in the Netherlands right after World War II. Even though I was not alive *during* the war, I vividly recall listening to my father's stories about the horrors that happened during the Holocaust. I remember walking with him over the ruins of the city in which he was born and raised, Groningen (see Figure P.1). I have stored in my memory in detail the atrocious acts of war I picked up on with my four-year-old ears. Is it a wonder that my firm decision, my vow to myself that I *had* to do something to make wars stop, was firmly engraved in my mind, even though I was just a little girl?

Figure P.1: Me at age four with my father

Little did I know that life would offer me an opportunity to contribute to the understanding of human behavior by having me grow up with a "lack of Sense of Self." Through the task of figuring out what was "off" in my life, I gained a deep understanding of what is "off" with the world and, with that, of what could be the healing procedure.

Now, more than half a century later, my vow is ready to start its work. My contribution to humanity is to help bring peace in the family, peace among people in general. My Sense of Self Method greatly helps to establish peace within the heart and mind of each individual. When we have a clear SoS, we can find peace within ourselves. Only when we have peace within ourselves we are able to solve conflicts with others in a non-violent way.

My findings are the fruits of my life experience and intense effort to understand the ultimate cause of my personal problems. The root cause of these problems (and possibly yours) is quite similar to the root cause of war. By studying the SoS Method, you will—I believe with all my heart—not only experience a decrease in the number and level of intensity of your own problems, and finally get a good night's sleep, but also contribute to a more peaceful world.

Ending the *war within* ourselves through gaining a Restored Sense of Self™ will lead us to happier and more productive lives. Finding our "inner home" may also help prevent *wars between* people, between nations. I truly hope that the impact of the concepts of this Method is clear and that it may help you and your loved ones to become more successful and live up to your potential.

The essence of this message is that once we gain the ability and the courage to honor our own spirit, we automatically gain an ease about letting others honor theirs, and no fighting is needed to establish who has the power. We can just be who we were born to be.

I truly thank you for having come to this point of reading of how this book was born. Now let us get ready to work our way toward our goal of less human suffering![2]

---

[2]For more on War, see Appendix II: **Considering War and a Healthy Sense of Self,** page 232.

WHAT THIS BOOK PRESENTS: THE SENSE OF SELF METHOD

This book offers a holistic (i.e., integrated) Method, as the foundation for a self-help model that aims at informing people that many symptoms human beings suffer from are rooted in a lack of Sense of Self. They show up as ill-physical, mental, and emotional health of a person, as well as in various social and societal dysfunctional aspects of our lives.

This work hopes to shed a light on how the development of a person into a healthy, fully functioning man or woman can be hindered, which then results in distortions in the person's psycho-emotional system. These abnormalities, on their turn, can result in physical, psychological, emotional, and social problems. This work is not a general Method of psychology but rather an expanded first-person case study of abnormal development. The Method is holistic (integrated) in the sense that it talks about the mind, emotions, and body as mutually interactive and interdependent.

Finding a (natural) solution to a severe case of insomnia was the immediate reason I began to question my motivations. What keeps me awake at night would not suddenly have disappeared during the day, I figured. If I could gain insight into *what I was all about* and *what I was ultimately after in my life,* I might get in touch with the cause of the insomnia. The book that lies in front of you is the result of my investigations—results that have grown into a widely applicable Method of human motivation. The Method is about Self and about different ways of Sensing the Self, and it shows how looking at your motivation is the key in understanding whether you have a healthy or unhealthy way of experiencing yourself. As you read through the chapters the importance of a healthy (Natural) way of Sensing the Self becomes obvious.

During my path of discovering the nature of the problem I was able to find solutions as well. To restore your Sense of Self is the next step into a better life. So that is where we are heading when applying the SoS Method in our lives.

This Method is not an abstract exercise; it is aimed at improving people's quality of life and the quality of life of the world as a whole. I want others to benefit from my valuable findings as an aid in solving their own life issues. I also hope to elicit interest among scientists to do research on my Method and to integrate it into the existing approaches to various problems. (To express interest in doing research, contact me at research@healthysenseofself.com.)

If you take an academic interest in this work please feel free to contact me with any questions or suggestions. I am planning to set up a "Train-the-Trainer Program" and would be delighted if you would help make this

Method widely known. It is beyond my one-person capacity to do anything like testing and experimentation or building statistics, even though that would of course greatly enhance the Method's credentials and impact.

The purpose of this work is

1. to help people recognize whether they have a Substitute Sense of Self,
2. to find the cause of why and how this could happen,
3. to have people accept and face their condition based on these insights,
4. to eliminate the power of their unhealthy past in their present, and
5. to ultimately replace their Substitute Sense of Self by a Restored Sense of Self.

I would like to spend some time on how the specific terminology that is used has come about. You need to know that my ideas and conclusions are original to me, as I had no particular education in psychology. I am not a psychologist, and the psychological concepts I needed to verbalize my findings were not available to me, so I made up my own words for what I found inside my mind. At first, I chose these words intuitively, based on educated guesses of how the specific inner process or result of an inner process could be best described. I so desperately needed to label certain concepts that I didn't have much time to consider if I used the right word: it would present itself to me and I would use it right away. However, that created difficulty when I later decided to describe the Method seriously. In the end I reinvented my jargon on a more rational basis.

The SoS Method will remain a living work in progress for some time to come. I invite you to share your thoughts, thus helping to turn this educational work from a Method into a practical healing method and giving more people a chance to improve their quality of life.

I salute our journey together. I invite your participation. Please share whatever you think can help implement a healthy SoS for all. To those who want to use the Method for healing purposes: Healing through a self-help method is hard work; I hope that this Method will help you heal faster and with less pain along the way.

This book presents

• the SoS Method with extensive explanation, examples, and details;
• several methods for self-assessment; and
• suggestions, exercises, and education for recovery: gaining a Restored Sense of Self (RestSoS).

WHO MIGHT BENEFIT FROM WORKING WITH THIS METHOD?

It is likely that you will be able to improve the quality of your life if any of the following describe you:

- Something is "off" but you are unable to find what it is.
- You know you are not living up to your potential.
- Doctors and therapists don't make you better.
- You have relationship challenges: marriage, children, social.
- You are addicted to work or other activities or behavior.
- You have a terrible time staying sober.
- You are in pain physically or emotionally.

My insight is new, original, and highly unconventional. Who would think that there are people walking around in this life without a SoS? What does that actually imply? Please don't toss out the idea too quickly just because you think it is unusual and therefore probably doesn't apply to you. Or just because you don't like the idea of applying it to yourself—the degree to which denial plays a role in all this is impressive. There are many people, including the majority of Americans, walking around *without* a healthy and Natural SoS.

We now know that the solution is to restore or strengthen your SoS. Then we are no longer ruled by unhealthy and (in hindsight completely obsolete and unnecessary) subconscious motivations, which too often can be the cause of many problems and pains.

Educating ourselves about, and then healing, our SoS might alleviate an impressive array of problems. An astounding variety of ill health, lack of well-being, general or specific dysfunctions, and in general feeling miserable seem to all come down to the root cause of lacking a healthy SoS. Some of these problems and pains include but are not limited to the following:

Headaches

Fatigue

Anxiety

Insomnia

Depression

Marital problems

Relationship problems in general

Addictions of many kinds

Relapse during recovery from addiction to substance use

Anger issues and rage

Work-related problems

Being held back by "invisible glass ceilings"

Too much drama

Not living up to one's potential

Being high-strung

Lack of focus or learning problems in children

The symptoms and problems show up differently for each of us and vary with our circumstances. The strength of the SoS Method is that it functions as an umbrella for a great number of ailments and dysfunctions. In other words, the root cause of a lot of dysfunction and disease may, I believe, be greatly relieved by having a Restored Sense of Self (RestSoS).

No pills, potions, doctor's visits, new religion, or new technology is needed, though some people might require assistance or professional help. You are your own expert. That fact, together with understanding and applying the SoS Method, can give you great tools to solve a variety of issues you might have and deeply enhance your life!

WHAT IS REQUIRED FROM YOU?

Getting to the answer to your challenges requires your open-minded willingness to look around inside your mind and feelings and be honest about what you find. I offer you suggestions of what to look for. If you find what I think you will find, you can apply to yourself the suggestions and solutions that worked for me. The Method is logical and easy to understand. There are stories and examples, and the basics are repeated on a regular basis. Once you get the ideas, you are well on your way to your own healing!

There also is a chance that you already have a healthy Natural Sense of Self. In that case you might want to read the book out of interest or to help understand your clients or even your friends. There is much to learn that can help you do better business with people once you have a clearer view on where they might be coming from.

As you read this book and process the Method, you might start to understand what happened in your life. You will probably realize that you would benefit from restoring your Sense of Self and be interested how to go about doing that. In Chapters 11 and 12 you will find practical exercises and ways to train yourself in what is predominantly a reconditioning process. And as your SoS grows, you will be surprised to find that not only you, but also your family and friends, will be happier!

List of Benefits

Less stress

Better overall health

A more relaxed nervous system

A better functioning digestive system

Sleep better

Less panic attacks

Fewer migraines

Less depression: feel better, think clearer, feel more alive and engaged

No suicidal thoughts or acts: more joy of living, happiness, success

Less substance abuse; healthier habits

Less addictive behaviors; more moderation (shopping, sex, Internet, TV, gambling, food, etc.)

Less motion sickness

Less prone to accidents due to lack of focus and erratic behavior

Less prone to (professional!) injuries (musicians!) due to more relaxed muscles

Less eyestrain

Decreased fear of failure (stage fright)

No "self-sabotage"

More inner peace

More patience

More self-confidence

Comfortable with facing your Self; more self-accepting

A better balance of head and heart; genuine and integrated feelings

Better equipped to deal with criticism; less over-reactive

More common sense, more realistic, more "real"

Sense of your own limitations, boundaries, potential, and talents

More likely to achieve any goal (Direct Motivation)

Less controlling of others and of situations

Feeling comfortable in your own skin

Comfortable being in most crowds

Comfortable being by yourself

More compassion, empathy, tolerance; less hostility

More self-accepting, which leads to accepting others

Better relationship skills (friends, family, coworkers)

Lower divorce rate

Stronger ability to focus

Better child rearing

Fewer rages and family upsets

More respect for children

Increased learning abilities for your children

Less uncontrollable behavior (e.g., temper tantrums)

Less violence and verbal abuse

Less war

More comfortable with self-expression

Ability to self-realize and live life to the fullest

More success in business and other creative endeavors (Direct Motivation)

Better equipped for teamwork

Better social skills

Better communication skills

Overall higher quality of life

More likely to have a clear preference, taste, opinion, and standing up for it

Know what you want

Better flow in your life

Fewer issues with money

Less compulsiveness

More capabilities to commit

Better chance to find, give, and receive love

Better aligned with one's blueprint

1 | Introduction to the Sense of Self Method (SoS Method)

Wʜᴀᴛ ɪꜱ ɪᴛ ʟɪᴋᴇ ɴᴏᴛ ᴛᴏ ʜᴀᴠᴇ ᴀ Nᴀᴛᴜʀᴀʟ Sᴇɴꜱᴇ ᴏꜰ Sᴇʟꜰ? Tʜᴇ Qᴜᴇꜱᴛɪᴏɴ ɪꜱ hard to pose, let alone to answer. How is it possible to experience the lack of something you do not know exists in the first place? In the Preface, I extensively described how I found out that I was lacking something other people seemed to have. Let me give you an example of a situation that helped me to see a small light that was going to grow and become a beacon in the jungle of darkness.

"Please don't be mad at me," I kept begging my husband every time I yelled at him to vent my annoyance when I was unable to fall asleep. "In reality I am not angry at you, but I am angry at the fact that I don't sleep. I can't keep myself from getting upset and I need to let it out."

He understood, and so we went on like that for many years. However, at some point he said, "I do not quite understand you. Are you not the one in control of this anger? You either choose to or choose not to be angry. Then, if you do, you choose how to express yourself." I simply could not find within myself any power, force, or will that was capable of such choosing or not choosing. Based on this and other similar conclusions I deduced that he must have something inside that I did not have. So I started to pay attention and look more closely into this.

When a **Natural Sense of Self (NatSoS)** does not develop, the result is that another type of structure develops in its place, the Substitute Sense of Self (SSoS), which makes up for the missing part in us. In a later stage, this lack is hard to discover because, technically, one could say that nothing is lacking because something else took its place. The lack of a SoS was masked by the presence of something else, a SSoS. So even though I didn't really experience a lack of something, I call this condition a lack of SoS because the SoS that

Natural Sense of Self

The lifelong subconscious sense of being a real, independent person who develops according to Nature's plan and timing, if the infant receives the necessary positive responses from the parent.

Lack of (Natural) Sense of Self

The person never developed a natural, ongoing, inner knowing that they are a "real," independent human being.

Ego-References

Subconsciously accepted requirements to feel and behave in certain ways, and achieve certain results, in order to feel approved, as a substitute for feeling like a "real person."

Annihilation

A strong perception of being overlooked, not being seen and heard, not being taken into account, not having any impact in one's environment, which is experienced as non-existing.

should be there *is not there*; it is missing. We do not notice the symptoms of the lack of a SoS, but we do see and can identify the symptoms of a SSoS, which reveals the lack of a (Natural) SoS. The symptoms of the SSoS indicate the condition of a person as having a lack of SoS.

In other words, even though the many symptoms of disease and dysfunction are the immediate result of a SSoS at work, the presence of that SSoS ultimately is caused by a lack of SoS. So in a way one could say that the signs and symptoms of disease and dysfunction are caused by a lack of SoS. It is important that you have a clear understanding of this.

CHARACTERISTICS OF A LACK OF A (NATURAL) SOS

In case of a missing SoS, we have no sensation of having a home in our very own being—no anchor that keeps us from drifting and settling down, no source to base our decisions on, other than the criteria of the SSoS.

People with a **Lack of SoS** are, among other things, highly sensitive to criticism and extremely irritable. They have a great need to perform to perfection because they have to live up to self-imposed expectations, called **Ego-References** (more on those in Chapter 6). A deeply felt restlessness leads them to extremes in many aspects of life, for example, not settling down, not being able to stay with one partner, or not staying in one field of study. There is a continuous changing of jobs, an inability to be a good (consistent) parent, and a lack of focus and consistency. In short, people with a lack of SoS do not know where to go or what to do or why to do anything. It might appear that they are extremely motivated, but deep down they are driven by their compulsive behaviors that are based on their fear of **Annihilation**.

DETECTING A LACK OF (NATURAL) SOS

Drawing conclusions from my self-exploration was hard. Identifying a lack of something when you have no information on what that something looks or feels like is almost impossible. The lack of SoS is therefore inferred and/or detected through the presence of a SSoS or the presence of the workings of a SSoS, if you will. In other words, the presence or absence of the signs and symptoms of a SSoS was and still is the only way to recognize a person's type of SoS.

In order to find out whether or not we have a lack of SoS we need to list the issues we have—the types of ailments or dysfunctions we are plagued by. Next, with this list in our hands we take a moment to visit Appendix I to review the Comparison Chart (page 224). To help you identify a Lack of SoS pay attention to the presence in your life/body of any or several of the symptoms that you find in Figure 1.1. This overview highlights some of the items in the Comparison Chart to self-assess your, or other people's, SoS. These symptoms and/or dysfunctions may originate from lacking a healthy SoS but often result from the stress and exhaustion that accompany a SSoS.

Figure 1.1 is a shortened list of some of the symptoms a person ruled by a SSoS due to a lack of SoS may experience. If any of the following problems or pains pertains to you, your loved one, or your client, chances are that the SoS Method will be highly relevant and helpful to you.

A BRIEF SUMMARY OF THE SOS METHOD

This Method presents a new and integrated approach to the understanding of an important part of the human condition, and offers potential improvements. My point of departure is that body, mind, and emotions are continuously in communication with each other during all developmental and maturational phases, which then results in the way each person is whatever he or she is in the world right now.

Symptoms of Lack of Sense of Self	
- Emotional Roller Coaster	- Unreasonable Anger, Violence
- Excessive Need for "High"	- Unmanageable Chronic High Stress
- Fear to Face Your Self	- Chronic Sense of Failure
- Out of Touch with Reality	- Controlling Behavior
- Inner Turmoil	- Prone to Motion Sickness
- Absence of Straight Focus	- Fear of Crowds
- Compulsive, Obsessive Behavior	- Easily Aggravated, Offended
- Insomnia	- Highly Sensitive
- Panic Attacks	- "Fluttering" In Stomach
- Migraines	- Absence of Happiness + Love
- Suicidal Thoughts	- Cramped Muscles
- Relationship Problems	- Issues with Money

Figure 1.1: Symptoms of a Lack of Sense of Self

Here is what I believe. Each of us is born with certain qualities and characteristics of who we are when our potential is optimally manifested in life. It is crucial that a person live under conditions that enable this process to take place. In other words, if there are few obstacles to your developing a healthy mind and body, then your life circumstances allow you to live up to your potential. What happens though, if there are too many obstacles? What happens to your potential when your development, as it could naturally go, is blocked or distorted by certain life circumstances (which seem to be the rule rather than the exception)?

I always felt I could have been so much more successful in doing what I have done, if I hadn't been forced to look within to find what was off with me, and how to change into a person who has her act together. If only I had been so lucky not to have been distracted by doing the things for the wrong reason, and to have spent all that energy and focus on my profession or even on being social, I would have been good at it and it would have been worth my education. Or perhaps, I would not have chosen to become a professional musician at all and would have found great satisfaction as a psychologist. I would have had, possibly, a lot of people who wanted to be my friend because I had something to offer instead of being needy and fearing rejection.

One of the most important things that develop in human beings is a SoS. This Method is about what happens when the kind of input needed by infants in order to develop a Natural Sense of Self is insufficient in amount or inadequate in kind—and about the suffering that results from that situation. The Method is also developed into a Self-Healing Method and tools are given to recover from what otherwise would be a lifelong predicament.

If the growth/health-promoting input is missing for an infant, a survival mechanism kicks in to help the body, mind, and emotions compensate for that lack. This Method is also about describing those compensations that turn into compulsions to establish an imitation Sense of Self, the suffering that imitation causes, and how to overcome these compulsions and their ill effects.

Such compulsions are natural, instinctive responses by the infant to this unmet need during the critical period of development of a SoS. Through engaging in a trial and error phase, the young person establishes an Early Childhood Survival Strategy (ECSS) that leads eventually to the development of a SSoS-oriented System.

The SoS Method deems the absence of a Natural Sense of Self to be a root cause of many ailments and dysfunctional lives and of the failure of so many of us to manifest and live up to our inherent potentials.

THE IMPORTANCE OF A SOS

This Method maintains that:

- the development of a Natural Sense of Self is a core aspect of healthy, normal psychological maturation.
- the maturation of SoS is subject to either healthy or unhealthy development based on behavior of the primary caregiver toward the child.
- a lack of a Natural Sense of Self in a person leads automatically to dependency on a SSoS for self-experience, which is one of the root causes of many aspects of human suffering.

To improve the human condition, it is crucial that all people be educated in developing, strengthening, or restoring a Natural SoS in themselves as well as in their children.

HUMAN SUFFERING refers to the array of lack of well-being, from personal unhappiness to war. It includes physical disease, from the common cold to serious illnesses; conflicts and disagreements; psycho-emotional ailments of all sorts; depression; insomnia; mental challenges such as learning disabilities, bipolar disorder, attention-deficit/hyperactivity disorder; and possibly many more. Human suffering implies family dysfunction, child abuse, and possible cases of sexual aberrations, suicide, violence, crime, and war!

It might be unrealistic to believe we could eradicate all aggression and violence, all disease and dysfunction, and all conflict and war from human behavior, because some of it might be evolutionarily innate to the human species for survival of the fittest. Whether we like it or not, humans are part of the kingdom of animals, and animalistic traits will probably always pop up in our behavior.

However, within that limitation, my own experience leads me to believe that much of the human suffering could be reduced or eliminated, if every person were thoroughly in touch with his or her "Self." A greater prevalence of that core aspect of psychological maturation would lead to more responsible and more self-respecting behavior (and therefore more respectful of others) more often in more people. Based on my inner research, I have come to believe that if everyone had a healthy SoS, everyone's quality of life would be enhanced, and world peace would be within reach!

Therefore, I regard the message of this book as being of the utmost importance. I would like to invite educational systems and their leaders to consider integrating the insights and recommendations of this Method into the curriculum of elementary schools or even nursery schools. *Parents and educators need to become thoroughly aware of this core aspect of psychological maturation.*

Ultimately, I have a vision that the awareness, knowledge, and skills provided by the SoS Method will ripple out to everyone everywhere and help people establish a healthy SoS in themselves as well as in their children. Once established in these two generations, it will take increasingly less effort to make the world a better place for future generations.

So you see, the importance of the *primary caregiver* in this process is major!

THE IMPORTANCE OF THE PARENT/CAREGIVER

Throughout this book, by "parent," "caregiver," or "primary caregiver," I am referring to whoever does most of the care of the baby from birth on, whether that person is a relative or not. These terms are used interchangeably. At later ages, these positions can include teachers, nannies, sports figures, religious leaders, and other authority figures who function as influences on a child's SoS.

A SoS is something that either develops or does not, and that process depends fully on the nature of the input from the primary caregiver. And because the SoS is so foundational to the functioning of a human individual on all levels of living, I state that the role of the caregiver (mother/father function) is crucial to the world. The people who are with the child from birth on (and before) are the ones who make the greatest impression on the newly born individual. They are the ones who determine whether a healthy Natural SoS develops in the child. With that, they, unknowingly, more or less determine this person's quality of life and the impact he or she will have in the world.

Responsibility for "Being There" for Your Children

A caregiver's most positive contribution to society includes having the skill, patience, and psycho-emotional healthiness to relate to her or his children in a responsible and truly loving way. To that purpose, ideally, women and men would spend time working out their own problems before they engage in parenthood to make sure they can be fully present and "there" for their offspring, not only physically but also psychologically. Only those who feel they have come to terms with their own issues are able to make way for and lovingly care for others.

This book presents a rather utopian vision of possibilities in child care, but I am pointing in a direction and, as I mentioned before, "the map is not the territory!" If each caregiver could live up to just 5 to 15 percent of this ideal image, there would be a considerable change for the better in this world.

If anybody can make a change in what people become later on in life, it is the primary caregivers (kindergarten and elementary school teachers included), because they are in a position to make or break children, the consequences of which will stay with them well into adulthood. Caregivers' behavior toward children largely determines an essential characteristic of the children. Will they grow up to be helpful, of service to others, tolerant, and forgiving because they are blessed with a Natural Sense of Self? Or will they be frustrated, violent, and full of suppressed rage because getting connected to their own Self was thwarted, which resulted in them feeling "not allowed to be," which led to the unhealthy SSoS taking over their lives?

Sense of Self, its healthiness or unhealthiness, is, according to this Method, the crucial determinant of that difference. Just about anyone can be a parent in name only. Biologically, becoming a parent is not hard, but *being* a parent, especially in today's society where everyone needs to also become his or her own person, develop skills, and bring in money, is extremely challenging.

However, if we truly want to change the world at large, more caregivers would assume responsibility and gain insight into themselves. They would learn to "introspect," to look inside, get to know themselves, and find out who they actually are. They would then stand a much better chance of lovingly bringing up a next generation after they first deal with their own issues.

An Influence Throughout Life

As a child grows up and becomes more autonomous, the direct influence and impact of parents'/caregivers' behavior on the child normally diminishes. This is true for children who have developed a reasonable healthy SoS, but for those in an "**Enmeshment**," an unhealthy degree of dependency continues through adulthood and even into old age, even though the parent's or caregiver's influence has become less visible, less obvious, and therefore less traceable. The continuation of this unhealthy relationship is often facilitated by modern ease of communication (see Chapter 7 for more on Enmeshment). Too often, for example, grown children become terribly stressed when visiting their parents, because they know they are not the parents they want them to be, and they feel the need of their parent's approval and validation. It's often similarly stressing when parents come to visit. A grown woman, for example, may start to clean and organize like a madwoman because her house never seems to be "good enough" for her mother. If you point this out to her, she might prefer to not look at her own behavior and to be in denial of the truth

Enmeshment

An unhealthy relationship between child and primary caregiver. The child's identity and motives are merged with the adult's, associated with extreme dependence on approval.

and mention futile things that justify her behavior. But when the stress level she experiences is so much higher than is justified by the actual event, it is likely that deep down inside she feels her SSoS is at stake.

At any age, grown children whose parents are alive can still be needy; they can still hope that by facilitating their parents' caprices and that they might finally get their deepest wish come true: being unconditionally loved and feeling accepted the way they are, being acknowledged as a valuable human being.

Even if an ocean lies between parents and their grown children, parents' influence can be just as present as ever within the child's inner life. The parent's standards and criteria still reverberate in his or her head and form what I call the **Virtual, Internalized Parental Voice (VIPV).**

Even recently I fell into the trap of thinking I had to be a certain way, in order to be a good mother to my children. However, I ran into a conflict with how I felt I really was. I was convinced I was a failure as a mother if I had projects going on for myself. To resolve the conflict I had to look closer into this issue that was causing some sleepless nights for me. Through thorough introspection, I found that I was using my caregiver's criteria. Being unable to live up to them because of my own agenda brought me mixed feelings of fear and anger. Distinguishing what you really think of things yourself and to put aside with peaceful conviction the other voice in your head is not as easy as it might sound.

Unfortunately, most adults in this situation are unaware that they have internalized their parents' criteria and reasoning and even let their parents' expectations run their lives instead of developing their own standards.

THERE IS NO PERFECT SOLUTION BUT . . .

For many of the problems and choices we face in life, there simply isn't the option to find a one and only best solution. Sometimes we need to set priorities or give in to the limitations of our personal circumstances. But one thing every caregiver *can* do is this: *Consider your children as independent, autonomous human beings and not as extensions of yourself!* Having a healthy SoS yourself enables you to do just that. If you feel that is a challenge for you, then please find the courage to undertake the steps necessary to work your own way to a healthy Restored Sense of Self. This will enable you to create a better future for yourself, for your child, and for the world!

In a nutshell, that is the purpose and goal, the hope and the vision, of the SoS Method and the activities of our company, HealthySenseOfSelf.

Virtual, Internalized Parental Voice (VIPV)

The often-repeated verbal and non-verbal messages through which parents talk to their children becomes (almost) hardwired in the child's mind so that it is perceived as an unquestionable truth (about and) by the child.

2 | Self and Sense of Self

Before we can understand how we come to fail to develop our Sense of Self (SoS) and make an effort to regain it, we must take a step backward and define what the Self is and what it is that makes up the Self. We also need to take a closer look at what is meant by "sensing" in "Sense of Self" and what Self and Sensing the Self are not.

WHAT IS THE SELF?

The Sense of Self Method proclaims that strengthening or, if needed, restoring your Sense of Self is a key to reducing and/or eliminating many aspects of human suffering. So what does this Method consider the "Self" to be?

The **Self** has been an object of study and wonder for philosophers and psychologists for many centuries. If you want to learn how traditional psychology views the Self I refer you to the many good books about this subject. It is neither the purpose nor the scope of this Method to review and incorporate other relevant theories on this subject. The reader can compare or relate the underlying approach to what is already out there if he or she so wishes.

In the SoS Method, the Self is considered to be composed of six layers that, each in their own specific way, need to undergo a healthy and adequate development so each can contribute to a fully functioning healthy unit of interactive layers that we can compare the Self to. Note that the ability to sense this Self itself also depends on the opportunity or circumstances a person (child) has to effectively have those layers unfold their potential and do what they need to do at the time that it is meant to happen.

Even though the process of developing a healthy natural SoS is meant to go smoothly, all too often people encounter obstacles that hinder this process

Substitute Sense of Self

A psycho-emotional structure that develops as the backbone of the psyche of those children whose caregivers relate to them as an extension of themselves, and that leads to a compulsive drive for achievement-based approval.

from taking place in a healthy, natural way. Please note that this is a crucial moment in the development of the young person and exactly the reason why a situation can be created in which the person identifies with other ways of giving his or her psyche a structure and what I refer to as a **Substitute Sense of Self (SSoS)**.

Imagine that we are putting the Self under a microscope. Pretend for a while that the Self is an object that we can magnify to better study its structure. What we then see are its six separate layers. Think of the layers as functions of the Self.

Here is how I have named them:

1. The basic (white) layer of the Unconscious Spiritual Self,
2. The second (red) layer of the Incarnated Self,
3. The third (yellow) layer where the Self is experienced as a Conscious Thought-Form,
4. The fourth (green) layer of the Psycho-Emotional functions,
5. The fifth (blue) layer of the Social Self, and as the crème de la crème
6. The sixth (white) layer, the Conscious Spiritual layer of Self (see Figure 2.1).

I have chosen this image because now that there is differentiation within the Self that carries labels, it is easier to shed light on what happens when things go wrong and where exactly that aberration takes place. Understanding the interactivity of the layers in the selves of both the mother/caregiver and the child combined with insight on the reverberations of this interactivity within the structure of the Self of the child enhances understanding the Sense of Self Method.

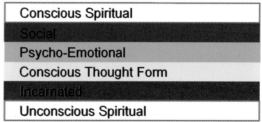

Figure 2.1: Layers of healthy Self

With the labels in place, we can better understand how much impact a lack of adequate development has on the rest of the layers of Self for the child because the layers are not isolated. They interact with feedback loops, and the nature of the interaction depends on various health-promoting or dysfunction-promoting factors in development.

Figure 2.2 briefly suggests how each layer of the Self affects all the others in an "upward" direction. Perhaps more important to remember is that these effects also work in a downward direction.

Lack of Sensing, Not a Lack of Self

Before moving forward, I want to make it very clear that it is not a deficiency of Self that I consider the root cause of many ailments and dysfunctions in our daily lives but an inability to Sense the Self. The development of the ability to Sense the Self was obstructed during the crucial moments in a child's upbringing.

I wish it were possible to quantitatively measure the degree to which a person is (or is not) tuned into his or her Self. We could then measure when and to what degree that process is actively working in each individual person. I wish that we could attach numbers to the degree to which each person experiences their Self. We might be surprised to learn how greatly those numbers would vary, with the low numbers being found in many more people than we would think, specifically in people who have many problems in life.

In the following explanation of the layers of the Self, and throughout this chapter, note that in these explanations the terms *being*, *identity*, and *core essence* are used synonymously for Self, and the referent of "I" stands in for the phrase "I exist."

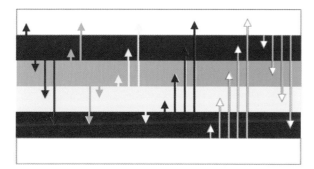

Figure 2.2: The influence and dependency of the layers of Self on one another

The Layers of the Self

Layer 1: The Subconscious Spiritual Layer

The Self is carried by, and rooted in, an ultimate nonphysical awareness that we rarely consciously "sense"—shown in white in Figure 2.1. In this layer, the Self is "something that exists"—the Being, the most primordial identity, the core essence, the pure awareness prior to any object of awareness. It is the referent of "I" in "I exist." Most religions and spirituality point to this Self.

"I am."

Layer 2: The Layer of the Incarnated (Body) Self

More specific and close to conscious awareness is the Self that is awareness of our physical existence as a living creature, of being within a body, of being incarnate (shown in red in Figure 2.1). We share this Self, and the sense of it, with animals.

As infants, we are immediately confronted with the body's demands and joys, which bring our existence to our recognition. We strongly react to these sensations, and if responded to in an adequate way, they help us begin to develop a healthy Sense of our Self. We spend quite a number of years learning how to manage our bodily needs and wants. Receiving tender love and care physically is certainly welcome; it reinforces the development of a sense of well-being that gives us confidence in being in and with that body and helps us to (very subconsciously) recognize and accept it as "Me."

"I am alive in this body."

Layer 3: The Layer of the Self as a Conscious Thought-Form

In this layer of our Self, shown in yellow in Figure 2.1, we experience that we are not just a living creature, but that we are human with the basic functionality, essence, potentials, and limits of a human body and human being: a human organism with a human psyche. This Self is more conscious—a "thought-form"—than the second layer of Self, although the sensations when sensing it are difficult to put into words: "I am a human being, a member of the human species." From this layer arises our awareness of being a distinct and separate being from the entity that gave birth to us. The cut of the umbilical cord reverberates in this layer and awakens our sense of being unique. The development of this layer coincides with the child's growing up and discovering the "mine" and "not mine."

"I am alive as a (separate) human being."

Layer 4: The Psycho-Emotional Layer

With this layer (shown as green in Figure 2.1), we experience life, others, and ourselves on an emotional level. Our specific, individual self-essence—our unique psychology, emotions, dispositions, inclinations, talents, weaknesses, strengths, and challenges—become part of our daily awareness of ourselves as a unique human being. We use and observe these elements of Self and relate to them directly as "me."

The concept of "I," born in Layer 3, gains qualities and characteristics. The "I" grows and gains more content; the psyche and the emotional body develop as well. A growing sense of me-ness distinguishes the individuals from the you-ness of others: "I feel . . ." and "I want . . ." and "I believe . . ."

"I am me."

Layer 5: The Social Layer

Also observable in our ordinary awareness is our social Self: the social aspects and characteristics of our individual being. It enables us to function in society because it consists of, and influences, our relationships with friends and family, our associations at work, our roles in society, and so on.

The Social Self, if well-established and well-sensed, helps us contribute to the world. A Social Self that is able to function independently from others offers us the confidence that we, as a sensed Self, will not disappear when things go awry and the outcome is not what we had aimed for. We recognize ourselves in a particular role, function, or status and are able to function interdependently.

"I am me in relation to you."

Layer 6: The Conscious Spiritual Layer

The sixth layer of Self is not considered a necessity for everybody. Many people consider our existence on earth the beginning as well as the end of life. There is no need for them to include a spiritual reality because it is not tangible to them. So the sixth layer is for those of us who relate to this concept. It is the Conscious Spiritual function of Self, and when it shows up we have closed the circle and fulfilled the task of making the Unconscious Spiritual Layer, the beginning of us as a person, conscious. In other words, it emerges into the conscious awareness of those of us who find that the Self is not simply what is encapsulated by the physical body. This larger Self as an identity includes the preceding layers, which in turn are experienced as part of the "Ultimate."

"I am part of something (divine) that is bigger than myself."

Healthy Layers Form a Healthy SoS

When the layers of the Self function correctly and are recognized (at the appropriate degree of awareness) by a person, the Self functions as the home and resting place for the spirit or essence of the incarnate "I." From this place, the person forms motivations and values that give shape to his or her life.

I like to compare the Self with the concept of the tonic chord in music: The melody starts from it, develops from it, and returns to it. Even if the complete chord is never sounded explicitly, it, as the root of the melody and harmony, is present throughout the piece, giving it functionality; in fact, it *determines* the functionality of the other pitches used. In just that way, a sensed Self provides functionality to a person's consciousness, his or her psyche. Everything else flows from it, and it holds up the whole of everything else.

THE SENSE OF SELF

Sense of Self

A conscious or subconscious awareness of existing independently as a unique and potentially autonomous human being and of what intrinsically comes with it in your daily living.

When we are appropriately aware of each layer, we have a **Sense of Self**. Being subconsciously aware of our independent existence as a definite, unique human being forms the backbone of the human psyche; it indicates to us on an ongoing basis that we exist and that we know who we are and that we experience our own Being. In sensing our Self, we can develop along one of two paths:

We develop a Natural Sense of Self (a healthy way of sensing our Self and our Being),

or

We develop a Substitute Sense of Self (an unhealthy distorted way of experiencing our Self and our Being).

A third possibility—the Restored SoS—is attainable through working with the SoS Method, which helps us analyze our SSoS and correct our detrimental views and behaviors. By understanding and righting what went wrong, we can achieve a way of experiencing our Self that is close to a Natural SoS. This concept, and how to achieve it, will be discussed later in this text.

The Natural SoS

A **Natural Sense of Self (NatSoS)** is the most rudimentary and natural awareness of our own Being and of our be-ing alive. In this fortunate situation, every layer of the Self is healthy and, having developed correctly as we grew, performs satisfactorily according to its intended function. A Natural SoS is an abiding, unshakeable, subconscious awareness—the sensation of being an autonomous human being, ultimately independent of others, especially from our parent or primary caregiver(s). Having a Natural SoS does not refer only to physical independence, which obviously does not happen until adulthood, but also and most importantly to psycho-emotional independence. Having a Natural SoS can be considered the anchor of a person's be-ing. It is our ultimate inner home, or more exactly, it is who, what, and where we mean when saying or thinking "I" and "me." It is the place from which we act and are motivated.

Natural Sense of Self

The lifelong subconscious sense of being a real, independent person that develops according to Nature's plan and timing, if the infant receives the necessary positive responses from the parent.

This type of SoS feels natural to us, by which I mean unquestioned, unquestionable, foundational, basic, and intrinsic, because it has always been with us and it has grown with us as we age. It is so natural to us that we do not even need to become *consciously* aware of it, that is, to refer to it by words, by name, or by labeling it because of its steady, ongoing presence.

What people with a Natural SoS have in common is one important, automatic characteristic: the ability to be at rest. A Natural SoS provides us with the one and only safe haven we can expect to have in life: No matter what we do or what we do not like about ourselves a person with a Natural SoS can always rely on the security of the "I am" bedrock it provides. Being rooted within us, it cannot be affected by superficial, or surface, matters. With a Natural SoS, internal peace and confidence are the rulers of our being even when the world around us is in turmoil and chaos.

A Natural SoS makes us aware that we are a distinct "someone" different from other "someones." It allows us to fully *be* ourselves and enjoy being alive as who we are. It opens us to experience joy and personal satisfaction and allows us to be free to experience what we truly feel, to relate to others authentically without unhealthy filters, and to feel compassion. A natural Sense of Self is a blessing that permits us to focus on the content of our lives and "get things done" (without being distracted by an eternal search for the Self).

The Substitute Sense of Self (SSoS)

When a Natural Sense of Self does not develop, another structure develops in its place: a Substitute Sense of Self. It makes up for what is missing within us. Or it could very well be the other way around: Because another structure develops in the growing infant, there is no room for a natural SoS to develop. When a healthy (i.e., Natural) SoS is lacking automatically the foundation develops of, what later turns out to become, a compulsive drive for achievement-based approval to enable the person to experience a fleeting imitation of the lacking Natural SoS.

If an ongoing sense of autonomous existence does not develop, an inner vacuum is created that leads to an intolerable terror. Subconsciously, a person then adopts various unhealthy strategies for getting positive feedback, be it physically, emotionally, verbally, or nonverbally, from his or her caregiver or parent. This feedback becomes the closest to a healthy regard that the person can obtain. These unhealthy, subconsciously self-imposed strategies include various requirements (conditions) for feeling or acting or behaving in certain ways to get recognized. Through successfully meeting these requirements or conditions, people feel good about themselves, which is comparable with receiving a sort of validation that they "exist" as a Being. I consider this to be a substitute way of experiencing the Self, or, in other words, a SSoS.

The SSoS is the central part of a complex collection of psycho-emotional motives, goals, feelings, needs, desires, habits, and behaviors that, as a whole, is called the SSoS-oriented System (see Chapter 8). This system operates a great deal of the person's psyche and behavior, and has a profound influence on his or her health, relationships, work, environment, children, and spouse—in general on life itself. It causes a great deal of (unnecessary) suffering for the person who is ruled by it as well as for the people in this person's direct environment. But now that we are able to identify the condition and label it, it can, fortunately, be addressed and, with enough determination and effort, be healed.

The Layers of the Substitute Sense of Self
This section is rather complex and is not critical for understanding and applying the SoS Method. If you are not highly academically interested I recommend you skip this part.

When a Substitute Sense of Self is in place, the layers of the "Self" are affected in particular ways. Let us zoom in on those layers one more time to explore what the trauma has done to them. Let us look up close at what the Self looks like when unhealthy or distorted.[3]

---

[3] For further and more detailed information please visit our videos and graphics showing the unhealthy relationship of the (layers of) Self in relationship to the caregiver, and the interactive influences among the many layers of Self. Please visit www.healthysenseofself.com or go directly to http://bit.ly/SoSVideoBlocks.

In Figure 2.3, we see how the layer of the Conscious Thought-Form (yellow), the Psycho-Emotional (green), and the Social (blue) layer of Self are stunted, distorted, and/or warped when the SoS does not have a chance to develop normally. They become abnormal when governed by the SSoS-oriented System. Note that the first layer, our spirit and that "given" at birth, is unaffected. What the development of a dependency on the SSoS to the layer of the embodied Self is hard to tell but if we use our imagination we could get a sense of the invisible changes that take place in our physical body and that later in life might result in afflictions of some sort.

The following are some brief comparisons between the healthy and distorted forms.

Layer 2: The Incarnated Self (the Body)

Most modern cultures emphasize that we are (mainly) our mind and our mental accomplishments and neglect a healthy attention to our physical presence. Later in life, in order to become a whole person again, we often have to relearn that we are also our body. Even if we do pay attention to our body, it is often in exactly the way our caregivers paid attention to us when we were infants: as means to ends, not as distinct beings worthy of honor, attention, and care to our body's individual, unique needs and wants. Being out of touch with the authenticity of our body's actual needs and sensations can become the root of illness.

Layer 3: The Conscious Thought-Form

When we are without a Natural SoS, this layer is particularly vulnerable in the growing child. It is during this time that the seed is planted for a healthy separation of the child from the parent/caregiver. We need to get, in this crucial period of the development of this layer, a glimpse of the idea

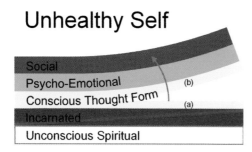

Figure 2.3: The damage done to the layers of Self of a person with a SSoS

that we are a separate person and that we have an (potential and beginning) identity ourselves.

If this process does not take place we become dependent on obtaining that visibility by complying with our caregivers' wishes of how they need us to be. If the caregiver is unable to give us, or mirror to us, the intrinsic notion that we are not dependent on the degree to which we fulfill their wishes, then what we have learned so far is what we keep on doing. We keep working on fulfilling their demands and feel a short satisfaction ("Feel-good-about-Self" [FgaS]) when we are not rejected. But we experience the terror of not existing in the eyes of others unless we are able to live up to the expectations. We develop a great fear of being invisible, a ghost with a body, so to speak. Others see us, but we are ignored, discounted.

In Figure 2.3, note that the yellow layer is divided. In a SSoS-oriented System, children can experience a tear at this level. They become "enmeshed" with their caregiver (see Chapter 7 for a fuller explanation of Enmeshment) to the point that they identify their physical and psycho-emotional layers of Self more as parts of their caregiver rather than as parts of themselves. One could say that these children come to associate a large part of their Incarnated Self, Conscious Thought-Form, and Psycho-Emotional constructs as not belonging to them but rather as belonging to their caregiver. This may seem a blunt statement. Therefore much of this book is devoted to further explanation of how this (third) layer of self is affected by childhood deprivation of healthy acknowledgment as a unique human being and to studying the impact of that reality on a person's life.

Layer 4: The Psycho-Emotional Layer

This layer is especially hard-hit as it can be completely overwhelmed or co-opted by the developmental disability that a lack of SoS really is. This layer of Self governs one's mind, emotions, motivations—all that is experienced as "me." It is disrupted, distorted, and contaminated by the unhealthy functioning of other layers and specifically by the invasive activity of the caregiver's attempts to be and stay the center of the child's existence. The consequence of this leads to further destruction by means of the implementation of detrimental forces such as **Indirect Motivation** and Ego-References (see Chapters 6 and 7, respectively).

Layer 5: The Social Layer

People who are dependent on the outcome of their achievements and the high standards they have to live up to need their circumstances to cooperate

Indirect Motivation

The motive for doing something is not what it appears to be; instead, the real motive is to get the temporary emotional state that substitutes for a lasting sense of being a "real" person.

with those tasks, so they want to be in control. They cannot afford for things to go awry because that leads them to experience high anxiety or rage. They may even become violent or depressed. What we see, on the other hand, are people who might be insecure and not forthcoming with others because they are not grounded in their own being. People's social behavior is imbibed with influences from their contaminated fourth layer, the Psycho-Emotional layer, of Self and their split layer of Self as a Conscious-Thought Form.

The SSoS—A Natural, Inevitable Development

Even though the development of a Substitute Sense of Self is not the way it is supposed to go as it can lead to a variety of ways of lifelong suffering, its development is completely natural and inevitable. There is no blame to lay on the child, whose choices are driven by a force of nature and are made quite below the level of conscious awareness.

A person lacking a Natural SoS has, figuratively or metaphorically speaking, no structure, base, or safe haven to return to. This person is comparable to a ship without a set course, rudder, or anchor and thus is at the mercy of the waves of the ocean.

It is like this: If, for the development of a healthy SoS, acknowledgment of the parent/caregiver is needed but has not been provided, a painful void exists. Note that in a child's mind, acknowledgment and approval are being mixed up. So this void acts like a Black Hole. It sucks up everything that looks like the acknowledgment he or she needs. Any outcome of an action or behavior that looks like it would qualify for approval is used to feel good about him- or herself. That is the only viable goal in the life of a person who is ruled by a SSoS-oriented System.

Over time the person turns the observations and conclusions on how to fill that hole into strategies that become internalized and habitual behavior. In this way, a SSoS is *automatically* generated within the person's subconscious

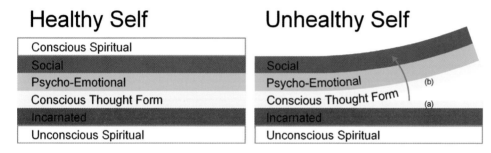

Figure 2.4: Layers of a healthy Self versus an unhealthy Self

mind. So it is the nature of the human psyche to fill the void that is left when the child's interpersonal environment does not support the development of a Natural SoS.

DEFINING SENSING

As mentioned previously, the central tenet of this Method is one's ability to sense, or to have a sense of, one's Self. But what does "sense" or "sensing" mean in this context?

Our five (or six) senses make us aware of things. In this context, the term *sensing* means to notice or detect by way of our senses (sight, hearing, taste, smell, touch) consciously or perhaps subliminally—that is, without being conscious that our senses are registering something. Thus, to sense the Self means being more or less consciously aware of one's Self. Some people believe that there is a sixth sense, which can be thought of as intuition, a "knowing without (consciously) knowing." For this Method, this type of sixth sense isn't relevant.

If people are unable to sense their Self, then they have no way of knowing where to find that place where they can be at rest. There is no way of knowing that there even is such a place. All they know is that they have to work (hard) so they can feel good about themselves for a short-lived moment.

Experiencing the Self can occur in two ways: through a direct or an indirect relationship.

A Direct Relationship with Your Self

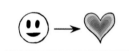

Direct Relationship with Self

A healthy sense of being your own purpose, which includes personal empowerment and relying on your own criteria.

To experience existing independently from the outcome of one's actions and behavior, a person must have a **Direct Relationship with the Self**. That experience includes a person having a deep inner knowledge that he or she *is* a visible person just like everybody else. There is no doubt in these people's minds that they can and will be seen and heard by the persons in their surroundings if they wanted that to happen.

There is a deep-felt sense of "I" as an independently existing being that completely supports the surface experience of "myself" at all times. In his or her subconscious, the person knows fully and continuously that he or she is alive and has the right to exist as who he or she is. This person never doubts that he or she has the right to occupy space and time in this world. The "I" is a given that is never doubted.

Having a direct relationship with the Self means that there is no need for other tools or tricks to getting the sensation of being (alive). Actions, activity, and behavior are realized because of their immediate and logical goal. For example, I help my neighbor because I want to do that for him. My agenda is plain and simple and has no hidden aspects (compare this to "I help my neighbor because my father will be happy and like me for it").

It means having good access to your authentic feelings, beliefs, needs, desires, preferences, and motives. No part of the Self is hidden from yourself or from others. There is no need to adopt anyone else's emotions, desires, or preferences or fake your own for any reason. You know that whatever you do or not do, your life (i.e., your sense of being allowed to be) is not at stake. This is the exact opposite of the experience of a person with a SSoS, who hides things, adopts too much from others, and fakes a lot.

This direct relationship with the Self is found only in those who have a Natural SoS or a Restored Sense of Self. People living with a SSoS experience an indirect relationship with the Self.

An Indirect Relationship with Your Self

If Sensing the Self only takes place through experiencing a state of FgaS based on positive outcomes of our achievements or the responses from others, we have an **Indirect Relationship with the Self**. People who need to cut themselves with a knife to experience pain that then gives them a sense of being alive have an indirect relationship to the Self and need to feel good about themselves as a memory of the craved approval that used to be essential for their well-being. An indirect relationship with the Self indicates rather a lack of relationship with the Self, because all that there is is a relationship with a need for approval, which then is taken for acknowledgment. So we could say that FgaS is in fact a deviated form of (craved) acknowledgment. To fill this need of acknowledgment is what the person is all about, so he or she identifies with the tasks at hand and the process of getting the desired outcome. It is not that the Self is not there! It is just not sensed. All the attention and energy goes somewhere else. It is that somewhere else that the person identifies with and takes for him- or herself. In other words, we could say that through coping mechanisms created and maintained over time, people identify with the SSoS as representing "themselves" because their concern is not about their life but about attaining the state of FgaS they have come to associate with approval from others, rather than from their own desires and needs.

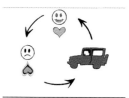

Indirect Relationship with Self

Sensing yourself as a "Self" only via achievements or the responses of others, giving you a transitory good feeling instead of a healthy abiding sense of being who you are.

A SoS Is an Action, Not an Object

Contrary to what the language in the preceding discussion may suggest, we do not really "have" a "thing" called Sense of Self. Rather, this SoS is an awareness, not an object of perception, and though the term *Sense of Self* is a noun, it refers to our continuously acknowledging the *presence* of the core of our being. People develop differing degrees of this presence to their own being.

These processes do not have to be consciously recognized as such when all goes well; it is when things need to be healed that a full awareness of these six layers is highly helpful. This is where recognizing and sensing these functions helps greatly to restore what should have developed further in us in the first place: a Natural SoS.

So it seems reasonable to surmise that if the *sensing* is absent, then, in the *subjective* experience, the *Self* also seems to be absent. It might be there, but if we cannot sense it, we will not know it is there. This is why the concept of "sensing" is important in this Method.

Self-Esteem Requires a Sense of Self

The use of the word *self-esteem* is popular these days, as low self-esteem is also often used as the root cause of many problems, but self-esteem and Sense of Self are not the same. According to *Merriam-Webster's Dictionary*, self-esteem is "confidence and satisfaction in one's self; self-respect."[4] In the SoS Method, the concept of self-esteem follows this definition, that is, confidence that is based on the opinions of others and/or the judgments of others that we have internalized. In this context, self-esteem is indeed built on events and things *outside* of our being—a healthy self-validation or pride in one's achievements or performances—and is not part of the profound Self.

So if we want to compare self-esteem, and its counterpart, self-loathing, to our SoS concept we just need to agree with the following truth: Before we esteem or loathe something, we must be aware that it exists. We must *sense* it. In other words, we cannot have low or high or whatever self-esteem if we do not sense our Self in the first place. Therefore, self-esteem is something that people with a Natural SoS can experience, but those with a SSoS cannot because they are unable to connect with the Self.

For me this lack of awareness of a Self may have been the reason that I remember my elementary and high school years as a blur. I may have performed well enough at school, but I was hardly there. I remember things and events not as individual instances but as an exhausting activity of keeping everybody satisfied. In fact, I am tremendously grateful to have been able to

---

[4]"Self-respect," *Merriam-Webster's Online Dictionary*, http://www.merriam-webster.com/dictionary/self-esteem (accessed September 13, 2012).

get enough insight to identify the hang-ups I was hooked on: fulfilling conditions and being apprehensive about the outcome. I hope that people, through gaining insights into their own lives though the SoS Method, will be able to truly connect to themselves and consequently own their lives, instead of running around like jugglers trying to keep their plates in the air.

LOOKING AHEAD

We now have an understanding of what the Self is, and what its components are. Next let us explore how a SSoS is created and what is involved in that process. We will explain how lack of acknowledgment in early childhood can result in missing out on developing our Natural SoS. We will understand how becoming the slave of fulfilling conditions in search for approval is the result.

3 | Environmental Input: The Developmental Decider

A STRICT SEQUENCE

When a Sense of Self (SoS) starts to develop in a person, and that starts right at birth, it follows a particular pattern with particular input at particular times. Children who do not get what they need at the right time grow up locked into compensations that are self-destructive and that cause all kinds of suffering and problems.

Before we explore the natural, healthy process of how a person ought to grow up and compare it with what happens when that process is distorted in one or more ways, here are some thoughts about growth processes in nature.

Every infant, seedling, or animal goes through a formation process. Even after it has sprouted or been born, its anatomical and functional systems are still forming. This process follows a strict sequence that is pretty much predetermined by nature and, as a whole, it is also being influenced by *the interaction* between nature and nurture.

The genes of each living being are its "nature" aspect. The circumstances in which the being exists are its "nurture" aspect. These two influence each other, such that genes or circumstances may reinforce the growth and development of a plant or animal in one direction or another. Some processes need to take place before others can. If some bit of a living being's physiology does not develop fully and appropriately at its given time—its "critical period"—the clock marches on anyway. When this critical time passes, the being is abnormal in some way, unable to live up to its full (initial) potential.

As it is with plants and animals, so it is for people. So much of who we are as people, and how our lives unfold, is initiated in our childhood. So let us take a brief look at what happens in childhood.

Humans do not stop developing after they are born. Development follows certain natural rules and certain patterns; for example, we crawl before we walk; we walk before we run; we babble before we talk. Another important but often overlooked rule is that certain kinds of input are required at certain times in the sequence for the development to occur as it is meant to. If the right input happens at the right time in the sequence, a child's development is normal and healthy. If a child does not experience the correct conditions, it will grow in an unnatural and defective manner. It might be alive, but it is distorted and weak, and it struggles to function.

For example, an infant, during this process of formation—which can be specific and unique to a particular critical period in the sequence—needs various kinds of physical environmental inputs, such as adequate food, water, and warmth, as well as specific interpersonal, psychological, and emotional

Figure 3.1: A tree thwarted in its development while being deprived of space

input. To understand fully the necessity of these inputs, it is necessary to real-ize that both physical and psychological inputs affect both body and mind.

The *natural* in Natural SoS means a person has a SoS that has developed at the natural time, in an adequate way, and in the natural order that the development of a human being requires. It indicates the development has been "normal"—that the human consciousness has been able to do what it is programmed to do, without encountering obstructions or Hindrances in facilitating the maturation process. If the various required inputs are not pres-ent or provided at the appropriate time, the development of a Natural SoS cannot take place, and the result is a person with a warped SoS.

When developed in a distorted manner, we often need others to support us.

A SoS is not something we are born with or that we develop automati-cally and inevitably, no matter what. We do have an inborn drive to develop it,

Figure 3.2: Crooked tree

but unless certain kinds of experiences (feedback) are provided and processed in infancy and early childhood, a SoS won't develop naturally and normally.

A core sense of an independently existing me-ness is part of normal, healthy human development, and our psychological development programs that into us. Normal development requires a specific attitude from the primary caregiver toward the child; this attitude needs to communicate certain information to the child about his or her "being." This specific attitude needs to provide to the child the building blocks for the development of a healthy SoS, and is called Mirroring.

LACKS AND LAGS IN INPUT IN THE SEQUENCE OF DEVELOPMENT

When a required environmental input is not within the optimal range and timing for the normal development of that particular species of living organism, the adult (if indeed the young organism even survives) is defective in some way. Its form is misshapen, distorted, or stunted. Its functional systems, physical and/or psychological, are weak and may work in abnormal ways. Because the necessary functions for supporting a normal existence are not operating adequately, this situation might lead to an earlier death. And during that life, there will be suffering from the abnormalities in functioning.

Many studies and experiments have been done to find out what happens if the crucial ingredients at the crucial time are lacking. One was a study by Rene Spitz of infants deprived of being touched at early stages of development. Basically, the infants withered physically and emotionally, and died very young.[5]

It may or may not have something to do with how I turned out myself but I know that my mother felt utterly inadequate to handle her firstborn baby (me). My father, who was nine years her senior and his ways being somewhat authoritarian, seemed to have taken over my care on specific instances. An interesting detail was that he had a Spartan philosophy concerning child rearing, a common approach in the Netherlands that had just been freed from the German invasion and domination. That meant that I was to be left alone in my crib, not taken up or hugged by anyone—just left there till the clock would show the next hour for me to be fed, all for fear that I would grow up as a weakling.

---

[5] Rene Spitz, Developmental Psychologist. The film *Psychogenic Disease in Infancy* (1952) shows the effects of emotional and maternal deprivation on the infant's development. http://www.youtube.com/watch?v=VvdOe10vrs4

We will take a look at the required environmental inputs related to the development of SoS further along in this chapter and the next; however, the conclusion here is that if children receive the required input for the development of a Natural SoS at the appropriate time, they can develop a Natural SoS. If these various inputs are not provided or are not provided at the appropriate time, these children's development cannot proceed normally, resulting in people with a warped SoS.

THE METAPHOR OF THE TREE

Plants and trees, because they are immobile, pretty much have to take whatever they get of the necessary environmental input. It is available in the right amounts and kinds at the right times or, if not, the developing organism has limited options for its attempt to get its needs met, and it grows crooked and ends up defective. For example, a seedling will grow in the direction of more adequate light, and it will put out roots in the direction of more water—even if these stretches and bends weaken the seedling (see Figure 3.3).

For human beings, the same laws are applicable. What they need is either available at the time it is required or it is not. If not, a person's growth is thwarted, and he or she becomes crooked in some way. Just like a tree, a human being will grow in the direction it perceives its needs are better met. Of course, people do not grow roots, but the formation of our brain, and its wiring, is stimulated in certain directions, even if this leads people away from their own innate abilities and characteristics. Children will bend over backward, psychologically and neurologically, to get what comes closest to the environmental input they need for development of a Natural SoS: to be acknowledged as a real person.

The roots of a tree are sometimes visible and therefore their degree of compensation for the young tree's deprivations can be observed and studied. Unfortunately, what happens in the brain of a person is an invisible process on the physical level.

To better visualize the compensations for lacks in input and lags in sequence that are initiated and executed in the human psyche and to see how that process brings about permanent changes in the structure of the brain, let us examine in more detail how it works for trees, all the while visualizing the human brain.

An infant experiencing deprivation, especially during a critical period of some aspect of its development, tries hard to get its needs met despite the circumstances because its very existence is at stake. As part of its survival

Figure 3.3: A tree making the best of its
circumstances while growing up

**Early Childhood
Survival Strategy**

*Infants and toddlers who
do not feel acknowledged
as separate (unique)
beings by their caregivers
subconsciously adopt
particular behaviors
that gain them approval
to fill in this unmet
need; this lays the
foundation for unhealthy
(Indirect) Motivation.*

strategies the human infant develops, by trial and error, a system to get its needs met—or get as close as possible to that. This behavior over time turns into a behavioral strategy: an **Early Childhood Survival Strategy** (ECCS; see Chapter 5).

The need to get feedback from the parent is most relevant in developing a SoS so that the child learns who and what he or she is. Without this, the developing person would have no way to comprehend any idea of Self. Comparing the way in which a tree forms to the way the human mind forms helps us to have a clearer mental picture of what happens in our psycho-emotional development as an infant and child when raised in specific input-deprived circumstances.

The branches of the tree represent the mental-emotional structures in our consciousness, or, more precisely, its physical manifestation as our brain's wiring. When a person learns something, or matures in some way, a neu-rological pathway is created in the brain that is either reinforced through repeated use, falls latent (when not used often), or gets overgrown and dis-appears (if not used again). For the sake of the comparison, I propose that the neurological pathways continuously developing in our brain, especially during infancy, be considered the physical manifestation of our mind, which in turn influences our entire psyche.

This description of brain processes is meant as a very simplistic approach for this highly specialized subject of brain wiring. I have chosen this image because it helps people recognize and accept certain growth deviations that might have happened in their own brain's wiring as they encountered obstacles or lacked essential nourishment for healthy psycho-emotional development as they were growing up.

So let us accept, for now, that there is a similarity between the growth and development of our brain's wiring, and thus with the development of our mind, with the way the shape of a tree forms. Just like us, it develops following its blueprint—nature—and its development is influenced by circumstances—nurture. (See the previous discussion in this chapter on nature versus nurture.) When there are a number of unfavorable circumstances, a person's develop-ment may become quite lopsided.

A seedling grows into a healthy, strong tree when all its conditions are favor-able (nurture) or even with less-favorable circumstances if it has very strong genes (nature). A seedling's natural inclination is to grow up straight, symmetrical, and as tall as it has the potential to be (see Figure 3.3). Sometimes a seedling finds obstructions on its pathway of growth: a building, a fence, other trees, or wires. When there are obstacles, its only way to develop is by bending to avoid them (see Figure 3.4). Changing its direction of growth permanently affects the shape of the trunk, making it not straight and tall but bent or crooked.

In some cases, this means that the roots grow horizontally and sideways instead of deeply into the soil. Some trees develop mostly to one side (see Figure 3.5). Their trunks may develop more branches on the side that receives a lot of sun and fewer on the shady side.

Continuous, strong winds often result in trees with branches and twigs on the leeward side only (see Figure 3.6).

Some trees are doomed to never live up to their proud potential of being straight and symmetrical, due to such outside influences. Roots, too, if unimpeded, grow naturally in certain directions so they can best balance the weight and shape of the tree (see Figure 3.7). A root may grow out of

Figure 3.4: . . . bending over (backward)
to avoid obstacles, this tree is making the
best of its circumstances while growing up

proportion in a certain direction compared to others, or if the tree is to avoid
an obstacle the root may be thwarted in its growth and a different one may
develop instead.

Now imagine the tree bending over backward to get its supply of nutrients that it cannot do without and how that affects the actual physical
body of the tree. That is exactly what happens in our brain as well. Imagine
that our brain's neurons (see Figure 3.8) are similar to the branches of a tree.
Specific brain wiring develops as we shift ourselves to fulfill unmet needs.
Some of that wiring inhibits the development of other neural pathways
and becomes dominant in areas in which it normally would not even exist.
What happens to the original blueprint of the person who would have fully
developed under better circumstances? Maybe some of you can relate to the

Figure 3.5: Some trees develop branches only on
one side . . .

question it evokes: Is that maybe what happened to me? I seem to be functioning far below the level of which I think I am capable.

Imagining the actual physical impact of what we went through also
sheds light on why it is so terribly hard for human beings to change a certain
behavior embedded from early on. I do not say it is impossible, but it takes all
your power to change. (This is discussed further in the chapter on restoring
your SoS; see Chapter 11.)

So the development of the human mind, it seems, can be compared
to the growth of a tree. By looking at all the different shapes and directions the trunk and branches of a tree shown clearly against a winter sky,
we might have more ease in imagining a visual representation of a comparable situation during the development of our own brain's wiring (our
entire psyche).

Figure 3.6: The trunk and branches of a crooked tree

Figure 3.7: Well-balanced development of the roots

Now would be a great time to explore by asking yourself some questions:

What were the obstacles that were in my way?

What was the climate like in which I grew up?

How did my inner brain-tree adjust to that?

What effect did that have on the shape and form of my mind and emotions?

How did that development influence the fullness of the unfolding of my
    potential and make me into the person I am at this very moment?

Draw how you imagine your own tree-mind grew. Obviously, there is no right or wrong way to do this. Just enjoy the process of creating this image of your own mental and emotional growth and development and enjoy whatever you might learn about yourself or whatever questions, impressions, and/or memories arise for you during the process.

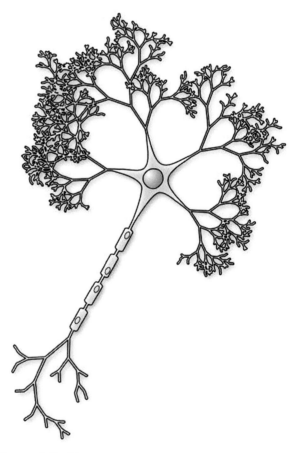

Figure 3.8: Neuron

Figure 3.9: If only our brain wiring was as visible as the branches of the trees in winter

Figure 3.10: Would your brain tree look like this?

Figure 3.11: Or would your brain tree look more like this?

Figure 3.12: Or maybe more like this?

LOOKING AHEAD

In this chapter, we compared the way branches of a tree are shaped with the development of the neurological pathways in our brain. We also discussed what happens to children's growth when they are deprived of essentials during childhood. In the next chapter, we will look at the most crucial element of our development: Mirroring.

4 | Mirroring: A Crucial Element

In the preceding chapter, we saw that in early childhood, many people are deprived of the environmental/interpersonal input necessary for the development of a clear, strong, healthy Natural Sense of Self (SoS). It almost seems as if that's what keeps the world from moving beyond the place it's in, with so many people affected by so many various types of ailments and dysfunctions. Not getting the necessary ingredients to develop a healthy Natural SoS is indeed a disaster for people's future lives because we need a healthy SoS to fully be able to be ourselves and for each one of us to develop into an independent, autonomous human being.

> Only when we have a healthy SoS can we fully be ourselves.
>
> Only when we can fully be ourselves can we function independently and interdependently!
>
> Only when we can interact on a not-needy basis can we effectively help make the world a better place.
>
> A healthy society consists of people who are psychologically independent so they can function interdependently and build community with others by assisting, supporting, and completing each other's lives and contributions.

So the fundamental difference between a healthy, normal or an unhealthy, abnormal SoS is the *right, or wrong, kind of input* during the critical period (infancy). Again: If the development of the awareness of being a separate and autonomous human being does not take place at the *right phase of a child's life*, the development of a healthy Natural SoS is forever prevented because the person does not have a concrete, or even a vague inner knowing, that "my life is about me."

As we have seen, a Natural SoS is crucial for healthy life functioning; it is the backbone of the healthy psyche. Its development depends on a certain kind of Mirroring input from the primary caregiver to the child, from whom the child learns how he or she is experienced by the other person, which translates into a sense of who he or she is as a human being.

Obviously, not every child gets the right Mirroring at the right time. What happens then? We could say that Plan B then comes in action. Plan B generates what this Method calls a Substitute Sense of Self (SSoS). This chapter describes how a SSoS develops, where it comes from, what it does, and how it feels. It describes the role of the parent or primary caregiver, the conclusions a child draws when its needs to build a healthy SoS are not met, and how these conclusions over time are internalized and identified with. This chapter indicates how to recognize a SSoS and how it differs from a healthy SoS. The chapter ends with a story to illustrate the deeper meaning of the nature of this predicament.

Mirroring is an unconscious feedback that parents, caregivers, or others provide to children in a specific crucial period of the child's development. It functions as a building block in the development of the child's SoS, and the way this process evolves is crucial to the development of his or her SoS.

MIRRORING FROM CAREGIVERS

As part of the developmental process, children must form a clear image of the fact that they are separate from their caregivers and others. Mirroring creates a nonverbal and gut-level perception, identification, and recognition of their Self. This self-image is not innate but initiated and reinforced by the way the child sees itself reflected in other people's behavior toward them. Because the primary caregiver is the person to whom children are most exposed, the mirror he or she presents is of major importance for the development of children's SoS. Based on the way in which the primary caregiver interacts with and relates to them, children make their initial conclusions about who and what they are. More specifically, from that reflection to the child of *what he or she means to the caregiver* or what impact his or her presence has on the caregiver's existence, a child deduces his or her function in the relationship.

This feedback, the mirrored image, is conveyed very subtly, and constantly, through gestures, tones of voice, what is said and what is not said, facial expressions, and actions done and actions not done. Rarely is it put into direct words, because adults are often unaware of being a mirror and conveying an image at all, let alone of what the nature is of the message they might want to

Mirroring

The subtle, mutually subconscious process by which the primary caregiver conveys to his or her child a sense of either being a means to fulfill the caregiver's emotional needs or being a "real" and unique person—a sense that the infant accepts as the truth of who it is.

give to their child. Interestingly enough, it is the degree to which the person (caregiver) who provides the mirror has a healthy or not-so-healthy Sense of Self that determines the healthiness of the Mirroring the child receives. As this factor plays a role in a child's life from birth on it crucially determines the foundation of its being and thus the quality of his or her life.

Now let us apply all this to the specific human need for the kind of interpersonal (environmental) input that enables the development of a Natural SoS.

IS MIRRORING ALWAYS ACCURATE AND NEUTRAL?

Most importantly, and ironically, the quality of this reflection depends on the healthiness or unhealthiness of caregivers' sense of themselves. Primary caregivers are not neutral mirrors, as real mirrors are. The way their child is experienced by them and the feedback they provide the child obviously depends greatly on who they are themselves and on what plays in their own lives as well.

Children, unable to distinguish between an accurate and a distorted reflection, subconsciously conclude that they "are" who this reflection says they are because they are not equipped to take into account whether the people doing the reflecting are caught up in themselves or have room and energy for other beings in their lives. The reflection is accurate about who the child is, as far as the child can tell. It is only much later that, upon investigation, we can learn the truth about what happened back then when we were little. Unfortunately, by then it requires a lot of persistency and hard work to change what has become hardwired in our brain.

The child who receives the "reflection" that it is a distinct unique human being with a right to its own nature, needs, and desires develops a healthy, natural sense of being/having a self.

A number of important caregiver behaviors can facilitate the development of a Natural SoS:

> *Acknowledgment of the child:* The child is acknowledged by the caregiver as a baby, toddler, and later, as a young child, through his or her listening and *actually hearing* what the child has to say, through his or her watching *and actually seeing* the child. At all times it is important to avoid using the child for—or directing the child to function as—an adaption of the caregiver's own emotional needs. In such using and directing, the specific purposes can vary, but the common denominator is that whatever is done (supposedly) "for" the

child is only serving the parent/caregiver and is not truly done for the benefit of the child. (Note: Indirect Motivation!)

Self-expression: The children are given a voice to express themselves as soon as they are able to have something to say—as opposed to being dealt with as objects that only have to comply with the family rules or the rules of the house. When house rules are part of a caregiver's hold over a child, they become a life-or-death matter for the child, oftentimes seeming to be of higher priority than the actual well-being or feelings of the child. This may lead to a strong sense of rebellion against authority, which can become a prominent theme in a person's life that does not serve him or her. ("He has a chip on his shoulder.")

Personal opinions: Children are encouraged to form their own opinions, tastes, and preferences at an appropriate age, as opposed to being blamed for having any personal opinions, tastes, or preferences, let alone ones that differ from their parents' or caregivers'.

Drawing out potential: Ideally, a parent or caregiver has an eye and an ear for the very essence of the child. The ideal parent considers raising and educating a child to be the task of "drawing out" of the young child his or her potential and helping him or her develop as an independent human being. This is as opposed to the parents/caregivers harping to whatever about the child pleases them, which is usually geared to either molding them into a copy or an extension of themselves or geared to having their child compensate for their own lacks.

"Being there": Parents acknowledge their children's presence by being totally there for them. This means that they are focused on their children and their mind is not elsewhere. It means they engage actively and fully in the interaction with their children in whatever is undertaken together. They wholeheartedly provide for their multitude of needs and mirror them accurately and compassionately.

Bending: Hinting at the earlier comparison of the growth and formation processes of trees we can paint the picture, literally and metaphorically, of parents bending lovingly over their offspring, making sure that the little ones grow psychologically "straight" (metaphorically speaking), with a healthy Sense of Self, with deep roots. That way they have a chance to branch out naturally and develop a rich fullness that is a tribute to life itself, and which will make the children, when grown, able and eager to express themselves without under-mining doubts and fears. (See the metaphor of a tree in Chapter 3.)

For children, being regarded by their caregiver as real, independent, au-tonomous beings with the right to exist as who they are, is the feedback, as previously described, that enables them to build a healthy Sense of Self. So the ability to develop that awareness and sensation of "being real, being like other people" can be promoted (or hindered) from birth by a person who is continuously around and functions as a primary caregiver.

You now have a good idea about what kind of parental behavior enables the natural flow of development toward instilling in their offspring a sense of "being a Self" who is separate from other beings—in other words, what kind of parental behavior results in a healthy and Natural SoS in their children.

THE DISTORTED MIRROR

As we saw in Chapter 2, infants have a normal, innate need to be acknowledged—to be mirrored—as unique and distinct human beings by their primary caregiver so they can develop a normal SoS. When the caregiver is unable to do the right thing and effectively acknowledge their child or children because of their being too wrapped up in their own problems and emotional neediness, we might have a problem.

The mirror, which in general is a silent, nonverbal process in which the children see their reflection, seems to convey to the children a different mes-sage. What it should be is "You are a being who has every right to exist and grow up independently of and equal to anyone else." But what the message can end up being is "You are allowed to be and to exist insofar as you please me and meet my needs. Who and what you are and that you exist in the first place is first and foremost dependent on this conditional relationship with me. You exist only insofar as I allow you to, which is when you do what I want you to do, or when you are the way I want you to be." In the latter case, children are taught that their existence depends on conditions the caregiver imposes on them as necessary to fulfill before the caregiver counts them as real, existing persons who matter (to him or her).

Like a funhouse mirror, the message can create a **Distorted Mirror** through which the children inevitably and naturally conclude that they are the reflection they receive from the mirror. Especially from infancy until the tender age of perhaps 14, we all expect mirrors to be accurate—especially as it comes from the parent—not funhouse distortions, right?

Distorted Mirror

The process by which the primary caregiver is unable to effectively acknowledge their child or children as he or she is too wrapped up in his/her own problems and emotional neediness, and the child inevitably and naturally concludes that it IS the way it sees itself reflected by the caregiver.

But how parents/caregivers become Distorted Mirrors deserves more attention now.

Becoming a Distorted Mirror

The development of a SSoS results from having a parent/primary caregiver who is unable to provide the child with the building blocks of a healthy Natural SoS at the critical time in the sequence of development. Several causes can create such a condition. In this Method, though, the focus is on one particular reason: The parent is self-absorbed.

I do not believe caregivers behave in egoistic or egocentric ways because they are innately bad. Rather, they behave this way only because their own needs as children were not met! This is how the eternal cycle of abuse keeps going on, passing down from generation to generation. Self-absorbed people are probably always operating from a SSoS because of their own childhood deprivation of appropriate Mirroring from *their* parents.[6]

What the reason is for some people to be more prone to becoming a victim of this situation I really cannot say, other than indicating the bigger picture. Can it be their specific genetic makeup? Is it environmental? Both?

Self-absorbed people have an excessive and unhealthy focus on themselves and are unable to focus on others. They think of themselves as the center of the universe and believe that everything turns around them and is about them. Many if not all of the characteristics of self-absorbed people are subconscious, and not necessarily easily visible to others, especially their children. Here are a few of these characteristics:

- They do not recognize that others are the center of their own existence.
- They consider it a given that things happen or should happen to meet their needs, and not anybody else's.
- Other people are experienced as "unreal" and not as separate, autonomous human beings with their own rights, needs, and characteristics.
- They only acknowledge and approve of people, things, and situations if they are perceived as potentially good to serve (overtly or covertly) the person's own (unhealthy and subconsciously operating) psycho-emotional needs.
- Other people are allowed in their environment only as a means to their own ends.

---

[6] Research is needed to confirm this, but I would like to suggest that people, who depend on a SSoS, are self-absorbed people; it is a part of the unhealthy manner in which they function.

- Other individuals are objects to be manipulated for the self-absorbed person's purposes.

- On the surface, self-absorbed people can seem very generous, kind, or giving, but under the surface, the reality is quite different.

- They do not have genuine interest in other people's (their children's!) stories and experiences: interest can be faked, but there is always a Hidden Agenda. Anything that cannot be used for this agenda is ignored or rejected. In their opinion it would be best if it were not there at all.

- Any problem that arises from outside their self-absorbed world is experienced as a Hindrance or a nuisance. It is slayed the moment it emerges. Considering what the effects are of this behavior for other people (their children, their spouses) is not within their scope.

- They throw a temper tantrum when they feel out of control or things don't go according to their plan.

- When they are in the position to exert their power they live at the cost of those around them as they upset the atmosphere with their sudden onsets of anger. They make for a household where people have to tiptoe around them.

- Self-absorbed persons often blame others (their children, their spouse) if things go wrong or even when they haven't yet gone wrong. They often anticipate what could go wrong and act on those anticipations, causing great emotional upheaval.

All these characteristics arise, subconsciously, from fear, as you will see.

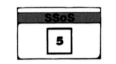

The Challenges of Being a Parent

The moment a person becomes a parent, a lot of attention and focus needs to go to the newborn. For a self-absorbed person, this is quite challenging and quite simply, hard or nearly impossible to do.

In the beginning, the baby is cute and the self-absorbed caregiver can handle it as he or she is often able **To Score** with the baby's cuteness for his or her unhealthy, subconscious emotional goals. However, as the child grows, its presence becomes more noticeable. The baby becomes more of a person, with its own many needs and demands. The growing child requires attention, other than the usual care. A self-absorbed parent is unable to allow or encourage the child's presence to grow, unable to focus on the reality of the child being his or her own person, equal in rights to the parent. This type of parent has

To Score

Being successful in using a Vehicle to improve on an Ego-Reference; a success that feels like gaining "points" toward the goal of getting parental approval, which results in the feel-good-about-Self as a Substitute Sense of Self.

a difficult time attending to the child and giving his or her energy, time, and good intentions. The parent's patience is short-lived because the process does not contribute to his or her own needs. All the caregiver wants is to focus on fulfilling his or her needs. Even if something is done seemingly "for the child," often a subconscious self-absorbed agenda exists. And no one can make the parent see this harmful agenda because his or her life is only about him or her; that's the parent's only concept of life. There is no love but self-preoccupation. But there is no self-love either, so how can this parent love his or her child?

Let me give you an example of such a (possible) Hidden Agenda from my own life. As a toddler and a young child, I frequently had ear infections. At some point, the mastoid bone was affected, and the doctor advised surgery to remove it. My father was opposed to the procedure, but my mother had the last say, so I was operated on. It was a nasty operation that had to be repeated a few times; I ended up having a big part of that bone behind my ear cut away. Looking back, it is debatable to me whether my having surgery was even meant for my own good. What it was supposed to do was to stop me from being sick all the time. I know that my mother had a hard time dealing with people being ill, including herself. I highly suspect that my well-being was not taken into account, as I have noticed it never really was.

Self-absorbed parents are unable to regard their children as anything but a pawn in the (subconsciously played) emotional games of their own lives. I call this "playing games" because their actions and world in fact have nothing to do with the reality of life in the world outside their small circle of awareness; the developmental needs of their children are part of that reality of life outside that circle.

Self-absorbed parents can never foster the development of a Natural SoS in their children because they put themselves continuously not only in the center of their own world but also in the center of other people's worlds while their child bends over backward in an attempt to get his or her need of acknowledgment as a being, as existing, met.

For a better overall understanding of the problems involved, I would like to refer back to the layers of the Self, as explained in Chapter 2. It is a graphical representation of the description of what can go wrong. The image shows how the children of self-absorbed parents will not develop a healthy layer of Self as a Conscious-Thought Form (Layer 3). A more detailed version of the image in clay (Figure 4.1) also shows how the Psycho-Emotional Self (the green layer) and also the Social Self (the blue layer) reflects the crippling of Layer 3. (See Chapter 2 for the layers of Self.)

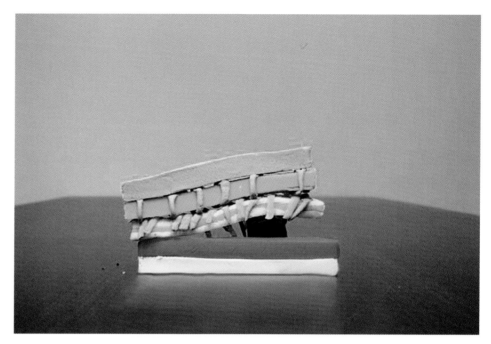

Figure 4.1: Layers of the SSoS

An Eternal Vicious Cycle

A parent who lacks a SoS and who is compulsively driven to fulfill his or her perceived survival conditions makes that his or her children have to facilitate the parent's Hidden Agenda—consequently there is hardly no room for their own input, whether that be wanting to have friends over for play, engaging in activities that the parent has no interest in, or being sick or demanding attention in any way.

These patterns of behavior are likely to develop into a vicious behavioral cycle that extends over generations. The parents are not able to focus on their child and acknowledge it as a truly existing human being with all the rights that come with it. They then raise their child in such a way that, when in the situation of being a parent themselves, they will be unable to pay attention to their own children. Again they are not free from dependencies on fulfilling the Ego-References of trying to be heard and seen themselves.

There is absolutely no bad intention involved here or even willful neglect. The whole Substitute Sense of Self–oriented System is kept in place by a compulsion that forces them to let these parents have their own needs prevail. This mind-set automatically leads (again) to the lack of acknowledgment of their children.

LOOKING AHEAD

In this chapter, we discussed Mirroring: the way our parents see, experience, and relate to us functions as a mirror to the child to base its self-image on. The Mirroring happens on a subconscious level but it affects the development of a Natural Sense of Self. In the next chapter, we will address the experience of children whose mirrors reflect a distorted image and we will shed a light on the coping mechanism these children subconsciously put in place.

5 | Approval, Fear, the Black Hole, and Annihilation

Black Hole

Metaphor for a subconsciously experienced, intolerably terrifying "invisibility"—as a "real person"—which, as a force of nature, sucks in behavior and motives to fill itself.

Annihilation

A strong perception of being overlooked, not being seen and heard, not being taken into account, not having any impact in one's environment.

WHEN A PARENT OR CAREGIVER IS UNABLE TO ACKNOWLEDGE THEIR CHILD AS a "real" autonomously existing person that parent fails to provide the foundation on which their child can build a healthy Sense of Self. The child experiences the resulting lack of Sense of Self, on a deep, primordial level of consciousness, as a painful void.

I refer to this void as a **Black Hole**. This void generates a gigantic power that sucks in any positive outcome of an achievement or behavior of the child that would have led to approval, which then is experienced as a Substitute Sense of Self (SSoS). Any situation that goes well in the person's life and that would gain the caregiver's explicit approval is used to fill the void of this Black Hole to create, if you will, a sort of balance in the system. At the same time though failure fear is a steady companion of this success as it is success not for the sake of itself, but for the sake of gaining a SSoS.

To get a full understanding of the rest of the developmental process, and the power of the unhealthy motivations that develop from this type of (Distorted) Mirroring, we need to take a close look at the child's inner experience of the Black Hole, an experience this Method calls "Annihilation." We also need to take into account and study the fear developed from having experienced this void, **Fear of Annihilation**.

EXPERIENCING ANNIHILATION

In this Method, the term **Annihilation** is an inner, usually not consciously defined, perception of feeling as if one is alive but does not exist to others. It comes down to feeling like a person without a voice or a face as a unique individual, and comes from not being acknowledged as an independent, potentially autonomous being. The person, sensing that he or she is not being seen, heard, or taken into account, feels invisible, or is reduced to a quasi-nonexistence.

The experience of Annihilation is not so much that of existing and then not existing because of dying physically. The ultimate terror of Annihilation arises from the gut-level experience of feeling invisible even though one is physically present—present as a body but not addressed and taken in by the community. It is as if a person's authentic essence/spirit is not able or allowed to come through to manifest itself in his or her environment.

Fear of Annihilation

Terror in anticipation of the experience of being unheard by, and invisible to, others.

Experiencing Annihilation is not recognized as such by the person at all; it merely manifests as a rising awareness of being "off" in some way, and as a result of being discounted, it comes down to a deep feeling of being rejected, of being denied access to the world of the others.

To label this complex condition, the term *Annihilation* is used, rather than death or nonexistence, for two reasons.

First, there always are certain fundamental layers in the Self that do develop or exist in any kind of childhood environment, no matter how starved for acknowledgment the child is. Thus, the child can be thought of as half-alive.

Second, because whatever sense of selfhood the child subconsciously manages to achieve is always disappearing along with the approval/good vibes that (unhealthy, Substitute) SoS depends on. The physical body dies only once. Annihilation, as described here, happens over and over again. By comparison, one could say that death is benign. The subconscious sense of not existing is experienced as terror. As we shall see, the motivation to avoid the experience of Annihilation is compelling.

Ideally the relationship between the infant and the parent(s) or primary caregiver(s) feeds the infant's sense of being acknowledged as someone existing as a separate person. This then contributes to the development of a healthy Natural SoS. This sense of being a Self is the opposite of the experience of Annihilation. If an infant's primary caregiver fails to reflect to the infant: "I see you as a being independent of me, no matter what you do or do not do," then a condition is created for a warped SoS.

What happens if a child's (person's) own needs and nature are NOT taken into account by others? The child may conclude it isn't good enough. And as it is, in that process, also being overlooked and ignored, it makes the child feel like being a ghost with a body—bodily alive but in the living hell of being invisible to everyone. An eerie suspicion of "I am not real. I have no real empowerment" may emerge in the child's or later the adult's mind. This vague uncertainty plus the strategies the child develops to try to overcome it or compensate for this feeling may stay with him or her for the whole of his or her adult life and greatly determine its quality.

I remember being present with certain groups of people and trying to mingle. I convinced myself it was normal to be overlooked and not addressed. I felt so unimportant to others, yet inside I knew I was worth a lot. I had no sense of when to come into a conversation or when to speak up in a group. I wasn't in touch with the part of your being that generates impulses and that, if you trust it, makes those decisions for you. If you have no SoS, there is no way you can rely on your intuition as you are not aligned with it.

FEARING ANNIHILATION

Fear of the experience of Annihilation arises in young children—and then over and over again while growing up and as an adult as well, lifelong—and stems from the circumstance of not being heard and seen in their essence and not being acknowledged as independent and autonomous persons. This circumstance, which once was a reality for them, is never recognized or confirmed, though. When a person (a parent) *is* with the child, feeds it, and gives it clothes, it looks like he or she cares for the child. In other words, it isn't really visible to an outsider, nor is it within the ability of a child to recognize that a parent merely tolerates the child and lets him or her come closer when the child complies behaviorally to the parent's wishes. That doesn't mean that this situation is less real, though.

I remember a situation in which, as a 12-year-old, I had an accident with my bicycle. I somehow had lost my balance and landed with my ribcage on one of the handlebars. I was in pain, but I do not remember a word of comfort from my caregiver and the trip to the doctor's office lives in my memory as a nuisance to my caregiver: "How could you do that to me?," was the non-verbal message. I don't think she really saw me.

It is hard for the grown person who has been in that situation to believe in him- or herself. There is always this uncanny sense that something is at stake: Annihilation. Now this Fear of Annihilation that lingers in one's life is the living proof of the defects in the relationship between caregiver and child. It is hard to put the finger on it later in life though, as this relationship is now only a memory.

It is the fear of not being visible as a Being, despite being bodily present, to others. The never-articulated subconscious belief is "I am unable to participate in life because nobody sees or hears me." Obviously, this leads to feelings of inadequacy and deep inferiority, and thus Annihilation becomes a constant threat and a constant reality. Fearing it, and the attempt to prevent the disappearance of anything remotely resembling a SoS, the SSoS becomes a dominant motive in life.

This fear, the seed for compulsions and addictions later in life, can be so intolerably terrifying and painful that it rarely reaches conscious awareness; most people who have it experience some milder version and do not realize what they are really afraid of!

This fear is also a profound motive to gain and keep the caregiver's real or virtual approval, which allows the "Feeling-good-about-Self" (FgaS) state to soothe the state of mind.

Fear of Annihilation in a person's psyche generates a powerful force that generates compulsions and addictions in desperate attempts to avoid experiencing it. Imagine how it would be if your *only experience of truly existing* were while you felt good about yourself?

Thus, the Fear of Annihilation is the fountainhead for many other fears, for example, fear of not being able to access the aforementioned state of FgaS that then functions as a SSoS. In short, the Fear of Annihilation is comparable to—and maybe even worse than—the fear of death.

In a person with certain early-childhood deprivations, fearing Annihilation never stops; it keeps the person in suspense (and in a "trance") for his or her whole life. It is a constant threat and a constant albeit unrecognized reality. The attempt to prevent Annihilation becomes—with the power of a force of nature—a dominant yet completely subconscious operating motive in life, and it generates an entire system of unhealthy, detrimental psycho-emotional habits, beliefs, needs, desires, compulsions, addictions, and motives. This system enslaves us until, and unless, we become aware of it.

FEARING THE FEAR OF ANNIHILATION

A person tries to avoid the subconscious but terrifying experience of Annihilation, and that forms the root incentive for the development of the SSoS-oriented System (for more on this see, page 56). Avoiding a feeling of Annihilation is the prime motive for engaging in interpreting approval as a substitute way of sensing the Self. The procedure is like a battle of life and death that explains why rage, sometimes murderous rage, can be the result when that drive is thwarted.

Insight in this type of mind-set may also shed a light on the inclination of people to commit suicide: It means that they are at their wits' end, that they are feeling profoundly inadequate to perform following the requirements of their Ego-References. Depression lurks when people find themselves in situations in which they perceive there is no way they will ever achieve their Hidden Goal. Reaching that Hidden Goal is their one and only purpose in life. So what is left for them if the path to reaching that goal ceases to exist due to changing circumstances, for example? This desperation is so strong that, even the conscious decision to stop living for that goal because we have gained enough insight in our inner workings to accept our predicament any longer, can induce depression or desperation.

Another commonly misunderstood symptom of the Fear of Annihilation is insomnia. Anxiety about living up to the conditions we set for ourselves and about functioning well and satisfying our Ego-References the next day literally creates more anxiety—and that keeps us from sleeping. Exhausted, we can't function well enough to "earn" our SSoS.

As time goes by the unhealthy SSoS-oriented System develops. Now another layer is added to this Fear of Annihilation. It is fear of experiencing the Fear of Annihilation. The dramatic part here is that the person does *not* fear a loss of well-being, as he or she is not even in touch with his or her own quality of life. But the Fear of Annihilation that is felt with and through its accompanying symptoms (insomnia, migraines, among others), is experienced as a huge threat to reaching the much-desired state of FgaS (i.e., SSoS). The person enters into a vicious downward cycle that is hard to escape.

When fearing the Fear of Annihilation, people's need to function in such a way that their SSoS can be satisfied intensifies greatly and adds even more pressure to how they perform. Accompanying this stressful state is a set of motives and behaviors specifically aimed at avoiding and preventing even getting near the primordial fear. A mere whiff of the potential emergence of that fear into conscious awareness evokes fear of experiencing it, and all emergency systems kick into gear to prevent increasing the Fear of Annihilation. This includes, but is not limited to, people's need to exert total control of their own feelings and behavior, their environment, and their circumstances as well as of others' feelings and behavior. When people fear their own behavior and their very own emotions because they might clash with an Ego-Reference-imposed behavior, emotions skyrocket and are hard to contain. Getting those emotions and the need to express them is absolutely against the requirements of the Ego-Reference. So here the person is on a downward spiral and is bound to crash.

APPROVAL AND ACKNOWLEDGMENT: AN UNFORTUNATE MIX-UP

What in fact seems to work best to reduce the Fear of Annihilation is approval. In a healthy parent–child relationship, approval means simply that the parent appreciates what the child has done (or has not done) and this approval does not affect any existential layer in the child. For the child/adult with a lack of Sense of Self, approval stands for much more.

Getting or not getting approval through achieving the desired outcome of the Ego-References is tied directly to a sense of feeling allowed to be or not. Having done well enough to deserve the much-desired approval allows the child into the Castle of Enmeshment (see Castle of Enmeshment, page 97, and Enmeshment). This is the moment where we have to become aware of the mix-up between the much-desired approval and the ultimate underlying issue: lack of acknowledgment. The child's mind, though, understandably, has confused the one with the other. For the reader, it is of crucial importance to be aware of this distinction between approval and acknowledgment.

So what is taken for acknowledgment by the child is simply the parent's approval that is based on his or her own (self-absorbed) criteria, but it touches the child on an existential level. This fundamental but fatal misunderstanding takes place over and over again: For the child, getting or not getting the parent's (narcissistically oriented) approval determines the difference in its experience of being alive or being annihilated. It means the child/adult is being seen and heard and temporarily experiences a right of existence.

Now we have a clearer view on the confusion that exists in a child's perception from since it was little. The relief from the terror of the Black Hole by means of getting approval does not give children/adults what they actually need: being related to as separate and autonomous human beings. All they are getting is what we might call positive vibes, or approval, from a Distorted Mirror—"You are OK because you are pleasing me right now"—rather than a healthy mirror of who they are—"You are [always] OK because of the mere fact that you exist. Sometimes you might do something right and sometimes you do something wrong but that doesn't reflect on your being allowed to be." Another crucial difference between approval and acknowledgment is that approval, through its temporal and conditional nature, is fleeting.

So despite this approval the Black Hole and the terror associated with it still exist. When the child discovers it can evoke approval and thus experience feeling good about itself temporarily, the Fear of Annihilation morphs into fear of losing this feel-good state. This is why people develop the compulsion of continuously working. It is about FgaS (as a SSoS) at the end of the day. This need to feel good about one's Self is ultimately rooted in *the lack of acknowledgment* of the child as a unique and definite human being, with a right to be for the mere reason that it already is that *no approval* can ever undo. It is just too sad that a child is not equipped to identify the distinction between the two.

As long as he lived, my brother had this hope that one day he and my father would go for a drink in the pub, together. My father though didn't recognize my brother's deep need of acknowledgment as a valued son and just didn't bother for 90 years. I still wonder how easy that relationship could have been going in a different direction. But then, if you do not recognize it because you are emotionally "not available" as a person, anything can happen. It was one cause of my brother's early death.

BECOMING HOOKED ON GETTING APPROVAL

Getting approval and being pleased by it, as a child or even as an adult is one thing, but how do we get addicted to getting approval? How does approval become the one and only thing that we live for? Below, you will find a potential order of things that take place for this to happen. Keep in mind that this process goes on in the life of a growing person and takes a good many years to develop.

First, there is the lack of acknowledgment for the toddler or young child that instigates the involvement of creativity in order to get the unmet needs met in another way.

Second, there is the perceived sensation of the child of being or having been at fault and having been the one that caused the missed opportunities to get what it needs: acknowledgment. ("If I would have been different I would have gotten what I needed, I would have been acknowledged by my caregiver. No doubt in my mind that she is there for me; she cares for me like all caregivers do for their children.")

Third, there is the relief of the Fear of Annihilation obtained by choosing behaviors that by trial and error have resulted for the child in reducing the terror. This seemingly unimportant process has a dramatic and powerful spin-off, and we can see a few things happening.

- Children feel *compelled* to do whatever the trial and error has revealed they can do to bring this relief.

- Because these actions provide relief from the Fear of Annihilation, children will *repeat* these actions continuously because the respite they provide is only temporary.

- As the outcome of their attempt to "better themselves" is neurotic, it is sabotaged continuously or thwarted in ways that are hard to pin down, but the children/young adults/adults now *try harder*. Because of the outcomes of their attempts to do the thing that would lead to approval are almost never reached (also because they are fictional!), the person's belief of "being at fault" is reinforced continuously.

  The need to try harder increases over time, and the desired result seems to recede like a slowly disappearing horizon.

- This pattern of trial–error–connection–conclusion early in life leads to the Early Childhood Survival Strategy and ultimately to the ego-references. It is repeated over and over, day in and day out. The conclusions drawn are formed and strengthened. A child's behavior becomes set in these ways. Ultimately, the person doesn't know any better because he or she has these habits, which were subconscious in the first place. But the initial goal stays at work as the ultimate motivator: children's Hidden Goal—acknowledgment by the parent by way of getting approval.

To reiterate, if children receive true acknowledgment from their caregiver, their Natural SoS will develop. If they experience a deficiency in receiving approval, though, their SoS will not develop, leading them to becoming governed by a SSoS.

Erica's aunt was highly flattered by the attention of a neighbor who was a good improviser on the piano. She flirted with him and seemed all eyes for him. Erica decided to study music but was banished from the piano every time she practiced in the living room. She was surprised that her music skills didn't have the same effect on her aunt as those of the neighbor. "Why doesn't she give me the same attention?" she wondered, and practiced harder.

All of this is the effect of the child's attempts to get its needs met, in some way or other, starting close to the moment of the missed developmental window or critical period of opportunity but, if not detected, lasting throughout life. An eternal need to repair the damage done seems to be the person's fate and becomes the only goal in life, and it never dawns on the person that he or she is skipping his or her own life altogether.

Substitute Sense of Self–oriented System

The entire subconscious complex of needs, behaviors, motives, habits, beliefs, goals, and fears whose only objective is to generate achievement-based approval, and which functions as an unhealthy base for being.

THE EARLY CHILDHOOD SURVIVAL STRATEGY (ECSS)

Once a child has drawn the conclusion that certain things have to be done or avoided in order to get its need for approval (acknowledgment) met, a piece of the unhealthy substitute way of sensing the Self develops. This specific way of functioning of the psyche is ultimately the fountainhead for the **SSoS-oriented System**.

Over time, the SSoS-oriented behavior becomes ingrained in a child's psycho-emotional makeup, influencing many if not most of his or her motives, choices, preferences, decisions, desires, feelings, beliefs, needs, and wants for life. The influence of the (fictional) perception that something crucial is at stake (the SSoS) is highly detrimental to his or her quality of life, because the desire to achieve approval overrules, so to speak, any authentic inclination, which is then abandoned and never comes to fruition. Here starts the drama of the person essentially skipping his or her own life.

The story begins with children desperately in need of a direct relationship with their caregiver. Then, when they are unable to be seen and heard by their caregiver, they try to get that need met in an alternate way: through getting approval that then makes them feel good about Self, which functions as a SSoS. The way they try to earn that approval is by meeting certain conditions preferred by the caregiver (e.g., "be mellow," "be nice," "don't make trouble"). It becomes these children's deepest desire to get the good vibes from the caregiver in person. In a later stage, this "feeling-satisfied-to-have-complied-with-the-conditions" state has gradually crystallized and has become the experience (sensing) of a (Substitute) Self. Still later, as the child grows up, lives somewhere else, and when ultimately the parent dies the degree of success in fulfilling the conditions itself becomes the degree to which people experience (sense) their (Substitute) Self.

Virtual, Internalized Parental Voice (VIPV)

The often-repeated verbal and non-verbal messages through which parents talk to their children becomes (almost) hardwired in the child's mind so that it is perceived as an unquestionable truth (about and) by the child.

THE **VIRTUAL, INTERNALIZED PARENTAL VOICE (VIPV)**

So the good vibes of the caregiver, when no longer available, are not even directly necessary anymore. The now-grown children judge themselves by their caregiver's criteria, which they take on as their own. This approval from the virtual parent, also called the internalized parent, includes criteria that were used by the now-long-gone parent. They use these internalized parental judgments as criteria to anchor themselves in their lives through the FgaS state that then constitutes a SSoS for them.

To include the presence of another voice other than your own in your Self may sound strange or even far-fetched. And truly, it took me quite a while to discover this aspect, but when looking into myself more deeply, I felt as if my parent was still present through my own voice, which really wasn't my own voice. The voice that was supposedly mine presented criteria copied from my parent, not generated by myself.

Early Childhood Survival Strategy

Infants and toddlers who do not feel acknowledged as separate (unique) beings by their caregivers subconsciously adopt particular behaviors that gain them approval to fill in this unmet need; this lays the foundation for unhealthy (Indirect) Motivation.

Babies, toddlers, and young children, living with a lack of input to develop a healthy SoS, instead will develop their **Early Childhood Survival Strategy (ECSS)** based on what they observe their caregivers like best. In that process they become totally dependent on their caregiver's judgment for the degree to which they should feel good about themselves, which then gives them some semblance of experiencing a selfhood. This is just how life is for them. When later in life their caregiver is no longer around, they can make themselves feel good by working hard to fulfill the conditions or expectations that have brought them approval in the past. We now know that these motivators are nothing but (a) the now virtual, internalized judgments of our caregiver or (b) our own reactions to our upbringing (for more information about this, see the information on reactionary Ego-References on page 90).

THE "FEELING-GOOD-ABOUT-SELF" STATE

Is "Feeling-good-about-Self" (FgaS) a State, a Thought or a Feeling?

In traditional psychology, thoughts are not to be confused with feelings. I learned this when going over the Sense of Self Method with Dr. Hal Dibner.[7] The more I thought about that, the clearer it became to me how the **"Feel-good-about-Self" state** was actually more a *thinking* good about one's Self. It is basically a positive self-judgment that, based on the SSoS-oriented System criteria, is taken for feeling (sensing) the Self.

"Feel-good-about-Self" (FgaS) State

A fear-based emotional state (or thought) gained from accomplishing what leads to approval from the parent, and which serves as a temporary and unhealthy substitute for a sense of being a "real" person.

Over time during childhood, this feeling or state of judging oneself based on the fulfillment of certain conditions becomes a Substitute (unnatural, unhealthy) way of Sensing the Self. This state of judging oneself to have complied with the (self-)imposed conditions, and therefore being OK, functions as the ultimate goal in life and leads to compulsive behavior.

For those of us with a Substitute Sense of Self, life consists of mere moments of "Feeling-good-about-ourSelves," like puddle jumping for children

---

[7] Dr. Hal Dibner Ph.D. (psychologist, Stamford, CT)

playing in the street, the dry pavement parts being the FgaS moments. The puddles need to be seen as the lapses of time spent on working hard to get the required positive outcomes and during which no Self is experienced. There is just an identification with the task at hand. Experiencing their FgaS state is their only reference to a Self as it is their only way to avoid feeling annihilated. Because of this, they perceive reaching this state as a matter of life or death. Because this state results from actions or achievements that produce approval, they cannot stop trying to get the best-possible version of their action or achievement. This leads to "over" doing actions and achievements: They overpractice, overachieve, overcare, and so on.

In other words, a FgaS state is a (false) positive emotion (judgment) that has become the key compensation in avoiding the experience of Annihilation. It becomes what this Method regards as an unhealthy, surrogate way to get in touch with and refer to what is perceived as Self. Experiencing this feeling state, based on real or virtual parental approval, is the Hidden Goal throughout the life of a person with a lack of a healthy SoS.

The Role of the "Feel-good-about-Self" State in the SSoS-oriented System

The FgaS state plays a crucial role in the structure of the psyche of a human being who has a Substitute Sense of Self. When I first set out to identify the importance it played in my life, I was still far from seeing the whole of this Method. I was not even aware that the only "feelings" I experienced were those related to my Hidden Goal and my SSoS-oriented System. The only feelings I was capable of were based on anxiety of not being able and/or in a position to make my Hidden Goal come true: being acknowledged as a valuable person in my mother's/parent's life and thereby getting a "virtual backbone." I experienced anger and desperation about possibly being thwarted or disabled in this process and I experienced fear that the FgaS state was always disappearing too fast.

These emotions were so violent and dominating that there was no room for anything that "stirs the heart"; no frequency was available on which this could occur. I always lived with the vague impression that something squashed my true (natural) range of feelings—that that something continuously squeezed out of my heart all the juices so I could not *really* feel something.

I thought that "Feeling-good-about-mySelf," which only happened when I fulfilled the conditions, was an exception, that it was really a feeling. Even working on fulfilling the conditions gave me an experience that simulated the FgaS state by anticipating it. So I was only relatively at ease when actively working on these conditions (Ego-References). Anything else that needed to be done or even anything else that was meant to be fun was experienced as anxiety provoking and interfering with my actual goal.

At the time I came up with the term *"Feeling-good-about-Self,"* I did not know that the FgaS state was actually more of a thought than a feeling. The sensation I experienced in this state was not clearly definable as a state of excitement or happiness. I would much rather describe it as a state of relative calm in the absence of stress and anxiety.

In my earlier-mentioned discussion with Dr. Hal Dibner, he pointed out to me that I must make sure not to confound thoughts with feelings. Looking into this comment, I learned that it is a common mistake people make when they haven't been trained to distinguish one from the other. Or—and this was quite exciting for me to discover because it ties into the insight I had long after coming up with the term *"Feeling-good-about-Self"*—"when they do not really experience feelings in the normal and healthy way."

So it turned out that, in my need to give structure to my psyche, I mistook a thought about myself for a feeling. I labeled experiencing a SSoS as "Feeling-good-about-myself." But, in truth, the FgaS state really is nothing more than a "thinking well about Self." When I comply and/or live up to my expectations, I validate myself, deem myself OK, and "allowed to be."

The FgaS state is, as has been said, crucial. But the term itself already indicates the problem and points to the solution (in hindsight, of course): FgaS implies a judgment about Self. A judgment about Self suggests a disconnect from, or a stepping out of, the Self in order to look at it. Some people have a healthy ability, a mark of maturity, to look at their Self and to self-evaluate. However, for me, judging myself was a permanent situation. It was an unhealthy disconnect from myself.

The moments in which I did not consciously or subconsciously engage in self-evaluation were rare. It is one reason why I am highly uncomfortable with receiving a compliment. Hearing someone say that I did something well turns into a quick FgaS but is immediately followed by anxiety. It is as if I already fear I cannot keep that standard going and I will lose my just-gained SSoS.

People with a lack of SoS, who are dependent on a SSoS for experiencing their Self, continuously monitor themselves. They perceive that their right to exist depends on the outcome of their actions or behavior, on their achievements in fulfilling these conditions. They need to continuously think *about* their Self to validate their performance, in the light of their hidden

Quality-of-Life level

A normal (healthy) degree of emotional reaction that is in sync with the degree of intensity of the actual effect on one's life and that is an indication of a healthy Sense of Self, as distinguished from emotions that strike down to the level of a person's sense of existence as a Self because the person is dependent on a Substitute Sense of Self for his or her self-experience.

agenda and ultimate goal. That way of relating to yourself is the most *indirect* connection to the Self that I can imagine. This indirect connection to the Self that *is* exactly the problem that the person needs to be healed from.

Therefore, the conclusion of my SoS Method, and the ultimate tool for healing, is to learn to *cut out* the element that causes the distancing of a person with the Self, to remove the interfering processes that create the indirectness in our relationship with things and with others. To that purpose, we need to cultivate an unshakable awareness that our "being present" is unconditional. We have to free ourselves from the obsessive need to have a feeling, a thought, or a judgment "about" our Self. We need to become convinced that we do not have to meet certain criteria. "I am OK as I am" is what we need to be able to identify with at all times.

Of course, that doesn't mean that you cannot or should not improve yourself. It means that those improvements are not having an impact on you at an existential level: With or without the improvements, you have the right to be. You can work on improvements because they bring you a sense of satisfaction or perhaps an improvement in your quality of life. You want those improvements because *you* want them but your life (Annihilation) does not depend on them. Those improvements are on, what we call in this Method, the **Quality-of-Life level**.

Real Feelings

Clearing up the roadblocks of the dependency on a SSoS on the path to truly sensing our Self, the experiencing of real *feelings* opens up to us. Real feelings are there for the sake of themselves. There is no validation or judgment involved. No longer will there be the fear and upset about reaching our Hidden Goal. Our caregiver's approval that used to be the only guiding emotions we knew loses its grip on us. The stone that squashed the juices out of our hearts is lifted. From now on, we develop a sensitivity to more-subtle feelings as a reaction of ourselves to what happens in the present, such as happiness that is triggered by a situation or an event or even joy for no reason.

The Ultimate Addictive Goal

A child who fails to develop a healthy SoS needs the caregiver's approval ever so badly. It is its only way to experience the FgaS state as a SSoS. To the outside world, a child might seem to be greatly cherished and cared for when, in reality, the primary caregiver fails to mirror seeing him or her as a separate being. Alone with the parent, when there are no outside onlookers, the child may be at the mercy of the caregiver's capriciousness and random behavior changes.

The moment the child thwarts the caregiver's purposes, the caregiver becomes angry, and the child senses rejection. Experiencing rejection causes feelings of humiliation and Fear of Annihilation.

It is important to understand that it is not the caregiver's negative behavior that causes the problem. If the child/young adult had developed a healthy Sense of Self, the caregiver's behavior would have no other impact on the child than a Quality-of-Life level disagreement. But because of the existing condition of a lack of SoS, the lack of approval is experienced as highly threatening as it potentially destroys the FgaS state and with it the SSoS, which makes it a life-threatening situation.

Let us say the parent is a musician and is dependent for her own SSoS on the quality of her performance. The child is there in her life, but not within her immediate scope of concern or even awareness. Even when not busy practicing, the first thing on her mind is, "How can I organize my household, my child, and myself so I can practice?" Remember the quality of her performance is a matter of life and death to her. In the meantime, the child is there physically, more an object, and the parent is barely aware that this little being has personal emotions, needs (other than food), and wants. It needs to be controlled and that happens by partly giving in, anticipating and ignoring its needs.

What would happen if the child has to interrupt her mother while she is practicing because she is hungry? When she interrupts her mother, her mother would likely scold her, telling her to be quiet and to wait until the practice period is over. Depending on the level of dependency or healthy SoS that has developed so far, the child might conclude that she does not have the right to exist at this moment, comply and sit quietly until her mother is finished. Or she might just accept that she will have to wait for a while but has already learned that there needs to be no doubt that her needs are going to be met. When the child learns that the impulses based on her own spontaneous desires are leading to rejection, the child is set up to be merely wanting to get that re-assuring pat on the head from her mother and the "compliment" of "You're such a good girl for not interrupting Mommy again." The approval the child is looking for fills the girl with a sense of feeling-good; by pleasing her mother, she need not fear the Black Hole/Annihilation that seemed to lurk earlier. Next time, the child will not interrupt the mother's practice and will skip her own needs for the sake of not having to suffer the Fear of Annihilation.

IN THE PRECEDING chapters, we have discussed what is required for a child to develop a normal, healthy SoS. The child needs to be related to by the primary caregiver as an independently existing unique human being, who has a right to be exactly who he or she is—as opposed to receiving sporadic signs of approval when the child is satisfying the needs of or pleasing a parent or caregiver.

Unfortunately, some (many?) parents are self-absorbed. They are unable to see and experience their child as an independent being with a right to his or her own uniqueness. Instead, they force their child to be or function as someone who is meant to help them reach their *own* (Hidden) Goal. Here we have come full circle, because it is highly likely that these are all goals on which, they subconsciously believe, their own Sense of Self depends.

LIFE IN A SSOS-ORIENTED WAY

Living in a SSoS-oriented way is a life based on fiction because it involves, although subconsciously, a fictional Self. People live the fiction that approval is a substitute for having a right to exist and that approval is necessary to have any experience of a SoS: "I won't exist unless I get approval." They live with this in order to experience anything resembling their right to exist.

This fiction feeds and yet arises from an unhealthy compulsive cycle. Because of their subconscious perception of having their existence prolonged and not annihilated, they need the continuous influx of feeling good about themselves while never being aware of the falseness of the construct.

The term *substitute* in this Method connotes that a SSoS is unhealthy. When a SSoS is at the steering wheel of our lives, when life is guided by and anchored in a SSoS, we go through life in an inauthentic way. We are not in touch with nor able to express the core of our own being, nor are we in touch with our repressed natural, authentic needs, feelings, motives, and desires.

Because the SSoS has taken the place of our never-developed Natural SoS, on a subconscious level we never feel that we are fully existing, which is a cause of ongoing anger and sadness. Because of this nonexistence of an **Authentic Self (Real Self),** feelings are blocked or dried up, which leads to the inability to experience joy or pleasure in normally pleasurable acts.

We are guided daily by what Vehicles will best help us fulfill our ego-references and achieve the FgaS state, we engage in activities that are not really of our own choosing. We may study music not for the joy of music, but to fulfill the desire of a caregiver, or we may wash dishes not because we enjoy a tidy kitchen, but to satisfy something else, perhaps our parents' insistence that the kitchen always be spotless.

So as you can see, in this process, although the body is not destroyed, eventually there is a near extinction of a person's spirit and psyche. The person

Real Self/Authentic Self

One's Self is experienced in the healthiest, most integrated way as an independent and autonomous Being; actions and awareness are based on living experience not contaminated by pathological motives. See Natural Sense of Self.

is always conforming to something external, never free to know and express his or her real nature; the real potential Self never develops, and once the SSoS-oriented System has settled in, it becomes his or her identity.

After years of constrained, contorted behavioral compulsions from their ECSS, children start to identify with the ego-referent behavior: The behavior is part and parcel of their SoS, which is a SSoS. Working to fulfill the conditions becomes not only their identity, but the only reason for living. Life for them becomes one big struggle to live up to all the (self-imposed) conditions to constantly renew this fictional identity. You can imagine how stressful this is, and what a sad situation, made even worse by the collateral damage of the side effects, sufferings, and problems.

When people do not notice this psycho-emotional pattern operating in them, they are bound to repeat it. These people are *not* in touch with themselves and are merely juggling as much as possible to experience the SSoS. The poignant drama here is that they are skipping their lives altogether and aren't growing and maturing. In addition, these people are not the masters of their own lives; they are slaves to the force of nature that is fulfilling the ego-references and achieving the FgaS emotional state. Life is not about them but about juggling the many. People caught in this SSoS-oriented life miss out on a life that is their "own." In a way, we could even say that their worst fear is true: They *don't really exist*! In the long run, that can cause many diseases and addictions, big and small.

Personally, I dare say that I must have missed out on quite a number of years of active presence while being the slave of my Ego-References.

In the grip of these imperious imperatives, the only thing we see about the world and people is our own point of view, which is all about fulfillment of our Ego-References. There is no room for another person to be truly seen or heard or acknowledged as a person by us. All people are merely pawns in the game of fulfilling Ego-References, which is no game but deadly serious. And through their actions and behaviors, others sense their inauthenticity because they are perceived subliminally as being uncaring, insincere, and distant—which, indeed, they are!

LOOKING AHEAD

Now that we know what a person with a SSoS is searching for—approval in lieu of true acknowledgment of our being—and what the motivating factor of this behavior is—Fear of Annihilation—it might be of interest to take a closer look at how this person's motivations are born. The following chapter will go into detail about direct and Indirect Motivation and the effect of it in a person's life.

6 | Motivation and the Substitute Sense of Self (SSoS)

INTRODUCTION AND OVERVIEW TO MOTIVATION

This Method states that understanding and purifying your motivation is the key to developing and maintaining health and a reasonable degree of happiness. In other words, understanding your motivation is a crucial first step if you want to tackle the task of healing yourself from the dependency on a Substitute Sense of Self (SSoS) and move toward Restoring your Sense of Self (SoS).

If you understand your motivations, you have a key to understanding yourself. Why do we do what we do, or avoid doing some things, often at all costs? If we understand what we are actually after, we come closer to seeing the whole picture of ourselves. By figuring out what our *ultimate* goals are, we get to know ourselves thoroughly and learn what we are all about. Self-knowledge is power! Knowing ourselves fully will enable us to make smart decisions that also benefit others.

Discovering Our Motivations Is Not Easy

In order to be useful, our discovering of our motivations, of this key, requires total honesty with ourselves. That might seem easy enough. It isn't. Finding out the truth about our deepest motivations is not obvious, nor simple or easy.

It is a challenge because we human beings are masters at denial. We might be ready to admit that we sometimes deceive others by pretending we are closer to our ideal self than we are. Try on the shocking admission that you might be going out of your way to deceive yourself, even for a whole lifetime! Yet that is what many of us are doing!

If you choose to move from deceiving yourself into the truth of who you actually are, then getting insight into your ultimate motivations is the way to go. This Method contains a great deal of practical information to help you dig down and get clear on your way to becoming healthier, happier, and more successful.

How Do Our Motivations Develop?

This Method presents a new and holistic approach to the understanding of the human condition and the potential changes that can be made. Our point of departure is that the body, mind, and emotions are continuously in communication with each other, which then results in the way each person is what he or she is in the world right now.

Here's one way to look at that. You are born with certain qualities and characteristics of who you are on a soul level. If there are few obstacles to your developing a healthy mind and body, then your life circumstances are allowing you to live up to that potential.

But what happens though if there are too many obstacles, and your development, as it could naturally go, is blocked and distorted by some life circumstances? (This actually happens to many of us.) Then nature seeks ways in which your body, mind, and emotions can compensate for the lack-of-growth and/or health-promoting life circumstances.

How does motivation develop differently in those two cases? In a healthy situation, we know motivations by describing the obvious reason why we do something. In the unhealthy situation, motivations become more convoluted. We develop complex patterns of subconscious motivations in nature's attempt to compensate for our thwarted natural development.

Labeling Motivation as Direct and Indirect

In this section, you will learn how unhealthy motivations develop. First please make sure you understand how a healthy, Natural SoS develops (see Chapter 3). We see how a child's motivation is formed by its circumstances and environment. Based on that understanding we will discover that motivations can be divided into direct (healthy) and indirect (unhealthy, the result of thwarted development), and you will learn how this comes in turn from and contributes to a healthy or unhealthy SoS. When you will be able to see the connection between a healthy NatSoS and Direct Motivation and how Indirect Motivation points to a SSoS you are on your way to healing!

Looking at indirect (unhealthy) motivation through a magnifying glass will require some new names for things we spot while looking so closely. Some of those terms include: *Ego-References, Vehicles, Hidden Agendas,* and *Hidden Goals.* You'll come to understand more about the essence of human motivation in general and about some specific concepts that are closely related to motivation, such as Hindrances, rage, rewards, and body language, and about how the SSoS as *the ultimate goal of Indirect Motivation*.

Why bother to learn and understand such things? Because, in this Method, ailments such as depression and insomnia, and dysfunctions such as abuse and violence, can be a direct result of thwarted Indirect Motivation.

WHAT IS MOTIVATION?

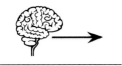

Motivation

In general, what creates an incentive or urge to do or avoid something. Motivation is the drive that determines behavior.

In this Method, **Motivation** is generated by the reasons or reasoning we have (consciously or subconsciously) for doing or avoiding doing things. Motivation is the force that drives us to act and the incentive for our behavior. It either refers to a reasoning or force that moves us to act and that is the incentive for our behavior toward a goal that is experienced as desired and that aims at satisfaction ("fun"). But the drive to do or not do something can also be much stronger and reflect our needs or perceived needs for survival ("need"). In this Method, motivation refers more generally to the reasons, either conscious or subconscious, we have for doing or not doing things. It provides us with an agenda of doing what we are motivated to do and provides us the goal of accomplishing whatever we are motivated to do. This distinction of motivation as being fun- or need-oriented will be addressed later in the chapter. You will find that in the process of becoming addicted to a SSoS the nature of your motivation switches from being fun-oriented to need-oriented. Motivation then changes from being a Quality of Life–level reasoning or force to a drive in which there is a perceived life/death affair going on, because of the Fear of Annihilation.

Why Is Knowing Our Motives Important?

Questioning my *motivations* and coming up with true, sincere answers was the key to getting insights when working through my own self-knowledge toward my healing. Once the insights were there, the potential for healing was created. "What exactly drives me to do what I do, or avoid so strongly what I don't want to do? What are the *real* reasons for my choices and behaviors?"

In this Method, we do not focus on the universal obvious motives of food, shelter, warmth, and so on. Instead, we look at other kinds of motives. We look deeply, beyond the surface: "Are my choices in life *really* motivated by what I *believe* my motives are? What is the real relationship between my goals and my motives? Am I really in touch with what drives me? Are the choices I make in daily life indeed directly linked to what seems, on the surface, to be my goal?"

You might assume you have free choice, but upon looking more deeply, you may discover your choices are not that easily reversible, not as freely optional as you might have believed they were. That's one clue that your choices are somewhat addiction based. Do you sometimes feel as if you're being driven by an invisible power?

I remember the many instances during the time I worked as a professional bassoonist when I was unable to stop practicing or preparing my reeds. It felt as if my life literally depended on the quality of my performance. In hindsight I can see why I was so compulsive in my preparations for a concert—I could not afford for others to think I was a bad musician and go home with that devastating feeling of having failed to perform well. It felt as if my spirit would evaporate until the next time when I would do well.

Knowing our true motives is important because not only do our health and well-being depend on *which* motives are operating in us, but it helps us to get a clear view on where we stand within the criteria of this Method. As stated before, there are two types of motivations: the one type stems from and leads to health and happiness (Direct Motivation); the other stems from distress and leads to all kinds of personal and social problems (Indirect Motivation).

This distinction will help you look into what might be the invisible power behind your motives, and where, in many people, that power might come from. When you know your *true* motives, you can develop strategies for improving your quality of life.

"Things Are Seldom What They Seem"

Consider these examples of differing motivations, which are hard to spot for the common observer.

> *Here we have two mothers and each take their child to a music school. Even though to an observer these two people are "doing the same thing," their motives might be totally different. One might be motivated to develop her child's talent and help the child be happy in the activities involved in that development. The other might be motivated to have a child who's a good musician because it reflects well on her as a parent.*

The outcome of the experience would therefore be different for all involved. The first mother and child would probably find satisfaction and mutual enjoyment. The second mother and child would probably have stress, fights, tensions, and mutual dislike. And the child might not only rebel at the activities, but feel disempowered, manipulated, resentful, and inauthentic. So why did I get started in music?

> *Two mothers are complimenting their children after a test at school. It looks as if they are doing the same thing. But their motives could be different, and the effect of the compliment could be different in each case, too.*

The first mother might be motivated by unconditional love and recognition of the child's intrinsic worth, so she is supporting her child's self-image as capable and loved no matter the test results. The effect of the compliment would be smiles on both faces, a deepening of their bond, and better mental health for the child. The second mother might be giving the child approval, which the child knows is only because of a good test result, a good performance. The child would be glad, but already worried about future failures. The mother might be getting an emotional rush from having a child who appears intelligent to the world, thus reflecting well on her own intelligence, which she isn't sure is high enough to get *her own* mother's approval. The mother's motive is to have the child do well on future tests.

For the second mother it isn't really about the child, and a nagging fear of future failure lurks for the child as well as for the mother through the child. The child is a pawn in the mother's game. The child senses she needs to perform well in order to get "good vibes" from the mother; the mother depends on the child for her "Feeling-good-about-Self" (FgaS) state.

Now consider this example. Erica's aunt has prepared a lunch for Erica and her young child and her husband, Paul. The weather was gorgeous and Erika, Paul, and their child went for a ride on their bicycles through the lowlands, the child in the front seat. The ride had been a bit longer than planned and the little one had fallen asleep on the bicycle. They were a bit late for lunch as well. On arriving home, Erica's aunt blamed her for being irresponsible and selfish for having taken the child on this ride and making it too long.

She kept going and put up a face of being personally insulted, which was the case because in truth she was upset about her (very casual) lunch not being regarded important enough to be on time for. The bigger truth was that she was upset because she feared that she could not deal with the trio being late, which would spoil her FgaS state. After all, that was why she had gone out of her way to prepare lunch for them. So she was scared for her own behavior, which made her blow up even more. It was neither about the lunch nor about the people at the lunch. It was not about the little one who had fallen asleep on the bicycle. These were all pawns in her emotional world that consisted only to satisfy her Ego-References. Of course her temper tantrum did not add to a pleasant atmosphere at the table.

(Indirect) Motivation Aimed at a Hidden Agenda

It isn't just to an outside observer that someone's "true" motivations can be hidden and hard to discover. Our true motivations are often hidden from our own conscious minds, too, and can be very hard to discover. Usually, in any situation, we can come up with a plausible reason "why" we have chosen to do or avoid something. That gives us the comfortable illusion that our behavior is "justified" and that the plausible reason is the *real* reason that gave us the incentive/motivation we needed in order to act.

Hidden Agenda

Having a subconscious purpose for a behavior, which is to fulfill an unhealthy need for feeling good about oneself, not the ordinary, obvious, predictable, expected purpose of the behavior.

In reality, however, our motives and choices are often far more complicated than what we see and notice. What really is at play when we feel motivated, when we choose to do or not do an action or display a certain behavior, is generally not as transparent as we would like to believe. Many of us have **Hidden Agendas** operating—hidden even to ourselves! These Hidden Agendas are our deeper and ultimate reasons/motives for doing or avoiding things.

So our motivation Method is based on the idea of a potential Hidden Agenda in our motivations. Unlike in politics, however, for most of us this is not a conscious process; it's our subconscious mind trying to fool our conscious mind, hiding its agenda from our conscious mind.

QUESTIONING OUR BEHAVIOR

By questioning my own behavior, I learned that there was a deeper layer to a lot of my seemingly normal, everyday behavior; you could say that my everyday decision making and planning was not geared toward the apparent result of the action but was subconsciously motivated by something else. Many years of introspection enabled me to make this subconscious motivation more conscious, which then led to my recognizing certain patterns of subconscious motivation and behavior. Over time, and based on these inner investigations, I learned that many aspects of the suffering I encountered in myself were related to these subconscious motivational issues. Thus, we need to look more deeply into the causes and consequences of "unhealthy" motivation.

Direct Motivation

Motivation that is ordinary, simple, and based in the present, with no Hidden Agenda of filling a subconscious need based in the past.

DIRECT MOTIVATION

Direct Motivation is the most normal, natural, and healthy kind of incentive for our actions and behavior. The motives for our actions or behaviors are straightforward. They are not necessarily out in the open or easily talked about, but there is a straight line from our actions or behaviors to our goal (see Figure 6.1).

Dɪʀᴇᴄᴛ ᴍᴏᴛɪᴠᴀᴛɪᴏɴ ɪs transparent to an observer because the goal that we have in mind for the activity we are performing is logical and straightforward. It is in sync with the activity. The goal is overt and leaves no ambiguity upon interpretation. When our motivation is direct, we have no agenda other than the one a person can observe or easily guess. The agenda is in logical relation with the goal that the content of the action or behavior shows or suggests. With Direct Motivation, we do something for the sake of itself, for the enjoyment it

Figure 6.1: The inner flow of focus and nervous system activity associated with Direct Motivation. This person shows a healthy (inner) activity in playing his guitar and singing his song. No other reason is involved than the fact that he enjoys what he is doing or perhaps wants to convey a message with his song.

provides, or for a practical reason. What we do is what we are trying to get: we are washing the dishes to get the dishes clean. The appearance of what we are doing and what our goal is are the same. We go to the grocery store to get food in order to be able to eat and live. Period. Direct Motivation has nothing to do with proving something or trying to get a FgaS as a SSoS. Direct Motivation implies that we already have a (Natural) SoS and therefore have a direct relationship with ourselves, as well as with the things around us and with others.

INDIRECT MOTIVATION

Indirect Motivation is most easily defined as actions spurred by a perceived need or want in your choices—a Hidden Agenda unknown to yourself! In the SoS Method, because this Indirect Motivation is perceived as a need, not a want, and is experienced as a must, or even a compulsion, we can think of it as a strong drive. Indirect Motivations can be thought of as the action or behavior geared only toward fulfilling the conditions for approval that will result in a "Feel-good-about-Self," the Holy Grail of the SSoS-oriented System, what everything is aimed at (see Figure 6.2). "Earning" the "Feel-good-about-Self" feeling temporarily hides painful fear and offers something to lean on for a while.

Indirect Motivation

The motive for doing something is not what it appears to be; instead, the real motive is to get the temporary emotional state that substitutes for a lasting sense of being a "real" person.

TO THE OUTSIDE world, we are focused on the action or activity, but inside, subconsciously, hidden from ourselves and from others, something else is going on. We are using these actions or activities only as a Vehicle to get us to a **Hidden Goal**.

Our motivation is completely oriented toward others' acceptance and approval, and to how others react to us. Over time, transference of the parent's function as the approval giver or withholder to other people ensures the child stays in the same dependent position toward others as it was toward its parents. A person's belief that the conditions from childhood need to be fulfilled to achieve the sense of being OK and safe results in an addictive dependency on the FgaS state. Thus, this addiction to the SSoS results in people working continuously on the specific actions or activities (subconsciously) chosen.

Hidden Goal

The ulterior goal that the whole of the SSoS-oriented System is directed to, and that is perceived as compensating for the effects of the lack of acknowledgment in early childhood.

Now you can see clearly that the actual goals of this person's behavior are not the content of the actions but the Hidden Agenda of the Ego-References!

The Hidden Agenda

A Hidden Agenda that operates within ourselves works pretty much the same as Hidden Agendas that we see often in politics: A specific thing is said or done

Figure 6.2: The inner flow of focus and nervous tension associated with Indirect Motivation. This person is playing and singing as well but from a different point of departure. He is dependent on the outcome of the level of his performance for gaining approval of his father for "being a good musician," of which the perception would then lead to being accepted by his father as a "real" person (son). In a later stage in life, considering that he would have lived up to his father's conditions (VIPV, or Virtual, Internalized Parental Voice), this would lead the player to the FgaS state that then functions as a SSoS. There is a lot at stake: his avoiding Annihilation! Does this take away or affect in anyway the performance? Most definitely.

by someone in order to create a situation in which it is easier to achieve that person's ulterior (Hidden) Goal. The real motive for the action is not what it pretended to be; the motive is really to get to the goal of the Hidden Agenda.

So a Hidden Agenda is an ulterior motive, an action or a behavior that is not openly admitted, known, or visible on the surface. It may even be that the conscious mind might not permit people to realize they are subconsciously operating with a Hidden Agenda as it is perceived to be in their interest to keep the denial of having any Hidden Agenda going.

An example is found in the following story: Erica's Hidden Goal was to please her father because she never felt truly acknowledged by him. She knew that her father wanted nothing more than to have his offspring follow in his footsteps. He was a respected medical doctor so Erica decided to study medicine as well. She convinced herself that it was what she wanted to do. It would have been silly for her to admit that she would do that to please her father in the hope of gaining visibility in his eyes of her as his daughter. That knowledge would have defeated her plan immediately. So her conscious mind chose to be left in the dark about her real motivation.

The Hidden Agenda in this Method is typically the desired positive outcome of an Ego-References. A person who is dependent on a SSoS paves his or her way to the Hidden Goal with Hidden Agendas of positive outcomes of his or her Ego-References. We call this specific action or activity a **Vehicle**. A Vehicle is usually an everyday activity or behavior that is initiated explicitly to perform the specific Ego-Reference and with an eye on the Hidden Agenda. It can be a task that needs to be done anyway as well as something that is done especially to create an opportunity to work on a Hidden Agenda. In the preceding story, Erica's Ego-Reference (and Hidden Agenda) is to be respected by her father. The Vehicle she chooses is giving him the message that she has decided "to become a doctor."

Vehicle

An activity or behavior that is subconsciously selected to serve as a tool or means to achieve the desired state of "feeling-good-about-Self."

So now that you know this, you might want to look around and wonder, because daily activities are (often, depending on whether a person has a SoS or is dependent on a SSoS) not what they seem to be. Often they are just Vehicles for completing a person's Hidden Agenda, which forms the real and only motivator of the task at hand (see Chapter 7). The degree to which the Ego-Reference is *fulfilled* depends on the level to which the task has been performed, because that degree is responsible for getting the approval-related FgaS state that functions as the needed SSoS. Failing to get there means that Annihilation is waiting.

So what we can state to be the case for people who lack a Sense of Self is that fulfilling Ego-References enables them to experience a SSoS. These people's motivations are indirect as they are always aimed at realizing their Hidden Agenda, and their overt agenda is just a Vehicle to do that. Their Hidden Agenda is their actual ultimate motivator and not their own well-being or purpose. It isn't hard to see how, once caught in this drama, they skip experiencing their very own lives.

For myself, what I realized after many years of introspection was that nearly everything I did was to *get approval*, either from myself or others—or more precisely, nearly everything I did was to get to *feel good about myself*. My motives were not actually to have a clean house, or to be well rested, or to be an expert musician, or even to make sure I was happy. Those were all Vehicles of my Hidden Agenda to *get approval vibes, which then would help me reach my Hidden Goal!*

This was interesting and quite shocking, actually: In the process of doing all those tasks, I performed them all reasonably well. I *had* to! How else would

I have gained the desperately needed SSoS? The real goal, though, in almost everything I did, was finding some sort of a way to get my parents' approval (and later in life, to get the approval from my "virtual, inner parent") with the ultimate goal of feeling acknowledged by them as a valuable member of the human species, a cherished and well-respected daughter. That goal, my own goal, was hidden even from me! Only I know the price I have paid for performing that well. Even though I performed well, my professional expertise was lacking that exact direct connection, and so it was not really good enough.

The Hidden Goal versus the Hidden Agenda

Using the two terms *Hidden Goal* and *Hidden Agenda* next to each other may be somewhat confusing. Here is some clarification.

Hidden Agendas are used for and aimed at getting to the ultimate Hidden Goal (compare to the FgaS state discussed in Chapter 5). The Hidden Goal is always to repair the damage done in the past of not having been acknowledged as a real, unique, potentially independent person by the caregiver, which has left the person with a lack of SoS. Children to whom this has happened think it is their fault—they should have been better in those aspects of their life that would have pleased the parent more. The Hidden Agenda is a way children (and later adults) can do better in a specific aspect or behavior, and the Hidden Goal is that they hope they now are considered worthy to be taken into account. Ultimately, the Hidden Goal is to be able to turn things back in time, and have the parent change his or her mind about you from negative to positive. To make sure that this time you succeed in being acknowledged as a real and definite human being with the right to exist the way you are.

Reaching the Hidden Goal unfortunately seems to never take place, as the culprit is not the (former) child but the caregiver, who would have to work out his or her own dependency on a SSoS before being able to allow any other person into his or her life. If the caregiver had a healthy SoS the child would not have been in the situation of having to work on improving him- or herself through working on the Ego-References throughout the rest of his or her life.

Layers of Indirect Motivation

To better understand the process of Indirect Motivation we can distinguish an order of things:

- There is the task to be accomplished.
- There is the Hidden Agenda to be completed.
- There is the Hidden Goal to be reached.

A few examples of Hidden Agenda are:

- showing you can be unselfish,
- showing you can be normal,
- showing you can have a good reputation,
- showing you can be always be on time,
- showing you can sleep well.

In order to prove these Hidden Agendas, we behave in certain ways:

- to meet conditions,
- to get approval,
- to feel good about ourselves,
- to experience our Substitute Sense of Self, and
- to keep all this outside of our conscious awareness (denial).

And to avoid feeling a most unpleasant fear of failing in any of those steps, we experience ongoing anxiety, stress, and rage, especially when we are hindered in some way, and we fear failure in performing whatever tasks we need to perform for the approval we seek.

INDIRECT MOTIVATION AND THE SENSE OF SELF

During the last 25 years, along my inner journey, I noticed that whenever my mind was playing the Hidden Agenda game, I was (subconsciously) trying to compensate for the missed chances in my childhood of developing a healthy SoS. However, the window for such development was closed, and the only thing I still could achieve was the FgaS state that I mistakenly took for a (Substitute) SoS.

If, for some reason, you are starting to resonate with what is being said here, this situation could be true for *you or for your loved one*. Mind you that you truly wouldn't be consciously aware that the bottom line for you is that you lack a healthy SoS, which then would result in the issues you currently have. With all the conditions (Ego-References) operating to achieve specific Hidden Agendas, you can lead a whole life doing things that appear normal but have specific Hidden Agendas. Your Hidden Goal, which ultimately serves to experience, however vaguely, your SoS, which comes down to the

FgaS state, is really the only thing that *actually* matters to you in all that you undertake and achieve. The normal results of your action of cleaning the kitchen—for example, a clean kitchen—may not really matter to you! At any rate, this question is not even within your scope because you live to fulfill your self-imposed conditions. A way to help you assess your own situation is by consulting the Comparison Chart in the Appendix.

The psycho-emotional dysfunction (absence of a Natural SoS) makes even the most normal-looking action or behavior in daily life into a cover-up for a Hidden Agenda. You think the goal of the behavior/action is the normal/obvious goal, *but it is not!* What is really going on? As described earlier, when people have a healthy Natural Sense of Self, their actual actions or behaviors have normal, intended, predictable, and obvious outcomes—the outcomes one would expect. For example, I wash the dishes to get the dishes clean, and perhaps because I want a clean kitchen and home because clean is nice. The behavior (in this case *not* a Vehicle!) and its desired outcome (the goal) are in a sensible, ordinary alignment.

When a person does not have a healthy Natural Sense of Self and is operating from a Substitute Sense of Self, a huge discrepancy exists between the task used as a Vehicle and the actual goal (the Hidden Agenda) of the action, activity, behavior, or behaving in a certain manner. The natural alignment is distorted, or we might say even perverted, so the Vehicle is not aimed at the expected goal at all but at the Hidden Agenda, which will bolster the always-disappearing SSoS. For example, I wash dishes to score points with (or against) my spouse, or because my mother will be happy with me, or because I "have to" do things in a way that my father regards as proper so he will not reject me. Or, I give my children music lessons because doing so makes me feel part of the music scene, and that is most important for me. Here, "I belong to the music scene" is my condition or Ego-Reference, which leads to my SSoS because perhaps "I will be looked on as 'an achiever' by my parents," so I "score" with them (satisfying the Hidden Agenda). My ultimate goal is not about the children, their skill, their enjoyment, or their love of music, nor is it about the ordinary benefits of their having music lessons. None of these objectives are really important nor motivating to me. There really is no room for these motivations in my mind as I live for fulfilling my conditions (Ego-References).

A sign of approval is the Hidden Goal, which then results in feeling-good-about-myself, which functions as a Substitute Sense of Self. I absolutely need that because I was not acknowledged as a real, "always existing" human being, so I was unable to develop a Natural SoS. So there is no need to say that the approval is not just nice to get. The stakes are much higher. The approval is necessary to give us a substitute for what we lack: an ongoing fundamental sense of Being that everyone needs in order to function appropriately as a human being. We are motivated to get this approval because without it, we feel we do not exist at all.

REWARDS AND "HIGHS"

It seems paradoxical that after having been (relatively) successfully in achieving a level of performance that would (have) led to approval and "Feeling-good-about-Ourselves" that we would crave a further reward of some kind. However, because nothing concrete has actually happened, this is understandable. A short approval—a pat on the shoulder, a compliment, or anything that resembles being accepted—justifies to those without a SoS, or so you would think, the huge attempt to achieve the approval. Not so though; it is not enough!

After the efforts and focus on this fictional goal used to temporarily attain the fictional goal, a gap opens up, a nothingness that seems like an abyss. "What is next?" seems to be the question. Although there is some sense of *accomplishment* that is satisfying, the real price is not showing up. On that moment, at the end of this journey, which often coincides with the day coming to an end, your options are to maintain the status quo or return to your previous, lower state. For the person with a SSoS, going back down does not bring her anything, and holding the status quo requires new stimuli that are desperately looked for. Going to bed is no option—we need a prolonging of the achieved status of actually having that SSoS, which we now (subconsciously) protect as if it were a matter of life and death. Woe to whoever happens to be the cause of the person's "high" or "reward" being thwarted. Rage, anger, and even violence can be the result. If nothing happens to make the person tumble down from his or her ecstasy, the person will (subconsciously) take care of that him- or herself by endlessly trying to prolong the need to be rewarded and take action on it: The situation is already artificial and becomes more vulnerable to interruption or exaggeration as it is extended.

The loving embrace of the caregiver, in acknowledgment and in respect of the wonderful person you are, and which wipes out all former misunderstandings, quarrels, and struggles, would have been the ultimate reward (compare: Hidden Goal). The need to be acknowledged by the parent as a valuable son or daughter, would have been filled by the parent saying: "Wow, I never knew you are such a wonderful person and I am so glad that you are my son (or daughter)." The real reward would be to have that gnawing sense of inadequacy and failing to be the one to make your parents happy go forever away! What would fulfill your deepest need on such a moment would be that your SSoS would turn into a healthy SoS. But that never happens. You do not get that need met. And you are not even aware that that is what you actually want.

So when something went really well and you have the FgaS state and your parent would have been pleased and maybe even let you into his or her life for real, there is a sort of suspense hanging. Your energy is still high and the lack of closure to this effort through getting the real reward leads to hankering for some sort of a high, and after that another one, and another one. That can be (and often *is*) in the form of a substance-derived buzz, such as from alcohol or drugs.

In my case, I would crash after a few drinks. I would become violently angry about something that had come my way—or even about the possibility of something coming my way—that would thwart this high. It would be enough to make me explode in rage. Then I would be terribly sad that I had screwed up the opportunity. I would then proceed by trying to make up for my behavior, not really for other people's sake, of course, and often I received only a little of my credit back. Then I would not sleep, and the next day I would be miserable and feel dirty. After a while, this would level out, and I would start my mountain climbing over again. (See the "Castle of Enmeshment" in Chapter 7.)

The presence of these emotional roller coaster indicates SSoS-oriented activity. The impulses are so strong that, even if you are somehow aware, or have some awareness of your patterns (during Recovery, for example), returning to a normal state when feeling so anxious to have to let go of the earned SSoS is extremely challenging.

THE HARMFUL EFFECTS OF THE ADDICTION TO (OR DEPENDENCY ON) A SSOS

Unhealthy motivations, like Hidden Agendas, are fairly common, and people employing them would not necessarily be called mentally ill. Not all Hidden Agendas are equally bad; it is up to you to decide to which degree they have taken over your life. The ones that aim to compensate for past traumatic experiences *tend to* lead to many kinds of suffering in oneself and in others, though. The actions, which function as Vehicles for our Hidden Agendas, are, as said before, everyday little actions and activities. Still, it all may seem pretty harmless. Not so.

Here are the harmful effects that stem from Indirect Motivation and indirectly from the dependency of a SSoS:

Addiction to the SSoS leads to compulsive task fulfilling behavior: When behaviors have a hidden (subconscious) agenda of getting approval, *they become compulsive and addictive.* If succeeding in achieving the agenda feels at risk, we can erupt in rage and violence, become overwhelmed by these emotions, and not know why! Or we can become chronically depressed, as well as suffer from disease, insomnia, and many other types of human suffering, including divorce. All of these can be traced to one root cause: being motivated by the Hidden Agenda of getting approval. By cleaning up your motivation, you not only improve your quality of life; you also help make the world a better place.

Physical symptoms: I am not a doctor so I cannot go into specifics. However, it seems to me that much physical distress might be the direct result of the dependency on a SSoS, including gum-disease for example and many more (see Comparison Chart and Map of Healing)

Fear-based symptoms: The various types of fear, including but not limited to anxiety, fear of failure, Fear of Annihilation, certain cases of Post-traumatic Stress Disorder, certain phobias, and general isolation.

Depression-related symptoms: Common depression. I have a hunch that there are many more symptoms that are the immediate result of the addiction to or dependency on a SSoS for your self-experience.

General dysfunction: There is a lot more to say about all kinds of dysfunctions we encounter on a daily basis in our lives as well as in society as a whole, violence, suicidal thoughts or acts, divorce, greed, bullying, frequent fights in families, and many more . . . The purpose of this book though does not permit going into more detail about those. For now we focus on getting the SoS Method verbalized and out to the world. It is our intention as the company HEALTHY-SENSEOFSELF to study all aspects of dysfunction and disease that could possibly benefit from our body of work here. We welcome any experts in those fields to join us.

Mental and/or emotional problems: Including, but not limited to: a lack of the ability to focus, heightened sensitivity to criticism, unstoppable urge to hurry up in everything you do, memory problems, learning problems (math!) for children, inability to experience feelings, problems relating to other people, and so many more . . .

A Ceiling on Success Because of Divided Focus

A split focus affects the results of our actions. The degree of intention that goes into any overt goal (the Vehicle) of any action is responsible for the degree of success in getting the ordinary desired result of the action. It is no wonder that the result of an indirectly motivated action is not optimal; the majority of focus is toward achieving the Hidden Agenda, not the overt ordinary result expected of such an action.

The situation is even worse. Because the Hidden Agenda's goal is fundamentally the experience of a fictional Self, we could say that even the effort put into the action *goes to waste*; it does not contribute to successful achievement of the overt ordinary result. When an action, nominally a Vehicle for the real goal, is not the true focus, the performance of the action, activity, or behavior is bound to be mediocre.

Here is an example. Giving a concert can be a Vehicle to achieving approval from a parent or caregiver of a person who is a parent herself (!) "Look Dad, my daughter is a wonderful concert pianist!" Do you admire me now? Or maybe the attempt is geared toward self and the approval comes from the Virtual, Internalized Parental Voice: "I probably am a normal musician like other musicians after all." Now it will not surprise you to hear that the result of this concert will be either a technical or an underachieved performance, but not one with artistic peeks as it is not at all about (the beauty of) the music. It is all about the person who performs to achieve her Hidden Agenda.

In the first instance of the technical performance, the musician may have worked hard studying the music and practicing the piece to perfection, but there is great fear of failing to earn the "Feeling-good-about-Self" of the Substitute Sense of Self. The musician is unable to "let go" and give an inspired performance.

In the second instance, by choosing to perform easy pieces, the performer could stifle his or her growth as a musician to ensure achieving the Hidden Agenda and attaining the FgaS state as obtainable only through the caregiver's approval. So here, too, the musician is not playing the music for its own sake but for the approval vibes of the real or virtual parent.

It is funny how interferences come up as clues, letting you know that you are not on the right track; for example, a singer develops a cold or a sore throat every time he or she is supposed to perform. I could give many of these examples, but finding examples in your own life will not be hard if this applies to you. After all, the concert—a fake goal—was not getting all your energy and focus; achieving the Hidden Goal was.

Here is another example: Imagine you are desperately in need of acknowledgment from your father, so you pretend to be interested in what interests him: computer games. You play them all the time (with his virtual approval in your unconscious mind), but you are really bad at them. Your mind is scattered, and you are not focused on the actual content of the game, which doesn't really have your interest anyway. Deep down inside you are focused on the anticipation of receiving his approval and that soothing of your need to "Feel-good-about-Yourself" which his positive attention provides.

Taking all of this in you might want to conclude that if all too often *your* efforts do not have the desired outcome, it is worthwhile to check your motivation. If 60 percent of your energy goes into the Hidden Agenda, only 40 percent is left for the activity itself, and that 40 percent is pretty much wasted. Success proves elusive because of this divided focus.

It took me a great number of years of practicing like mad on my bassoon while working as a musician in top-class orchestras before it dawned on me: "I play the way I am." In other words, I can't surpass, through practice, the level of my skill, knowledge, and success imposed by who I am—including the degree of healthiness/directness of my motivations or lack thereof. To take my playing to the next level, I realized, I had to work on myself and clean up my motivation. Little did I know that it would take me about 30 years.

If you have reached a certain level of expertise or success that you have been trying unsuccessfully to surpass, inspect your motivation. No amount of practice will help you overcome the handicap of having a Hidden Agenda that you do not know. The way you are functioning as a human being determines the ceiling on your expertise or success.

A Lack of Integrity—Body Language

As much as the processes described here happen on a subconscious level, there *are* clues that people notice. People's bodies give us information about their motivations, which we register consciously and subconsciously. Then, within a split-second, we react to the vibes we detect, sometimes even before a person speaks. Interpreting our fellow human beings' body language is part of our survival system.

We know when people are straightforward with their goals and intentions: They look you straight into the eye, and you get a sense of solidity from that. When people are indirectly motivated, they tend to look away, or sometimes they have a look in their eyes one might label as dishonest, cheating, and insecure. Their pupils are larger than normal, and their eye color might lighten or change slightly. Overall, they seem, very subtly, evasive and nervous. When they speak about an activity of theirs that is indirectly motivated, their message is not clear. They will not have much to say or are too loud trying to convince everyone.

Isn't it interesting to consider that even though nothing unusual seems visible, people do pick up on the lack of integrity of motivation? They might not get a clear sense of what is going on, but somehow they are inclined to drop their interest and ignore the content of what the person is doing, or ignore the person altogether.

Imagine listening to a singer. A number of things may happen: You are captivated and interested by what you experience; you feel engaged in the performance. Or it can be that "there is nothing going on" or that it is an "interesting experience" at best and you are not being touched by it at all. In the first case the singer gives herself fully in the performance. She is able to get out of her own way to perform the music, so to speak. She "facilitates" the piece and does not use it for her own (needy) purposes. When there is "nothing going on" the singer produces the notes but doesn't get to "perform" them with her own take on it. He is just giving a flat interpretation of the music, and chances are he does it to satisfy his own need to perform with a Hidden Agenda in the background of his motivation. The "interesting" experience most likely consists of a highly technical piece, performed more or less with skill, but it is clear that the person uses the music to prove that he can do it. There is no other emotion involved than the fear of failure of the performing artist. It is not about the music, it is about him. Performing that piece for him means earning his SoS. He most likely has a lack of SoS and spends his life to prove to his caregiver, who has "a thing" with music, that he is worth this person's attention because he is able to perform these pieces of music.

Underneath such a performance may very well lie the unspeakable pain of not having been acknowledged by the caregiver. Chances are that a person in utmost distress is trying to accomplish something that other people take for granted—being seen and heard—only because, for some reason or other, he or she was not treated appropriately and did not develop a healthy and normal Sense of Self. In our judging a person as egocentric, we can be so "off" sometimes. Most of the time egocentric behavior is trying to compensate for a big need or a great fear. Awareness of this is one reason for more compassion for ourselves and our fellow human beings.

Considering all these harmful effects, we can say that the natural selection of what makes it in the world and what doesn't is strongly related to the nature of your motivation! Where do you come from; what is your real agenda? We can eliminate a lot of suffering through detecting (our) falseness in motivation. Parents can prevent their children from falling into the trap of working for unhealthy (Indirect) Motivation when they make sure their motivation is healthy (direct) so they can model that to their children as well! To that purpose they must make sure that they have a healthy (Natural or Restored) SoS.

CHASING BUTTERFLIES: A TALE OF (INDIRECT) MOTIVATION WITH A HIDDEN AGENDA

This story examines the concepts that form the SSoS-oriented System through an objective and a tool to pursue the objective: catching butterflies with a butterfly net. From the outside, it looks like a fun and happy outing, almost a game, but the game is based on a never-ending gnawing compulsion. Note the use of the many Vehicles: The net stands for Ego-Reference, and, of course, the butterflies represent the Hidden Agendas. Enjoy!

Every morning, after getting herself and her house ready for the day, Lisa Losos would jump in one of her many vehicles to go out and chase butterflies. She had her pick among big trucks, vans, Jeeps, SUVs, and cars of all kinds and colors. She would determine which vehicle to use based on the circumstances of the day, the weather, and where she planned to go.

The net she used to catch the butterflies was highly personalized in terms of style and decoration. The butterflies she aimed to catch were all of the same family: the MOD-butterfly. They were quite plain, but Lisa remembered that her mother particularly liked those. Somehow, it seemed to give her huge satisfaction if she was able to catch one, even though her mother was long gone. She never wondered if she liked them so much herself, nor did she envision the option to catch other truly beautiful ones.

Each day she would lower the window of her vehicle of choice and hold the butterfly net out, and drive in whatever direction she sensed might be favorable for her enterprise. She was always full of hope and happily motivated in the morning, but in the back of her mind, the awareness loomed that she couldn't afford to come home with an empty jar. If she did, she felt terrible. She believed her day had been useless. When she failed, it made her feel she had no right to expect that people would consider her a real person!

So every time she caught a butterfly, she felt good about herself. And at night, when looking back at the day while contemplating her collection, she felt good about herself too. In some vague way, she felt she had lived up to an expectation. She had no idea of whose expectation it was but she sure felt so much better when she was able to live up to it—it was almost as if it gave her permission to consider herself a "normal" person.

She didn't make money selling her butterflies, nor did she eat them. Instead, somehow, the amount of butterflies caught reflected for her that she was successful as a person and that she was a valuable contribution to the world.

No wonder she worked like mad to make it happen, to come home with a jar filled with moving wings. In a way she was addicted to this way of living because every butterfly caught represented a certain amount of "Feel-good-about-Herself," a state she craved like nothing else in the world. Every little butterfly represented for her—even though she didn't realize this consciously—a permission to be in existence.

But there was more to this situation than feeling good. Some of the feelings were very unpleasant. The moment she caught butterflies, she became anxious that they would die overnight. If they did, they would no longer count toward her "Feeling-good-about-Herself." She'd stay awake watching over her catch of the day, that they would not die on her.

When finally giving in to the need to go to bed she would lay awake for long hours in anticipation of tomorrow's hunt. After all, it was a stressful task to come home with a jar full of butterflies day after day! It was a never-ending job. And there were moments in which she wondered how on earth to make it happen. Where would she find enough butterflies? How could she hunt successfully when there was so much else to do? What would happen if she did not feel well enough to go out hunting? What if she wouldn't be able to sleep so she would barely be in a shape to drive her vehicle?

At times she simply threw up her hands in despair, saying, "Enough is enough! I won't do it anymore!" But that thought was also far from reassuring. Anxiety would plague her during the night, and the adrenaline rush of fear would indeed prevent her from getting the sleep necessary to be fit and well-rested to go on the butterfly hunt again.

Then she would find herself in a vicious cycle of fear and desperate butterfly hunting. Her need to be successful at all costs led to compulsive behavior that, if thwarted, generated rage, and sometimes even depression, which aggravated her insomnia. The struggle to get out of the claws of those feelings would swallow all her time, which made her insomnia even worse. She wasn't consciously aware of it, but her whole identity was tied up in the success of her butterfly hunting; deep down she felt it was the only thing that gave her life meaning.

Can you imagine what would happen to Lisa if she ever woke up to a healthy Sense of Self? How would it change her life if she would have a chance to gain enough insight in what motivated her to continue being the slave of her behavior and activity? She might come to see that she had been skipping her own life altogether and that *all* she had been doing with her life was *chasing butterflies*. She finally would be (directly) motivated to make the necessary changes in her belief systems that had kept her hostage, so she could be the master of her life instead of the slave.

Learning the SoS Method and applying it to your own life or that of your clients might do exactly that for you!

Figure 6.3: A Vehicle, an Ego-Reference, and a Hidden Agenda

LOOKING AHEAD

In a healthy situation, we know motivations by describing the obvious reason why we do something. That's pretty straightforward. What you see is what you get. The reason, incentive, agenda, and goal are obvious to any observer. In the unhealthy situation, our motivations are convoluted and indirect. We develop complex patterns of subconscious motivations in our natural attempt to compensate for the thwarted development of our Natural SoS.

In the SoS Method, ailments such as depression and insomnia, as well as violent behavior, often are considered to be a result of a *thwarted* attempt to realize our Hidden Agenda. A situation in which the Hidden Goal (note the difference between Hidden Agenda and Hidden Goal) is no longer obtainable, and we may become seriously depressed or even inclined to end our lives.

To understand the difference between direct and Indirect Motivation is crucial as it holds the key to dismantling a great deal of unhealthy human functioning. Indirect Motivation arises from a complex, invisible, under-lying psycho-emotional structure of motives and needs. In the next chapter, I explore the unhealthy coping mechanisms we use to accomplish our FgaS state and experience our SSoS: Enmeshment and Ego-References.

7 | Ego-References and Other Unhealthy Coping Mechanisms

So, Indirect Motivation is the immediate result of the dependency on our caregiver's approval that our understanding as a child takes for acknowledgment. Now that we have a sense of the difference between Direct and Indirect Motivation, let us shed a light on the pathway that is responsible for the motivation to be indirect.

The word *indirect* suggests that, instead of a one-on-one connection of the person with his or her goal, there is something else involved in this process. I used to refer to this aspect by comparing it to a strategy in billiards: playing over the long edge of the table. Here you do not aim the cue ball directly at the ball you want to send to the pocket; instead, you aim the cue ball at either one of the long or short sides of the table.

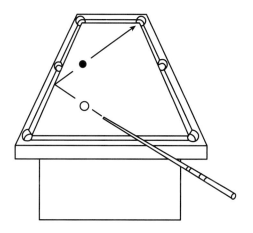

Our motivation becomes indirect when what we do, or rather, why we do it, serves to alleviate our Fear of Annihilation and our need and desire to be acknowledged. What we use as a source for choosing this way of relating are the observations we made in our early childhood, about how to behave or not to behave when (subconsciously) testing the reactions on us of our caregiver. The behavior that seemed to lead to the desired result of approval turned into one of our permanently attempted behaviors (Ego-References) as part of our Early Childhood Survival Strategy (ECSS).

So Ego-References refer to a set of required conditions to be performed at a high quality, and include specific behaviors and actions that we believe will satisfy the parent if we can improve our performance of them and that will get us the needed approval. They stem directly from the observations made in early childhood that are referred to in this work as the ECSS.

EGO-REFERENCES

The term **Ego-Reference** is central and unique to the Sense of Self (SoS) Method. It is a complex concept and part of the Substitute Sense of Self (SSoS)–oriented System. Most likely, Ego-Reference is a term that needs explanation.

In my years of introspection, I discovered that there was a strategy operating in my psyche but that functioned below my conscious mind. In studying my own motivation, I observed that this strategy would urge me to systematically improve certain behaviors that I felt at fault with and hated myself for. It would then give me the opportunity to "Feel-good-about-mySelf," a state that I craved. In order to be able to identify the strategy and keep track of it I had to give it a name.

I remember the absolute necessity for me to find a word that would do the trick, and instantly the term *Ego-Reference* came to mind. You have to understand that my research into my mind and emotions was not a well-planned one or a labor of love or leisure; it was a job that needed to be done to help myself to gain a deeply desired better quality of life. So I wasn't exactly prepared to take from a virtual shelf names for the concepts I wanted to label, names that would be commonly understood or even accepted in traditional psychology. But Ego-Reference seemed to cover the content: *Ego* could be considered to refer to that part of me that was *not* the path to truly sensing myself and that ideally was meant to make room for the healthy way of sensing "me." I used *reference* because it referred to the desired behavior I thought I had to perform, the required action I had to perform in an optimal way. If I could have put it into words, I might have said, "My Self exists only

Ego-References

Subconsciously accepted requirements to feel and behave in certain ways, and achieve certain results, in order to feel approved, as a substitute for feeling like a "real person."

in reference to these conditions and requirements and my activities in trying to meet them and my successes in doing that." Ego-Reference as a whole has everything to do with referring to the Substitute Sense of Self, mistaken for the real (healthy) SoS.

Each Ego-Reference, when worked on, is solely geared to win approval while soothing the fear for the perceived ever-present threat of Annihilation that is lurking. Ego-References are grown into solid, unchangeable strategies. You have to think of them as less dense items, with an energy that is still not hardened into, what it becomes in later days, the compulsion a person can't remove from his or her path because it has become part of him or her. So in general when we speak of Ego-References the child has already grown into an adult.

The specific desired behaviors are meant to result in the person receiving the right "vibes" from his or her caregiver. For example, a person may think: "I have to finish this work today," not so much because the work needs to be finished—which would be Direct Motivation for finishing the work— but because by finishing it early, I anticipate a sense of approval that will lead to me "Feeling-good-about-Myself"—which is the real motive for finishing the work.

To reiterate, Ego-References are those specific conditions we use to get the approval that will bring us the "Feeling-good-about-Self" (FgaS) state that ultimately is the substitute for our not having been acknowledged by the parent (and therefore having lost the opportunity to develop a Natural SoS) and that functions as a SSoS. They form the agenda points of the SSoS-oriented System in the pursuit of the Hidden Goal: to attempt to gain, long after their due date, the forever-lost building blocks for developing a healthy SoS: acknowledgment of the person as a unique, independent, and autonomous human being by the caregiver. These conditions to be fulfilled are called Ego-References because they are *what a person uses to refer to the person's substitute way of sensing their Self, instead of using their own being-ness as the referent to Self.* In other words, what started out as a strategic way for a child to get his or her needs met has now grown into a full-blown, but extremely unhealthy, irrelevant, and self-ignoring way of being.

Note that the child's **SSoS–oriented Goal** has now reached a new phase: The whole of the SSoS-oriented System has come into place, and it starts to rule and further form the (young) adult. In this system, the person, as he or she grows, builds on the earlier observations and strivings from childhood and, as a young adult, identifies this way of being as being him or her. Because there is no truthful way to get in touch with the Self the person is forever unable to develop any other way of existing other

Substitute Sense of Self–oriented Goal

The subconscious, ultimate goal—of convincing the parent to change his or her negative opinion about "me" into a positive one that gives "me" a feeling of "being a real, normal person."

than through fulfilling those conditions. Such a person always needs to achieve and has no inner place to rest. This exhausting, debilitating, and stressful lifestyle is the overture to the next phase: exhaustion, burnout, or disease.

Conditions That Become Ego-References

Which characteristics or behaviors become Ego-References depend on a person's individual specific circumstances. What the young child discovers when trying to adjust to the caregiver's demanding behavior or to the caregiver's responses to its own behaviors determines what Ego-Reference the person will develop. Each individual child discovers different behaviors (to do or refrain from) that evoke approval from his or her particular primary caregiver. Thus, each child develops actions and behaviors unique to itself and its situation, although there most likely are common patterns. It would be interesting to identify those by researching them more in depth. Chosen Ego-References might also have to do with the child's own specific temperament and inclinations and be colored by the particular conditions and requirements the child senses the caregiver is imposing on him or her. They can be, but are not necessarily, the caregiver's own Ego-References.

For example, whenever Erica, who had a hard time falling asleep, overslept, her aunt (who had raised her from when she was little) looked at her in a manner that said, "Why do you do this to me?" She would look at Erica with the look of an abused dog, which made Erica feel very guilty. It is not hard to fathom that Erica's Ego-Reference became "sleeping well." "I need to sleep well in order to get my aunt's friendship and approval, which would feel for her as if she was getting the keys to the castle." (This is a metaphor for her being allowed into her aunt's environment while feeling included. See The Castle of Enmeshment on page 97.)

Similarly, when Erica was sick or feeling under the weather and had to stay home from school, her aunt silently resented the situation, because it would give her extra trouble. It would be a Hindrance on her way to having a clean house and everything taken care of, which would give her the desired FgaS state. Another interesting detail is that Erica's aunt did not allow herself to be sick either. Being sick was something the parents of Erica's aunt despised as well. It possibly was even an Ego-Reference to Erica's grandparents. No wonder Erica developed the inner command to make sure she was OK at all times, which would lead her to pretend she was fine, even when feeling under the weather, lousy, or nervous.

Reactionary Ego-References

We also develop what I call reactionary Ego-References. They differ from regular Ego-References in that we use them for the opposite goal: to rebel. We are compelled to behave in the opposite manner we know our parent would like us to. For example, Peter engaged in reckless driving every time he drove from his parents' house or had one of his parents in his car. Even the thought of his parents made him behave in traffic in an irresponsible, potentially self-destructive way. He was not really present in his own body or else he would have thought about what could be at stake. If he could have thought with his own mind he would immediately become aware that he could get into a serious accident or hurt someone else. He was almost a grown man and he felt belittled by and resented his parents' nagging reminder to be careful. Once at the steering wheel of his car all he could feel was the reaction against what he intuitively recognized as an insincere and self-centered way of what his parents called "caring." They did not even really see him. Imagine these parents adding to their continuous repeated warning: "Be careful—don't drive too fast! We say it for your own good!" Subconsciously, Peter sensed that it was not about him they were concerned. They were more concerned about "their precious car" or about their neurotic way of being in control of everything so there would be no impact of anything unexpected on their lives. This was his way of rebelling against not really being seen by his parents as a separate and independent human being. He felt he was more of an obstacle for his parent's desire for a lifestyle without ripples. He did not really matter to them as the person he was.

Ego-References and Vehicles

As discussed in the preceding chapter, the term *Vehicle* is used to indicate an action, activity, or behavior that serves as a carrier for and an opportunity to work on an Ego-Reference. The action that functions as a Vehicle has two functions: It brings about an overt result and it serves to realize a person's Hidden Agenda, which is a positive outcome of an Ego-Reference. A person's focus is only indirectly on the overt goal; the person's real intent is to attain the Hidden Goal and/or the FgaS state, feeding his or her SSoS.

Here are some examples of behaviors used as Vehicles: household- or job-related requirements, paying a visit to someone, sending a card to someone, helping someone in any way, pursuing a certain education, educating children a certain way, going places, washing your car, being on time, and having a relationship partner, among others.

You'll find other examples of Vehicles discussed throughout this book.

Examples of Ego-References

Remember that Ego-References are held subconsciously. Considerable introspection may be required to discover that you hold the belief—accepted in early childhood—that you desperately need to fulfill these conditions and requirements. We can think of Ego-References as self-imposed conditions but we need to be always aware that this was the best that could have been done. It was a second best option. Note that Ego-References are rules with unrealistic demands of "always"—there is no allowance for circumstances. Holding on to Ego-References degrades these peoples' quality of life and makes them the slave of fulfilling the conditions.

    To get a better feel for what aspects of a person's life can become an Ego-Reference, here is a list of the ones I had. Based on my observations as a child (my ECSS), these were my crucial character and behavior issues that I needed to work on and continuously improve. These (self-imposed) conditions had turned into Ego-References. And as we now know, Ego-References are by nature compulsive as they form the cornerstones for a person's Indirect Motivations and as such for a person's entire **Substitute Sense of Self-oriented System**. Do not discard them right away, because the truth is deeply hidden under the surface of your daily life. Even if you do not immediately recognize any of these as yours, they still could be.

Substitute Sense of Self–oriented System

The entire subconscious complex of needs, behaviors, motives, habits, beliefs, goals, and fears whose only objective is to generate achievement-based approval, and which functions as an unhealthy base for being.

- As a mother, *my* family has to be positive and have a positive atmosphere at all times.
- I need to be in shape physically, emotionally, and psychologically so that I am always OK.
- I need to sleep well, be fit, be in a good mood, and look well-rested.
- I need to know what I want.
- I need to be on time.
- I have to have my act together.
- I need to achieve something in life, make something of myself.
- I need to stay away from getting angry, upset, irritated, or even annoyed.
- I need to avoid conflicts at all costs.
- I should never have or create problems for myself or anyone else.
- I have to make sure that I do not become sick or am not feeling well because it is not appreciated.
- I need to do things differently from other people and find a sense of being special.

- I need to be different from what and who I naturally am; I cannot just be who I naturally am.
- I have to stand out from the crowd.
- As a mother, I need to spend enough time with my children and husband.
- As a person, I must achieve great things in the world.
- As a housewife, I have to have my house clean and well-organized.
- As a spouse, I have to be in a good mood and never be angry.
- I must not complain.
- I have to be successful and admired.

Of course, other people's lists might be different, though some of these are quite generic and undoubtedly universal among people with a lack of SoS. Let it also be clear that we are not consciously aware of all these "rules" but by becoming aware of them we start to see that we are being forced to be careful all the time: we are walking on eggshells.

I have noticed that the need to get a good outcome to the ego-references increases with age. As the child and the parent age, we seem to be subconsciously aware that time to convince the parent that "I am a valuable human being" is running out. So not only do we try harder but the now-elderly parent may become increasingly more difficult to please.

When I visited my mother in the last decade of her life (I was in my fifties), I would not enter her house without bringing some flowers or a little gift. I never thought of actually making her a bit happy; I did it to get approval. (Ego-Reference: "not being selfish.") I had to keep up with my sister who gave her so many presents and flowers. I had to keep up so much that there was no room left for any spontaneity.

Other times, I felt I had to take her on a few trips to change the impression that I was leading a selfish life. My sister did it, so I also had to do it so I would not lose points. But due to the lack of predictability in my sleeping pattern I was unable to offer that as generously for it tied directly to another Ego-Reference, one that already was a hot item during my visits to my mother: I had to sleep well to actually be able to plan to take her out.

Ego-References and Inner Conflict

It is relatively easy to strive to fulfill one Ego-Reference, but what to do if two or more have to be fulfilled, and when they contradict one another? This complication leads to an **Inner Conflict**—a battle already lost, because a

Inner Conflict

In this Method, two or more competing but incompatible inner "mandates" to work toward experiencing a Substitute Sense of Self, which leads to high anxiety because there is a no-win outcome of the competition.

choice has to be made to fulfill one and ignore the other(s). Because so much is at stake in the fulfillment of an Ego-Reference, tremendous fear develops.

You may experience the following bodily sensation: a collision of nervous currents going in different directions, resulting in a perceived buzz throughout your body. There is not necessarily tension in the muscles. You feel as if your nervous network is under stress. Imagine a place in the sea where it comes ashore from various directions. It leads to a point where those streams meet and collide. That is how your nervous system feels in moments of Inner Conflict.

For me, that I learned to label Ego-References that made my behavior strategies recognizable has been a blessing. Often, it was still hard enough to identify the right Ego-Reference. But when I did, I would fall asleep like a baby. The mind isn't really worried and wasn't of great help in finding relief from the Inner Conflict. So I figured that the conflict played out on a deeper level.

My nervous system would indeed be under stress, because the impulses toward action were heading in different and often opposing directions. An Inner Conflict occurs when, on a subconscious level, people experience a confrontation with a big dilemma. This situation requires choosing between which of the two or more incompatible Ego-References to fulfill and which one to let go of, which generates a great Fear of Annihilation that manifests as a panic attack. There is no "good" choice available because, if

Figure 7.1: Inner Conflict

the Ego-References are contradictory, each moment allows only one Ego-Reference to be worked on. Consequently, only one Ego-Reference will be potentially fulfilled, which means that the others will be ignored at the cost of (perceived) Annihilation. The practical result of this situation is that, due to the lack of sleep and the stress, it is impossible to bring any of the Ego-References to a good end, which again increases anxiety.

In short, we are talking about an inextricable knot of perceived threats to the SSoS, and our bodies experience this particular knot accordingly. And as said, often no conscious thoughts or images help reveal the nature of the issue, namely, which particular Ego-References are involved and how they are conflicting. This situation can lead to a "blank night," a night of insomnia plus the unpleasant and exhausting buzzing feeling.

ENMESHMENT AND THE ADDICTION TO APPROVAL

Enmeshment

An unhealthy relationship between child and primary caregiver. The child's identity and motives are merged with the adult's, associated with extreme dependence on approval.

Enmeshment is an extreme entanglement with the caregiver. Figuratively, it is the failure of the umbilical cord to be cut. The caregiver has (had) an overbearing influence on the child and a strong demand to adjust to his or her personal needs and wants. There is no room in the caregiver's mind and heart to allow the child to be the way it is. The caregiver needs the child to be just so, so he or she can cope with his or her own controlled life. The caregiver depends on a "Feel-good-about-Self" that comes forth from fulfilling a variety of conditions. Not fulfilling these conditions creates anxiety and rage.

The child therefore learns in an early stage to cooperate with the caregiver's task to fulfill those conditions and in the process becomes enmeshed with the basic caregiver. There is no room for the child to develop his or her own criteria. Even though being two separate persons, the time in which commonly was worked on the caregiver's fulfillment of his or her ego-references has its price. It costs the child its authenticity. What develops instead is a lack of differentiation of values, criteria, possibly taste and opinions, motives, and goals—all the aspects of a person that make a person unique and different from others.

The caregiver considers the child worth approval when it doesn't obstruct his or her own neurotic goals. There is no interest and no ability in the parent to acknowledge the child as a real, independent person. The young human being, who has no concept of what is a normal or healthy relationship to the parent, becomes overly dependent on receiving approval from the caregiver as it intuitively senses that something of the sort is needed to get a sense of who he or she is.

Approval is also the only way the child feels allowed "into the castle" (see later in the chapter). Approval ultimately stands for "being allowed into the attention span of the caregiver" and that feels like acknowledgment. Only it *is not* acknowledgment. You could say that giving those vibes of approval to the child is a *conditional acknowledgment,* if there were such a thing. But there is no such thing because with this so-called conditional acknowledgment the child is not seen for who and what it is. It is only allowed close because it momentarily does not interfere with the caregiver's neurotic goals. We have extensively indicated the fatal mix-up of the child that subconsciously takes place, just because it is not knowable for it at that time, between approval and acknowledgment.

Approval is as close as a child can get to being allowed into the Enmeshment. And being part of that Enmeshment indicates that a child's quality of functioning is dependent totally on the vibes of "You are OK" or the absence of them, which leads to panic or desperation. The child's sense of existing as a person, as a being, develops in a stunted, distorted, neurotic, suffering-inducing way, with the child becoming dependent on what the other part of the Enmeshment (the primary caregiver) thinks or feels about him or her and about his or her behavior at any given time. What the child has learned does not change when he or she grows up, so we can rightfully state that the situation for an adult raised in this way stays the exact same. In other words, the child and the caregiver are enmeshed for life, whether the caregiver is still alive or not.

Here is an example of the way such an Enmeshment plays out in life:

Erica had moved away from her aunt's house to another continent as she had an intuitive drive to free herself from what she didn't know existed: an Enmeshment with her aunt who had raised her since she was born. She now had two children of her own and was determined to be a good parent to them. She and her aunt would call each other on a regular basis. These conversations were sometimes quite animated, but toward the end, there always was this funny situation during which she would walk on eggshells to make sure to stop the conversation at a point where they both would have this "Feel-good-about-Self." She felt she could only stop the conversation if she felt her aunt felt good about herself, so she knew she hadn't said anything wrong. You could say that all through her life she had felt responsible for her aunt's "Feel-good-about-Self" state, and this was still valid, even though she lived far away. At times she would call her back to ask if everything was OK; they would laugh about it, but it could be that something was said that made her doubt again, so she would call her back again five minutes later. When her aunt skipped a few days with calling her, she would panic and be deeply troubled, because in the last call, well, she had sounded a little annoyed. She might have taken offense. Of course, she was not at all interested in the effect of her words on her aunt, but she desperately needed her feel-good state as proof she was allowed into the Enmeshment. She and her aunt had one spine, so to speak. Without it, she did not exist—she felt annihilated.

Being granted access to the Enmeshment is the ultimate goal of the SSoS-oriented System because there the child can experience the part of its spine that is missing and feel whole (an illusion), if only for a moment. There it is that we feel we are allowed to be, that we exist, that we are seen and heard as a real being, just like "other people." I think you can easily see that "feeling bad about one's Self" is a powerful motivator to keep working on the achievement of the Ego-References.

When Erica moved into her house, she planted tomatoes and pepper plants in her big backyard because her aunt would have liked that, without realizing she never had given a thought to what she might have liked herself.

Being brought up in an Enmeshment causes the child, and later the adult, to be driven to please the caregiver via the earliest conclusions that then turn into the ECSS. It is like the child not only needs the caregiver's approval, but also needs that part of his or her identity, that missing part of his or her spine, that the caregiver holds conditional upon approval.

The Castle of Enmeshment: An Analogy

The following tale explores the difficulties and pressures experienced by one who exists in an enmeshed relationship with a caregiver.

Far away, in a country hidden in a valley covered by fog, lies a village called Struggletown. It's a village like any other, and most villagers live a reasonably happy life: they work, do what needs to be done, and on the weekends they usually find small pockets of time to do what they truly enjoy. Some people make instruments on which they make music to which others sing and dance; others carve wood or sculpt. There are philosopher meet-ups and horse races. Some women keep themselves occupied with embroidery and others play games with their children.

A small group of inhabitants, however, feels restless and unhappy. The people in that specific group are physically naked and under a lot of stress. They seem to be missing normal clothes, like the ones the other villagers wear, but they don't have the faintest idea why. They hardly ever come out of their hiding places and keep themselves compulsively busy with all kinds of soul-searching, hoping to get to the root of this problem.

Since their birth, these unhappy individuals have heard people whisper about the queen of MOD, who lives in the Castle of Enmeshment, on top of a very steep and rocky mountain. She has a factory in the basement of her Castle that produces plain, flesh-colored bodysuits. With artistic skill, the bodysuits are painted in such a way that they look just like normal clothes, but in reality the jackets, pants, skirts, and cardigans are like the faux-finish furniture and chandeliers on the walls of the Castle: only painted on.

Nevertheless, the people who have visited the Castle and possess a suit do not need to hide anymore as they can come down to the village and mingle with the other villagers as they look almost like them, though not quite. From afar, there is no visible difference between the clothes of the normal villagers and the fake suits from the Castle. Up close, though, the naked villagers fear the imitation may be visible. Therefore they have to make sure to not let anybody come too close, or worse, let anyone touch them, lest their outfits be discovered as false.

The queen of MOD put in place quite a number of specific requirements in order for the villagers to qualify for these suits. They had to travel to the Castle while making sure that the atmosphere and the flow-of-feel-good was guaranteed at all times. The flow-of-feel-good is a type of energy field that needed to be sustained continuously between the applicants for the suits and the queen of MOD. It was common knowledge that the queen depended on continuously being pampered by the feel-good vibes for her well-being. She made sure that everyone who entered the Castle felt the responsibility of meeting her needs in the matter. In fact, visitors who entered the Castle felt almost crushed under the pressure of having to manipulate his or her own feelings in favor of generating these feel-good vibes for the queen. Too much was at stake for them.

Halfway to the Castle was the House of Ego-References, where the naked villagers had to pick one or more tasks that they then were required to carry out to perfection, without complaining. These tasks consisted of certain behaviors: they had to avoid creating or experiencing any tension whatsoever; they must be happy at all times and could never be late. They were not to experience conflicts or disagreements with others. They were not to have sleeping problems and must have time enough to chat while completing their tasks to perfection. They could not be sick or have money problems and must never complain about anything, while making sure they performed better than the normal villagers did.

Occasionally it happened that, finally, a desperate naked villager was able to fulfill all these conditions and arrived at the Castle in good shape. Even though the task was very hard to accomplish, the villager looked fresh and fit, without any problems or lack of money, well fed with rosy cheeks and a smile on her face. Then the queen of MOD would open the doors to her Castle of Enmeshment and allowed the villager to enter.

This would be the moment the villager had been working for her whole life. It was like homecoming, and she let her guard down in total happiness. After all, that is what being home is all about: being able to be vulnerable. Often, though, this vulnerability proved to be a fatal error.

Interference or small Hindrances in the flow-of-feel-good was detrimental to achieving a positive ending to his mission. So, if the villager doubted in any way whether her task had been performed to perfection and her face showed that, the queen of MOD would immediately deny her further access to the Castle. Even though she would grovel, promising improvement, the door simply was not opened anymore and the poor villager had to crawl all the way back home to her hiding place. All that was left for her was to ponder new ways to plan the unavoidable next trip to the queen of MOD, holder of the suits.

Once inside the Castle, and all was going well, the fortunate villager was well received and experienced the desired hominess. The conditions remained the same at all times though: she must keep up the appearance of not having any problems and she must keep the flow-of-feel-good going so the queen of MOD could feel good about her Castle, her hospitality, and in short, herself.

After a few days in the Castle, the naked villager was provided with what she came for: the plain body suit that looked like a normal outfit.

The situation never is safe, though, and things can take a turn for the worst at any given moment: a Hindrance, an obstacle in the flow-of-feel-good, or the villager inadvertently making a mistake. Even the queen herself doing something that interfered with the good atmosphere was a reason for her to explode in a terrible temper tantrum and her yelling would shatter the windows of the Castle.

When that happens the villager would be kicked out of the Castle; her painted body suit disappearing into thin air as if by a trick of black magic. The shocked and shaken villager, naked again, would hide as quickly as she could, trying to find her way back to her dwelling while not being seen by others. She then would spend some days mourning the loss of her suit and of her efforts, after which she would embark on the journey to the Castle anew.

Meanwhile, the other inhabitants of Struggletown had no idea what was going on in the lives of the naked ones. They just sensed that they were different. They felt there was something "off" with them and so they didn't include the naked ones in their daily lives. Wearing their painted body suits didn't help in their desperate attempts to be one of them.

This made the body-suit people feel excluded and lonely. On top of that, they were under a lot of stress. They were walking on eggshells, trying not to make mistakes and to work hard to keep the appearances going because they were always at risk that their suits would be taken away from them.

At times when the unfortunate villagers would find themselves losing everything they had achieved just as they were about to enter the Castle, by just making one stupid mistake, they would break down and be overcome by rage. That would cause them to commit crimes and bad acts toward others. On occasion someone would even kill herself or her family. Or out of desperation they would burn down their own or other people's houses. The queen of MOD, as holder of the suits, was never their target, although she would be the one who deserved it. They needed her.

There was one naked villager, who had spent an enormous amount of time and energy thinking about his peculiar way of living. He had been rejected by the queen many a time. He found himself exhausted and at his wits' end when he was struck by a mind-altering thought: "What if I just make my own clothes, just like the other villagers do," he pondered. "It is strange that I have never thought of that solution before, but I guess my mind wasn't set up to envision that possibility."

He recognized that ever since birth, his people had been the naked ones. They were brought up with the unquestioned idea that they had to get their clothes through fulfilling tasks and conditions for the queen of MOD. They had to earn their clothes via performing the required actions and behavior in ways the queen demanded. So they got their clothes in an indirect way instead of buying them or making them directly. "So we focused all our attention and spent all our energy on pleasing the queen. It never occurred to us that we had the option of providing clothes for ourselves, and the real ones too! We actually can meet our own needs in a direct way! I can wear whatever clothes I choose."

He pondered this new concept for a long time as he sensed the vastness of the impact of this insight. Then he concluded, still in awe, "I guess our minds just were not able to generate the concept of that possibility because it wasn't put in there in the first place. What creatures of habit we are!"

The villager had to collect all his courage to face the fears of going through town with his first self-made clothes. But as he grew more skillful in cutting the fabric and sewing the parts together, his fear lessened and eventually subsided altogether. He had broken out of the prison of his own mind and opened himself to normal life; he was finally free. He also had found his mission in life: teaching the other naked ones to make their own clothes!

When a child is brought up in an Enmeshment with the primary caregiver, he or she doesn't develop a full sense of being an independent person, fully separate from the caregiver. It might be said that the child looks with the eyes of the mother or hears with the ears of the father (if he is the primary caregiver). The child makes choices in life about what to do, based on what he or she believes would be most successful to score with on the scale of points to please the parent.

The child never gives up hoping this parent will look on him or her with a benevolent eye and grant the child allowance into the Enmeshment, an image that I use to convey the concept of "having the right to be in the eyes of the caregiver," which can be thought of as co-codependency. In other words, it is the child's deepest desire to be allowed in the direct environment of the caregiver's undivided attention and feel one with him or her.

Being brought up in an Enmeshment produces the craving of the FgaS state, which the child experiences as an unhealthy (creating so many harmful effects described in this book) but desperately needed (because of the Black Hole and Fear of Annihilation) SSoS.

LOOKING AHEAD

Throughout the last several chapters, we have covered a lot of information. We covered what happens when developing a Natural Sense of Self is stunted. We found out how the Fear of Annihilation in its many manifestations leads to Indirect Motivation and to develop the behaviors that must ensure that we can achieve some approximation of what we need—acknowledgment.

In the next chapter, we tie it all together and explain the SSoS-oriented System we have subconsciously constructed to sustain the way we have developed our Sense our Self based on misleading observations in early childhood.

8 | Tying It All Together: The Substitute Sense of Self–oriented System (SSoS-orSyS)

The Substitute Sense of Self (SSoS)–oriented System is a collection of goals, desires, beliefs, motives, feelings, and perceived needs operating on a subconscious level. The system serves to give a surrogate structure to our inner life. The best way to visualize the SSoS-oriented System is to compare it to an army.

All the different squadrons have mobilized to attack the enemy, each by means of its own special force and expertise. In a person, it is similar: All of a person's functions and capabilities are set in one direction. That goal is, we know now, repairing, compensating for, or putting in place the missing input that should have led to acknowledgment of our personhood.

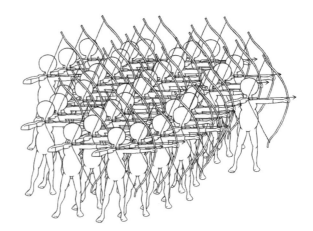

Figure 8.1: The army of the SSoS-oriented System

In review, we develop a SSoS-oriented System through the following experiences:

1. We receive Mirroring from a Distorted Mirror (i.e., a caregiver/parent who is self-absorbed) that states, "You are not unconditionally OK," which makes us believe that we are not worth being taken into account the way we are.

2. From this Mirroring, we perceive that we are deficient in some way and that we are to blame for not being acknowledged as a unique human being with the right to be the way we are. We experience Annihilation (our spirit is not acknowledged). We don't develop the spine for our psyche, a healthy Sense of Self (SoS). We develop Fear of Annihilation and become totally absorbed in avoiding Annihilation.

3. To avoid feeling annihilated, we observe what pleases the parent and adopt complying to these aspects, turning that adaptation into our Early Childhood Survival Strategy (ECSS).

4. With repetition, we begin to identify with these observations and they become Ego-References.

5. We use Vehicles as an excuse or as a cover-up to perform the Ego-References.

6. Over time we strive to fulfill our Ego-References; each time with a need to complete it better than before, with one specific agenda in mind that we are not aware of—approval from the caregiver/parent or, if he or she is no longer with us, from our Virtual, Internalized Parent Voice (VIPV).

7. When we bring our Ego-Reference to a good ending, we experience our Hidden Agenda, in other words we experience the "Feeling-good-about-Self (FgaS)" state, which functions as our SSoS.

8. Because the FgaS-state is fleeting, we have to begin the process over and over again in order to make sure we can experience it as if it were permanently available. Each time we are more determined to succeed in achieving our Ego-Reference's goal. It is this unknown goal that drives us. We are not consciously aware of it and mistakenly take it for a reason for living.

9. We also develop a fear of experiencing the Fear of Annihilation.

10. We suffer from many other SSoS-oriented fears, ailments, and disorders.

A SSoS is kept in place in the person's psyche only through constant re-creation through this complex system of dependencies, conditions to be met, motivations, the Hidden Goal/Agenda, emotions, and behaviors.

INSIGHT INTO THE WORKINGS OF THE BEHAVIOR OF A SSOS-ORIENTED PERSON

Figure 8.2 is a graphic representation of the daily ups and downs of a person's moods and behaviors. In order to get an understanding of what the reasons are for so much upheaval we need to look at the elements that play a role in this behavior (see Figure 8.3), which are described in the section on The Complex Emotional World of the SSoS-oriented System that you can find below, on page 105.

Figure 8.3 represents a closer look at the thoughts and feelings the person goes through. The person is always aiming to satisfy the Ego-Reference, but is constantly thwarted and encounters obstructions that lead to frustration, anger, a crash, feeling bad about one's Self, and starting all over again, or, in case of success of the FgaS, there is the need to extend that moment, to not

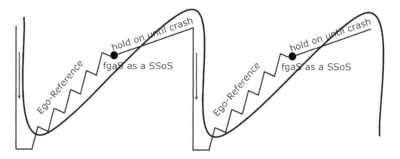

Figure 8.2: The ups and downs of a person's moods and behaviors

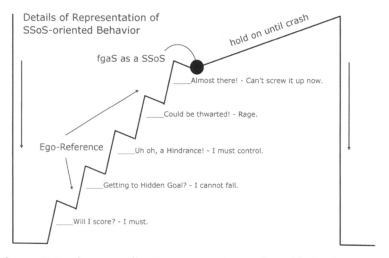

Figure 8.3: Elements affecting a person's moods and behaviors

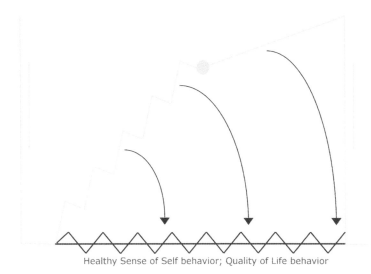

Healthy Sense of Self behavior; Quality of Life behavior

Figure 8.4: The ups and downs in a healthy person's moods and behaviors

let it die, which eventually leads to a crash by a quarrel or not sleeping and the need to start over again.

Figure 8.4 is a comparison of the chaotic mood swings with a representation of a healthy balanced lifestyle. There are the ups and downs at the Quality-of-Life level, but overall there is steadiness and a feeling rooted in one's life.

THE COMPLEX EMOTIONAL WORLD OF THE SSOS-ORIENTED SYSTEM

How can we start to understand the psycho-emotional makeup of a person who is governed by a SSoS-oriented System for self-experience? I refer to my own experiences here, but a detailed, "linear" description of all emotional aspects that were at play within me when I was still totally Substitute Sense of Self–oriented is hard to give.

For me, it meant that the emotions in the family where I grew up must have been quite overwhelming. In fact, as a young adult, I felt a distance between myself and most of the common things people seemed to be preoccupied with—things that would upset them or make them happy. I had made a decision not to be bothered by them and to focus on how to do things differently. Later in life though, when I became a mother, I needed to review this strategy because there was no escape from the trivialities and logistics in life at that point: I had to learn to deal with it all.

There are two predominant emotions in a person who has a SSoS: the Fear of Annihilation and the FgaS state. Fear is the basic motivation for doing what it takes to get to a FgaS, and they seesaw back and forth. When one is high, the other is low. There is never a stable situation, because the FgaS state never lasts for long before it fades and requires the next "fix" of approval. When it fades, the Fear of Annihilation gets stronger. (Note that a FgaS state does not survive a good night's sleep—hence, insomnia.)

THE SOUP OF SSOS-RELATED GOALS AND EMOTIONS

The complexity of all the emotions that a Substitute Sense of Self generates in a person is best compared to soup: Everything is in it but you do not recognize the individual ingredients. So I've decided to describe my psycho-emotional makeup as if it were soup. Everybody's soup tastes differently, even though many of the ingredients might be the same. My goal in creating this description is for you to get insight into what "laws" are at work when you combine some of these psycho-emotional ingredients:

- Normal quality-of-life events and emotions;
- "Holy decisions," such as "I am never going to do this or that; I am always going to be such and such; I'm absolutely going to do things in a different way compared to my parents; I am going to be different from everybody else.";
- The two sides of Ego-References: the normal Quality of Life motivation, for example, "not wanting anger in your house," plus the SSoS-oriented motivations for not wanting to be angry (for Fear of Annihilation);
- Multiple simultaneously existing but incompatible Ego-References that lead to Inner Conflict;
- The "elephant in the room" of feeling good at all cost (as a family-wide Ego-Reference and Hidden Goal). I refer to the unspoken agreement (in my family of origin) that every family member makes it his or her top priority to behave in such a way that other members are provided or can preserve their FgaS as a SSoS;
- Fear of encountering reasons to be angry, and the continuous conscious and subconscious drive to be on the lookout to avoid those. (See the issues of control in the following discussion.);
- Fear or one's own feelings/behavior;

- Fear of "screwing it up." There is perceived to be so much at stake (Quality of Life–level family peace next to the [much stronger] SSoS-oriented goal), but we are distressed and puzzled because we are not aware of that, or of what is at stake (nor is anybody else). All we are aware of about ourselves is that we are "high-strung," that our temper is not always contained, and that in some vague, undefined way, we sense a temper display puts us back to zero, having to start from scratch. Start what, we don't know!

- The unavoidable crash of the SSoS-oriented activities and behavior (see Figure 8.2).

We are still talking soup here:

The need to control and the constant presence of fear, stress, and the overzealous effort to do things the right way function as the binding ingredients for this soup (comparable to the function of corn starch). Throw into this pot of soup as herbs-of-the-season some random ingredients like the parental expressions such as

"All is wasted now" ("We had a pleasant evening, but in the end things turned sour. But all is wasted now.");

"You are always the one to screw it up" (a too easily made accusation);

"You blew it again";

"I'm walking on eggshells";

"If you are this or that way, everybody will walk out on you";

"Make sure you are not giving in to others and stay true to yourself, but I guess it is hard when you have no self";

and other similar expressions.

Put this on the fire of the Hidden Agenda (to bring the Ego-Reference to a good end), stir it really well while heating it to a boiling point, and serve it to your loved ones. Do you think they will like this soup?

Principles at Work in Making Soup

Let's elaborate some more on the analogy of soup so you might get a clearer sense of the mood and mind-set of a person who is dependent on a SSoS for experiencing his or her Self. There are a number of principles at work:

- Dependency on the outcome of an Ego-Reference leads to heavy control.
- Ego-Reference plus Ego-Reference equals Inner Conflict.

- Inner Conflict leads to blaming others, rage, depression, and insomnia. A person's circumstances spiral downward. The need to repair the circumstances (make up for it by going overboard) and to control others and the circumstances even more in order not to "do it again" increases stress and fear.

- Self-sabotage continuously thwarts a potential good outcome to an Ego-Reference.

- Anger, rage, insomnia, and/or depression due to the thwarting of the Ego-Reference adds more stress.

- Stress plus fear equals more need to control.

- Stress plus need to control equals more stress; ultimately there is a point that the body and/or mind can't handle it anymore and falls ill from exhaustion, fear, and depression.

HARMFUL EFFECTS OF THE SUBSTITUTE SENSE OF SELF–ORIENTED SYSTEM

Where a Natural Sense of Self provides a stable point of departure for a person, a Substitute Sense of Self is a complex, unstable, and chaotic psycho-emotional-behavioral structure. Even though it functions as a unit to hold onto in life, due to the lack of the presence of Self as a guide, in reality it results in a great array of suffering for the person and for the people in that person's environment.

The harmful effects of a Substitute-oriented System are widely varied and can be severe, such as the following:

- Anger and rage
- Fear
- Suffering
- Inauthenticity
- Stress

We look into how and why each of these problematic side effects is generated.

Anger and Rage

Anger and rage come from the subconscious thoughts "Why can't I get things the way I need them to be?" or, in terms of the SSoS, "Why can't the world be such that I can achieve a good outcome to my Ego-References feel-good-about-my-self as a Substitute Sense of Self and get the respect and acknowledgment of my caregiver?" Now think of a young mom, at the heart of her family, dependent on things to be just so, so that her FgaS state is facilitated. How much chance is there that she gets the situation to work in her favor? What happens if she doesn't?

We are talking here about a woman whose Ego-References are her first priority. This means that all circumstances need to be just "so" in order for her to use those circumstances as Vehicles to manifest her Ego-References with the guarantee that there will be a positive outcome. Take into account what is perceived to be at stake, and you will understand that there is no room for failure. Anything in the way is a **Hindrance** or an obstacle and leads to anger or rage, which can be a gateway to violence or its counterpart, depression.

Hindrance

Any obstacle that can lead to anger or rage, which can be a gateway to violence or its counterpart, depression.

So anger and rage are always lurking and can emerge at any given moment in a person with a Substitute Sense of Self because, often, life includes Hindrances to the good outcome of an Ego-Reference, be it through the words of an unwilling or noncomplying family member or through circumstances that are not "just so."

If one of our Ego-References is to avoid being angry, we are living in a complex situation. On one hand, anger builds because our Ego-Reference is being thwarted, and on the other hand the pressure of not expressing our anger builds as well. Managing this buildup is like a volcanic eruption to be controlled. It is not surprising that in spite of the perceived consequences (lack of approval equates rejection), we are only able to hold in all that tension to a certain point, and at the point of saturation—*boom!*—the anger spews from us, as lava from an erupting volcano.

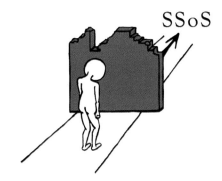

Figure 8.5: Hindrances on our way to a SSoS

This is the reality of the life of a SSoS-oriented person; once in this state of anger, sometimes a minor irritation, the infamous "straw that breaks the camel's back" is enough to make the person snap. Or sometimes a minor source of anger, such as trying "to talk out" a situation, results in an unforeseen eruption of stress and anger.

After many years of marriage, Erica knew that, once she detected in herself, symptoms of being frustrated with her husband, it would come out sooner or later. In order to prevent that, she would sit down with her husband "to talk it out." After many years, her husband's behavior had also been shaped by the repeated quarrels for no obvious reason, as he called them, and he had become pretty defensive. So in spite of all of Erica's good intentions the talk usually did not go the way she had planned, which made her even more frustrated. Trying to avoid being angry at the cost of her SSoS, she needed him to react in a positive way to her cause. The reality for Paul, though, was that he felt powerless and at his wits' end about how to do things in a way that would be good for Erica, while still staying true to himself. The result was a heated discussion that often would culminate in drama. Quite the opposite of what Erica's intention was in the first place. However, at this point of both people feeling at a loss about what to do in the situation, the Fear of Annihilation that turns into unbearable stress breaks free and is unstoppable. This is the moment

Figure 8.6: The straw that breaks the SSoS—or camel's—back

in which people can lose control over their words and actions. This situation then opens the door for even well-intending men or women, to commit acts of violence, or behave in a destructive way either verbally or physically, or both. When one is in this state, children or spouses get beaten, road rage occurs, and atrocities are carried out.

It cannot be stressed enough: Violence often is an expression of ultimate powerlessness. Given the nature of life, people might get angry or even *very* angry. even when really present to themselves and to their lives. However, blind rage that leads to violence can, in many cases, be avoided when the person becomes aware that the subconsciously experienced, false but perceived life-or-death threat of an unfulfilled Ego-Reference underlies their impulses and behavior.

Consider the following: In the summer of 1971 at Stanford University, Professor Zimbardo conducted an experiment on the psychological effects of imprisonment. A group of 24 healthy, intelligent, middle-class male students, without any particular psychological problems, was selected to participate. The group was randomly divided into two groups: guards and prisoners. The experiment was to last 13 days but had to be shut down after only 6 days due to atrocious behavior, cruelties, and power plays. The explanation was that prisoners and guards had lost their sense of reality.[8] I dare to question here whether they ever had one in the first place.

A bold statement maybe, that I cannot back up by evidence; however, I vividly recall the intense experience of my own emotional distress and my fits of rage about seemingly minor, unimportant things. Most fortunately, my husband managed to deal with my unreasonable anger, my need to justify my requests, and my need for utter control. Even so, I did get thoughts of despair, wondering if life would be worth living any longer, where I felt like Sisyphus, whom the gods had condemned to rolling a boulder uphill only to have it be thrown back into the valley over and over again.

Experiencing any kind of obstacles on our path toward achievement of any of our Ego-References can lead to irritation, anger, and/or depression. If we are thwarted in our compulsion to live up to the requirements of the Ego-References, we may also experience terror because the Fear of Annihilation lurks around every corner. This fear often results in rage or fury.

---

[8] Visit www.prisonexperiment.org to learn more about this experiment. It should be noted that there were several ethical concerns raised about this experiment, but these should not diminish the results regarding what anger and rage lie within each of us.

Fear

There is the ordinary everyday Quality-of-Life (QoL) fear. It is by the nature of our existence justified fear as things are not controllable. Even when we do not have "an existential attachment" to the outcome of things we still have wishes and needs for desired outcomes. It is no more than normal to experience apprehension and a certain degree of justified fear when a situation is anticipated or desired. For more on QoL level of experiences, see page 154.

However, a person with a SSoS has many more fears, all of which stem from the root Fear of Annihilation. In order to get the best result while acting out to fulfill our Ego-References, and because we have no room for failure with our SSoS at stake, we need to be in control of all the circumstances related to fulfilling our Ego-References.

These fears are related in a complex way, and it is impossible to overestimate how dominant the role is of the many kinds of SSoS-related fears in the life of a person who depends on a SSoS. Those fears exhaust the person, due to the continuous high level of stress.

Because it is hard for a person to label and get insight into these fears, they are experienced as vague and undefined. These fears are a psycho-emotional load and are probably the ultimate cause of many physical, mental, or emotional symptoms that, over time, can develop into physical and mental disease and dysfunction. Some of these fears include

- fear of our own emotions,
- fear of our own behavior,
- fear of failure (stage fright),
- fear of not being able to function, and
- fear of change.

These fears are very strong, and the way they manifest intense, because of the life-or-death level of Annihilation. People whose living is ruled by a SSoS have a desperate need to get to the required outcome of being good enough to get approval of the real or virtual parent—one's "being" or not "being" is perceived to be at stake, which explains the unreasonable fear.

Imagine this scenario: Erica is on her way home, and her husband has agreed to have diner ready for her at a specific time. He can be a bit picky when he is the cook because he values good food and the quality of food is time sensitive. But he is an easygoing guy who doesn't want to harm a fly. Erica decides on her way home to pick up her boots. She leaves in a timely fashion but encounters a lot of traffic on her way to the shoe repair shop and becomes anxious. She convinces herself that it isn't her fault that traffic is so unexpectedly heavy, and she wonders if she should call her husband. It isn't easy to call while driving, and she is afraid she will get an ocular migraine at the last minute, when multitasking, just when things were going so well. So she decides not to look at the clock. Slowly it starts to dawn on her that it would be better for her husband to know that she will be late so she calls him (note that reality kicks in only after the inner upheaval has been processed). It is a bit late when she calls him, and already he has started to prepare the meal. Erica squirms and feels badly. She wishes she could make him see that it really wasn't her fault. She excuses herself a million times for not being on time (not because of her husband's cooking, but because again she has failed to live up to her Ego-Reference).

The point of this story is that there is too much emotional intensity compared to the reality of the moment. There is in Erica, deep down, a Fear of Annihilation that causes her to overreact.

Now let us go more into detail about the various types of SSoS-oriented fears.

Fear of Our Emotions

This discussion will focus mainly on one particular behavior of which we are afraid: getting angry, and/or feeling as if we are being compelled (by something inside us) to get angry, against our will. Fear of being angry is one of the strongest fears, because anger is an explosive, destructive emotion that usually has a lot of impact.

But there are other fears as well in response to having certain qualities or characteristics as Ego-References. Fear of not liking something or somebody. When you decide you want to be nice to your husband—not because of who he is, but because that calms your fear of abandonment—you want to make sure that he behaves in ways that you *are able* to like him. If he behaves in a way that you do not like, you are on the inner battlefield. So over time you anticipate this situation, and you fear the fact that you might not like what he is doing before he is doing anything. You fear receiving a present for fear that you will not like it. You fear making an appointment for fear of being late.

Fear of Our Behavior

Emotions lead to behavior so these two fears are related. If we fear our emotions it is because we fear our behavior. The behavior is just one step closer to the manifestations of the emotion. It is more real. When we feel we have to display a behavior that works against our Ego-References, we experience fear in a way that works against our own safety.

Say that your parent's approval is your ultimate goal because it is associated with feeling safe. Doing something that goes against that brings up fear. You do not recognize that because you are not consciously aware that you are trying to live up to certain conditions. But it brings you to agony.

Here is an example: Your Ego-Reference is to never be angry. That was what you concluded to be the best way to get your parents' approval and feel they would let you get close to them. Now your husband does something that makes you mad. You are scared he will leave you when you show you are upset. It is not about your husband, who you do not want to get angry. It is about your Ego-Reference of not wanting to be angry that you have learned to cultivate. Because deep down, you are scared your husband might walk out on you when you get angry. But he behaves in such a way that you cannot let it pass, and there is conflict. What do you do? Here you are scared of your own emotion, of your own behavior.

People who rely on a SSoS do not have an authentic Self; they have only a SSoS-oriented System, which provides their criteria and operates on autopilot as their default. They do not have a will or opinion of their own. Their will and their best judgment for how they would choose to behave or ought to behave, if present at all, is run by their Ego-References. They are not present with their own selves; they are only fulfilling conditions as they have learned their "life depends on it."

There is another aspect to the Ego-Reference of "not wanting to be angry." The moment we have this feeling of not being able to deal with something the Ego-Reference "I don't want to get angry" creates anger in itself that can culminate in rage. *We* are upset to come across something that will make it extremely difficult for us to be successful in satisfying our Ego-References, and our life (of being acknowledged as a real person) depends on it. So deep down we are furious that that is happening to us, which aggravates the anger that is caused by the outside event. Just as the emotions experienced when we are "being late" are greatly overreactive, so it is with being angry—only the effects are normally much more noticeable.

All this plays out at a subconscious level; we only sense great apprehension for what life will throw at us, and we try to stay away from conflict. Avoiding conflict is, of course, a challenge for anyone, even for those of us who function at a Quality-of-Life level. But having it tied to whether or not you are worth being taken into account, which is the deeper belief of a person with Ego-References, makes it a matter of life and death. Being afraid of showing anger ends up creating a ton of unnecessary upheaval for ourselves as well as for others. Anticipating the results and effects of these emotions on others and ourselves, we then become afraid of our own behavior, as if we *are the victims* of it, are not in control of it, which is the truth, in the state we are in (not in touch with our own being).

We are unaware if there is a situation that is perceived as a threat to satisfying an Ego-Reference and have a strong urge to protect whatever level of performance (toward achieving the Ego-Reference) we've reached. So our worst nightmare is that something will happen to thwart our efforts, and we realize this something could be our own behavior.

So that's what's going on behind the scenes, leading to the SSoS-dependent people's fear of their own behavior.

Fear of Failure

People who are dependent on a SSoS have a heightened fear of failure. For them Annihilation is at stake and that is one good reason to be concerned about failing to reach their goal. But there is one other, even more potent reason, for this high level of failure fear: Whatever these people do, they are not really present in their own grounded Self.

Everything people undertake, as has been said before, is geared toward their Hidden Agenda. Only 40 percent of their energy and intent goes to the project at hand. So they do not function for the full 100 percent and that is why it takes them so much effort. That is why they have to spend so much time on their undertakings. And that is also why they intuitively know that they do not have the best point of departure to be successful in what they are doing. Fear of failure in itself undermines the performance of a task as well. So here we have three reasons why people with a lack of SoS are much more prone to fearing they are inadequate in what they are doing. But let us focus on a very specific type of fear of failure: stage fright, or performance anxiety.

You will find that stage fright is rooted, for a large percentage of people, in fearing Annihilation. Let me describe the processes underlying what happens to some who are performers. But bear in mind that we can just as well substitute "presence on stage" with any other situation in which we feel we have to "perform."

You have an upcoming performance. You are well prepared but anywhere from a day (or several days) to five minutes before the event begins your hands become clammy, you start to shake, you are nauseous, and if you are a singer, your throat starts to act up.

The following is an example from my own life: During my years in the orchestra I made several attempts to develop my voice as a singer. I took that very seriously because I thought I enjoyed singing. But every time an opportunity arose to give a small performance on the Lieder (a German art song) I had worked so hard on, the day of the concert, I had no voice. Was this accidental, I wondered? I hadn't overused my voice or anything—I just came down with a cold. The Universe works in mysterious ways, but I got the message at some point.

As a performer you may be worried (sick) you are going to forget your lines (as an actress or a professional speaker), slip and fall (as a dancer), or have "a frog in your throat" (as a singer). In short, you are scared out of your wits for not getting the desired outcome. Where does that so suddenly come from? Some people even say, "Oh, that is normal. Everyone has stage fright."

Fear is always rooted in a cause and with such a strong reaction there must be a lot that is perceived to be at stake. Now, don't get me wrong, if you are endowed with an intrinsic sense of knowing who you are and that you do not depend on the outcome of your activities nor on what others think of you, you can still be a bit tense. But if you chose to be a performer, you would most likely be excited and thrilled as well. You need the adrenaline rush to get you on the tip of your toes to create that special performance—whatever it is you do.

If you do a job every day and for a great number of years, you get used to certain tensions. So I still have a hard time deciding whether or not I am a performer. Part of the fun of being on stage is being seen and heard, which was a need I definitely had. I also love music and knew how to work on it to get it technically in good shape. However, what was missing, in hindsight, were the emotions of being moved by the beauty of the piece I was playing. It happened, when we were playing with the whole orchestra, but to let that come from my own core was an ability that was overshadowed by my absolute need to do a good job to go home at night with "a sense of belonging" and a FgaS state.

But for those performers who have severe symptoms of stage fright please consider the following: It may be that you are in need of acknowledgment by means of admiration and applause and that your SoS depends on it. You may be dependent on a SSoS, and through your performance, you aim at getting the "craved-for" FgaS state. In other words, you use your performance as a Vehicle to get your fix of feeling good about yourself. What you may not be aware of is that your virtual psychological backbone is at stake and that is why you are so anxious. Without knowing it might be a matter of having the "right to exist" for you and not being able to make it to that goal is something you want to avoid at all cost. What really is at stake for you is the fear of being annihilated, discounted as a real person among other people.

People train and study yearlong, marry specific persons, and choose specific jobs, not because of sincere dedication and interest, but to use these things as a Vehicle to get to their Hidden Goal. From the outside nothing is visibly at stake, but deep down inside, and oftentimes hidden to themselves as well, there is a deep fear that they are not going to reach that "holy" goal.

"What could be my 'holy' Hidden Goal," you want to know? Dive deep within yourself and ask yourself these questions: "What in my life would I want most of all? What am I all about?" And make sure you are totally honest with yourself!

What do I think will come up for you from deep down? You will see that your fear of failure really has nothing to do with the content of your performance or activities, but is related to that buried hope of getting to your Hidden Goal—your only goal in life.

The sad thing is, though, that although the fear is not directly connected to the content of your performance or activity, it still affects it a lot. The result is a double disadvantage: The presence of the existing sense of fear contaminates your activity, which makes it hard for you to concentrate on its performance. The bulk of your intention, let us say 60 percent, goes toward achieving the Hidden Goal and is not aimed at the actual performance.

So what remains? Forty percent of your energy is what remains available to create your top performance. On top of that: even though the audience can't put their finger on it, they somehow sense that what you are doing on stage isn't about giving them a wonderful experience, and they lose interest pretty quickly. Performing from a place of Indirect Motivation is a struggle of the highest intensity and its reward only a mediocre result.

So investigate for yourself and ask, "What is at stake for me during a performance?" It might surprise you how much you do not know about yourself. Addressing that issue is what allows you to concentrate fully on your performance, and since now nothing is at stake other than the beauty of the event, your fear of failure will have dissolved to make place for the thrill of the moment.

Fear of Not Being Able to Function

For a person with a SSoS, due to the resulting high stress and tension and a system in overload, there is a tendency to become ill and have symptoms that then paradoxically sabotage the SSoS. So even though part of that fear (of failing to function) is totally neurotic, there also is a legitimate reason for it. Because of the increase in the amount and intensity of symptoms of dis-ease, which pop up with distressing frequency, "not being able to function" is a constantly lurking condition that makes things even harder for the person than they already are.

On top of the fact that achieving the (Hidden) Goals of the SSoS-oriented System (all the time and over and over again) is impossible, there is an extra obstacle in getting a positive outcome of attempts to fulfill the ego-references: One's intrinsic fear of failure sabotages any effort. The higher one climbs, the more the fear of failure manifests itself in various appearances: teasing thoughts, solo syndrome, and smooth-floor syndrome, among others, which are discussed later in the chapter. These undermine attaining the goal.

Fear of Change

Change—moving, taking on a new job, and change in general—is challenging for people with a Substitute Sense of Self because they do not want to spend time on things other than their Ego-References. Change looms over them, offering mostly Hindrances.

A big part of the life of a SSoS-oriented person is therefore spent *anticipating the perfect setup* for fulfilling his or her Ego-Reference. Doing things to clear the path so we *can* spend time working on the Ego-References is already a chore and needs to be efficient, and with change we lose control over the circumstances in which we can complete Ego-References. To manage change we anticipate what could happen next. Rather than change, SSoS-oriented people are compulsively controlling their environment and themselves to avoid change.

Suffering and Stress

The dependency on a SSoS creates constant stress, which in turn promotes suffering. The perceived life-or-death situation that underlies motivation raises stress levels to absurd heights. Objectively, one could state that the stress levels are in no way congruent with what would be reasonable and to be expected when looking at the person's external stressors. It therefore is clear that there are internal stressors at work and that they need to be dismantled. For an example, see the story about having an Indirect Relationship with Self on page 21.

Not being able to take refuge in the shelter of our own Self, we continu-ously are after feeling safe, feeling alive, getting a sense of belonging—all feel-ings that were missing in our childhood and that prevented us from being able to develop a healthy SoS. Yet the attainment of who we believe ourselves to be after childhood requires constant vigilance and continuous manipulation, and this produces constant frustrations and constant anxiety—stress.

Many, if not all, Ego-References are difficult to achieve or are not feasible because of their fictional nature. Think of Ego-References as comparable to wanting to be perfect; it sounds nice, but it is impossible. We cannot make sure we will never be angry or will always be on time. We cannot anticipate whether our body weight is going to be acceptable for our parent, or that we will have the exact ideal, "cute family" our caregiver would like to see us have (so they can "Feel-good-about-Themselves"). Yet we keep trying to fulfill these mistaken beliefs—because that is a way to get our parent's approval.

The sad truth is that the fulfillment of the Ego-Reference conditions becomes our identity, and we are not in a position to actually notice and objectively evaluate the realistic or unrealistic nature of what we are attempting to accomplish. Hence, trying to accomplish these unrealistic goals creates stress and suffering in our lives.

Compulsiveness and Addictive Behaviors

The driving force compelling the creation and re-creation ad infinitum of the Substitute Sense of Self is as strong as any other survival mechanism. The obsession with fulfilling the Ego-References leads to neurosis and to compulsively driven behaviors. The behaviors are much more subtle than an obvious, classic compulsion of, for example, incessant hand washing. The behaviors tied to the Substitute Sense of Self are attached to and inseparable from everyday activities. The Black Hole is exerting its force on the motivations involved in the SSoS-oriented System.

Over time, the positive reward of getting the caregiver's attention, the nice vibes that reach us through this as well as our relatively higher level of (perceived) well-being (FgaS), positively reinforce the behavior. It becomes more and more automatic, more subconscious, and more desired by the person herself, until earning this (FgaS-)state through what we are doing becomes a person's identity.

We should not forget to mention the other end of the spectrum of this SSoS-oriented behavior though. There is a continuous interference by the aspects of the neurosis and problems a person has. They are continuously dragging down the positive attempts to realize a person's agendas of the Ego-References. Any SSoS-oriented score point is reached with the utmost difficulty and an effort that is much more demanding than normal as those negative characteristics of the neurosis painfully work in the opposite direction of the person's desired FgaS state.

For example: I want to prove to a specific person (or even to myself: VIPV) that I can be on time (for SSoS-oriented reasons) but I have a hard time sleeping and I know it so I am scared that I will not sleep. I get upset with what is in my way of going to bed in a "relaxed" way, be it a quarrel or an overflowing bathtub. Anything works as a Hindrance in getting to achieve my Ego-Reference's goal and aggravates me. I am high strung and can't deal with it. I blow up, which makes me feel-bad-about-myself and leads to insomnia, etc.

To get the SSoS in place is a need that brooks no compromise. It is a compulsion-generating drive because the SSoS is a structure that is an absolute requirement for the person's sense of being. The function of a SSoS for this kind of person's psyche is comparable to the function of our spine, which sustains our body; it is something that simply cannot be missing without causing total collapse—not to mention the terror of the Black Hole that is lurking always in the background.

The motivations involved in preventing collapse and keeping the terror at bay, therefore, are felt as irresistible compulsions, which lead to an addiction to the FgaS state. Anything compulsively sought has to be renewed repeatedly, aimed at relieving a pain (physical or emotional), yet it is damaging to our quality of life as a negative or pathological addiction. Life lived in this way is not geared toward a person's true well-being, and the person's expression or manifestation leads the person to do many things detrimental to his or her true well-being. Life is lived in emergency mode to prevent what feels like potential disaster, so priorities are shifted, and the person is a slave to the priorities of the SSoS-oriented System.

It should be abundantly clear, from what has just been described, that we are dealing here with just such an addiction.

Everyday Situations Turn into "Performances"

The invisible drama of a person who is ruled by a SSoS-oriented System is that nothing is what it seems to be. People are merely "performing" their lives instead of really living them. The performance either leads to a FgaS that functions as a SSoS, or it makes the person feel bad about his or her Self, which immediately generates the next task to do it better or plunges the person into depression or worse. The following are examples of how everyday life situations turn into performances and the result.

Smooth-Floor Syndrome

When I was a mother with two toddlers, I used to like it when at night before bedtime the house was organized. No toys or clothes on a clean, swept floor. Whenever I managed to achieve that, my husband and I would then (finally!) sit down with a book and spend a quiet evening reading, after the kids were in bed. Oh, what a delight! I can still remember the pleasant and satisfactory feeling of looking at this "smooth" hardwood floor of our living room.

The bad surprise (that eventually became predictable) was that I always had a night without any sleep at all after an evening like that. Somehow, that good situation was being used by my SSoS-oriented System as a thing for **Scoring** with, in the struggle to end the day with a FgaS state that functioned as a SSoS. Then, when I had this feeling, I didn't sleep. Please note that nothing on my mind was worrying me. There was no indication of any problem to be solved. I would lie there and just stay wide awake. I was tired but not sleepy—I would not fall asleep!

It was hard to figure out why that was. But ultimately I got it: It was a matter of life and death to hang on to that FgaS state that took care of my Fear of Annihilation. In other words, I stayed awake all night so that the achieved result of actually "Feeling-good-about-Myself-" as a SSoS would not disappear (compare with the story of the butterflies in Chapter 6; mine weren't going to die on me). My brain made sure to stay on red-hot alert as to "guard" the sense of achievement I had experienced the day before. I remember my husband would start to talk about tomorrow when I bugged him in the middle of the night, where I was still fully in today. I would stay in that mode until about 5 or 6 a.m. Then, when daybreak would convince me it wasn't today anymore, and that further protecting the SSoS was a lost cause, I would, 99 percent of the time, tumble into a deep sleep.

Desperately hanging on to the SSoS state that I would have realized in the day, or the fear not to be able to gain that state the next day is the subconscious process that I hold accountable for my insomnia of 25 years. There was a (subconscious) need to always make sure I had a Vehicle to earn a SSoS with, at my disposal. In this case, ending my day with a "smooth floor and a clean house" was my Vehicle, but I was unable to sleep because I perceived I could not afford to let go of it.

The fear not being able to function at all the next day, due to the insomnia, worsened my fear of insomnia, as you may well understand. A negative spiral of increasing anxiety is the result. Intercepting the perceived need of a SSoS, enables a person to break free from this spiral (I sense my body and I am

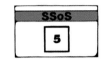

Scoring

Being successful in using a Vehicle to improve on an Ego-Reference; a success that feels like gaining "points" toward the goal of getting parental approval, which results in the feel-good-about-Self as a Substitute Sense of Self.

my body, so I am already! I am not going to be annihilated if I do not perform well. I am already so I do not need a SSoS. See the 12 steps!)

There are two different insomnia patterns caused by two different fears. First, there is the fear/need to make sure of having a Vehicle through which to earn the FgaS state again the next day, which resulted in my waking up too early (like at 3, 4, or 5 a.m.). The second is the fear/need to hang on to the feeling of success, which resulted in my not falling asleep at all until full physical exhaustion was reached. These fears are, in this Method, conceptually different, but both are generated by the SSoS-oriented System.

An Ocular Migraine Sabotaging My SSoS

When visiting my mother, from abroad, it was hard to balance "mother time" with "personal time." Once, during a visit to my mother in my adult years, I had done errands for her, and it had taken a little longer than I had hoped, but I was still on time. On my way back home I went through a lot of psychological stress, because I feared I blew it. I feared I'd have ruined whatever credit of good vibes I had collected with doing what was good for her, by being late. I agonized about not being on time but not about the fact that she had to sit there and wait for me—which is how a SSoS-oriented person works, unfortunately. I worried myself sick about the absence of the positive feeling this would lead to: (VIPV-) approval and a FgaS state. I would have to look her in the eyes feeling-bad-about-myself and feel annihilated. However, I was not aware of that!

My mother used to criticize me a lot for being late and call me egoistic. So being on time was an Ego-Reference for me. When I entered the room and saw her sitting there, relaxed and not—as usual when I was late—blaming me with that look of "What are you doing to me?" an ocular migraine ruined my FgaS state. It sabotaged my experience of being found OK.

The explanation? I had almost made it, and I almost experienced being allowed the FgaS state (as a SSoS). The stress of desperately fearing a last-minute problem/Hindrance caused overload in my brain and produced the vision problem. Then I had to either ignore it or give in and complain about the vision problem. Complaining would ruin the potentially good atmosphere, and preserving that atmosphere was a matter of life and death, for Fear of Annihilation. That atmosphere had to be preserved at all costs (compare this with the queen of MOD in the "Castle of Enmeshment")—it was "the elephant in the room." It was always there and had always been there. Thus, there was so much (perceived to be) at stake, hence the excess of stress that caused the overload on my brain, which generated the ocular migraine!

On many occasions when I had almost made it, this ocular migraine would pop up. It always occurred when I was about to score with satisfying an Ego-Reference. That is all part of the SSoS-oriented System.

Teasing Thoughts/"Solo Syndrome"

For many years I worked as a professional bassoonist. Whenever my part contained a solo, I, of course, would prepare well for it. When, at the crucial moment of performing, I was playing it well, I suddenly seemed to step out of myself and become an observer of myself, "teasing" myself with thoughts such as "What if you don't manage to bring this to a good ending?" or "What if you didn't count correctly here?"

Needless to say, it took the utmost concentration—even struggle—to effectively bring the solo to a good conclusion. Often, the teasing thoughts caused the quality of my playing to deteriorate. I could have easily done well if such teasing thoughts had not always been in the way, sabotaging my good playing.

Here's my explanation of how this self-sabotage happened. Partway through the solo, and because it was going well, my Substitute-Sense-of-Self System, with its gigantic Ego-Reference of being a superbly excellent musician, seized the performance to score on the scale of SSoS-oriented credits. This activated stress and fear, which interfered with the quality of my performing. It was as if the ground fell out from under my feet and the degree of concentration and effort I needed to bring things to a good ending was excruciating. All the fun and possible joy of being able to play that solo were drained from it.

By "ground," I literally mean the ground of my being because my being a Self had no firm footing within my psyche at that time of my life. So it depended on the fleeting sense of groundedness after each of my latest achievements. These teasing thoughts were the way the fear of failing to reach the desired outcome (the SSoS, not the beautiful music!) manifested. It was as if I were performing while living on a floating device on the ocean—there were no roots to the earth of my being; no steadiness in an inner knowing that I am and I know how to do this.

Teasing thoughts in general are ways to sabotage your SSoS. Even thoughts anticipating the possibility of having teasing thoughts can sabotage the performance of sleeping well, if sleeping well is an Ego-Reference, as it was for me! When I, during so many sleepless nights, would finally be on the verge of falling asleep, a nagging, anticipatory teasing thought would come into my mind: "What if this thought keeps me awake again?" Note that, desperate as I was, I did not want to sleep well *for myself* but to be "OK and normal," which was another Ego-Reference for me.

It was only much later in my self-discovery process that I learned that the teasing thought itself was only there when there was SSoS-oriented activity! Sleeping well then had become a performance (an Ego-Reference) to earn a SSoS (or even to earn my mother's "benevolence," cooperating with *her* struggle to get her to "Feel-good-about-Herself-" as *her* SSoS.

ERICA'S SITUATION: AN EXAMPLE

To see how all the elements discussed in this chapter affect a person, let us visit with Erica. We see her at a moment in the evening and her husband is not yet home. The following is a list of her Ego-References. She has to accomplish *all* the following goals in order to "Feel-good-about-Herself" and thus experience her SSoS:

- Have peace of mind (in order to be able to sleep well).
- Sleep well.
- Look fresh and fit in the morning and be in a good mood.
- Create no drama, problems, or quarrels.
- Be flexible about her husband's behaviors (because of her fear of abandonment).
- Be productive at her work every day.

Erica's aunt has warned her several times that she'd better live up to those conditions, otherwise her relationship with a significant other would be at risk. Erica didn't recognize that her aunt just reinforced on her the conditions that she would like to see realized by her niece so she would not get into trouble with her and be able to cultivate her own FgaS state. For Erica, this meant that, on top of having to please her aunt by living up to her ego-references, she also had to do that for fear her husband would walk out on her.

Today her husband has come home late from an evening meeting that was supposed to end at 10 p.m. It is midnight when he enters his home and finds his wife walking through the room like a caged animal. She immediately starts yelling at him, blaming him for being late and not taking her into account.

Not knowing what is going on, her husband doesn't understand her overreaction or her need to control his behavior. Imagine the bickering that follows suit. Erica excused herself for being angry and blamed him for being late. Then she explained to him how he should know that she can't sleep when he is not home or when she is angry, and then she squirmed, begging him not to abandon her.

What happened is that Erica's Ego-References were in conflict: She cannot go to bed for fear that her husband might not like her trying to control his behavior. Even if she does go to bed, she knows that she cannot sleep before he comes home and goes to sleep as well, as she needs things to be OK. So she's caught between two completely incompatible needs: She needs to not cause him any problems, or make any demands, or cause any drama by asking him to be home by her bedtime, or by being upset when he isn't, but she also needs to sleep well to be in good shape and do well at her work the next day, and she can't sleep well until he gets home and "everything is all right."

In other words, she has an Inner Conflict because two (or more) main Ego-References are demanding opposite behaviors from her: "I must sleep well" and "I must not speak up and cause quarrels." But if she does not speak up, she won't sleep well. In either case, the need for her husband's approval and for his Mirroring that her behavior is OK means to her that "Everything is OK; I am safe; I won't be annihilated."

You might say these could be ordinary, everyday Inner Conflicts. Yet there is a significant difference. These games are played on a (perceived) existential level. For these conflicts, there can be no compromise between the two sides, because both seem (subconsciously) like matters of life or death. So on nights like this, and on many other nights, Erica lies in bed, stressed, with a buzzing nervous system and no conscious idea of what is playing out within her. She is totally unable to pick up on what is going on within her own body and mind. She has too many different feelings that she is not consciously aware of. If she could express all those feelings, in words, here's what she might say:

> "I don't agree with his coming home so late, but he doesn't listen to me. So I don't come across clearly, and I am not being taken into account. [Note that her Hidden Goal is to be taken into account.] That shows I don't really exist, which equals I feel bad about myself; I have no Sense of Self [not a real natural one], so I don't really exist. I have to do everything in my power to change that. I can't sleep when I feel bad about myself. I need to feel good about myself [the SSoS]."

> "It's late and I need to go to bed [to sleep well]. If I will start arguing right now, if I openly disagree with him when he comes home, he'll disapprove of me, and then I won't sleep because I won't have

a good feeling about myself and I won't feel safe because I've been
inflexible [being flexible with her husband's actions]."

"I can't create drama because I can't afford to lose this guy because I am
not supposed to create problems. I also depend on his approval to
get my [Substitute] Sense of Self, and without him, I wouldn't be
able to feel good about myself at all."

"I'll feel like a nobody if I can't do good work tomorrow. I am a worka-
holic, and if I don't do good work I feel bad about myself. If I
can't sleep I will be unable to function and gain for myself a good-
feeling-about-self state [SSoS]."

"I feel dirty and ashamed if I don't sleep well. Everybody can see it from
my face [looking fresh in the morning and being in a good mood],
and then I feel I don't belong to the workforce, and therefore I'm
not a real person."

It's important for us to understand that the actual content of the issues is
not what really matters to Erica. *None of this is really about sleeping well or about
arguing with her husband.* They are Vehicles for achieving the Ego-References
of the Hidden Agenda and living up to the imposed conditions they represent
that then might lead to the "Feeling-good-about-Self" state instead of feeling
the agony of the inner void of no Self. The outcome for Erica is a total crash,
a feeling bad-about-Self state, possibly depression for a few days, and insomnia
because of being unable to gain a SSoS. In the best-case scenario, she will start
again and gradually try to complete the SSoS-oriented System.

The situation appears even more painful when we realize that Erica's
life isn't about her life at all, nor is it about her husband's life, for that matter.
It is only about maintaining the SSoS-oriented System's function, and she
has become a slave to her own survival strategy. You can well imagine that
in a no-way-out Inner Conflict like this, Erica's body is in an extreme fight–
flight–freeze state. She simply cannot comply with all the current demands
of the SSoS-oriented System in her situation, because they dictate opposite
behaviors! A state of panic might arise about losing the FgaS state, and the
source of this panic is Fear of Annihilation. So she might have a bad case of
insomnia. She might also have a panic attack or even a fit of extreme (unreasonable) anger, rage, or violence.

With enough time and help in understanding what is going on inside
herself, Erica could become conscious of the conflicting expectations and
feelings. She could do the hard inner work of understanding the true nature

of these Ego-References. Then, they could be laid to rest and would stop disrupting her life and ruining her quality of life.

That is what the insight and understanding of HealthySenseofSelf's Motivation Method aims to offer to *you*.

LOOKING AHEAD

Now you can see how the pattern leading to the development of a SSoS repeats itself and affects you greatly. With it comes the accompanying un-healthy dependency on the fulfillment of the Ego-References instead of rely-ing on a Natural SoS for your being and doing. From one generation to the next, children whose caregivers do not have a Direct Relationship with Them-selves but instead are dependent on the fulfillment of all kinds of conditions for their SSoS, develop into the same kind of self-absorbed person who created us in the first place. Unfortunately these patterns are bound to be repeated.

Now that we have learned about the SSoS-oriented System and its harmful effects, we can take steps to look at what it takes to change our con-dition. In the next chapter, we look at several common problems—depression, insomnia, and addiction—through the lens of the SSoS-oriented System.

9 | Map for Healing Your SoS; Depression, Insomnia, and Addiction—A New Look at Common Problems

The SoS Method asserts that many ailments are the direct result of a lack of Sense of Self. If a Natural Sense of Self is not developed there isn't really a way to experience your Self in a direct way. Instead you are subconsciously compelled to complete one never-ending task: to fill up the void in your psyche, that exists due to the inability to refer to your Real Self in an effective way. Day in and day out, you do your very best to "earn" your parent's approval as that makes you "Feel-good-about-Yourself," which then functions for you as a surrogate way to relate to yourself (SSoS).

If you have a Natural SoS or a Restored SoS, then *you do not depend on the outcome of your actions for your Sense of Self. Regardless of outcomes, you always know who you are and that you have the right to be-as-you-ARE.*

In the preceding chapter we described the harmful physical, mental, and emotional effects of the SSoS. This chapter presents to you a Map for Healing your SoS, based on the concepts used in the SoS Method. It encompasses a totally new interpretation of many common problems and pains. Time will be spent on providing you with guidance on how to look at this map and the ideas that are represented in this map. The chapter furthermore focuses on three of the most common problems of our time: depression, insomnia, and addiction.

INTRODUCTION OF THE MAP FOR HEALING YOUR SOS

In previous chapters you learned that the SoS Method describes that a Lack of Sense of Self (LoSoS) leads to a dependency and/or addiction to a SSoS. This condition can be a root cause of disease and dysfunction. What is important to understand is that this root cause existed before what so far have been considered the actual causes for these diseases and dysfunctions. We find it on a deeper level of a person's whole body makeup, and it is to be considered as a basic condition that allows disease to take place. In fact this condition of a lack of SoS, sooner or later, will lead to disease if nothing is undertaken to change this process.

To make understanding of the interactivity and connections that exist between the SSoS-oriented concepts that are at play in this process easier, I have graphically mapped them out.

Consider this first: you either start life outside the womb with *an adequate mirror,* held up to you by your caregivers, or with *an inadequate mirror.* In the first case, you, most likely, will not need this Method or this Map as there will be no sign or symptom of what this Map depicts. With an adequate mirror, you are able to develop a healthy Sense of Self, which results in people who experience their Problems and Pains on a Quality-of-Life level. While you won't lead a problem-free life entirely, as such is not the nature of life in general, you do not add unnecessary stress to your difficulties with a SSoS-oriented reaction to it. In other words, you do not have that complication that makes the problems you face harder to solve.

When your caregivers turn out to be inadequate mirrors to you, you enter the realm of the concepts depicted on this Map, which this work is all about. You then grow up developing a SSoS, not a NatSoS. That means that you come to depend on a SSoS that includes the Ego-References you identify with, and that are supposed to lead to (parental- or virtual parental-) approval, or FgaS as a SSoS. For the person who experiences the cycles of the SSoS-oriented System as depicted in this Map, getting to the FgaS as a SSoS is a matter of life and death.

For a person who grows up without an adequate mirror, that has consequences later in life. They will experience high anxiety during the whole journey of achieving the Hidden Goal (SSoS) through fulfilling the Hidden Agenda (goal of the ER).

This kind of anxiety is not present in the lives of people who have been adequately mirrored throughout their development, and therefore have been able to develop a HySoS. While it is normal and natural to have a QoL fear from time to time, in certain situations, in the lives of the people who depend on a SSoS, this (normal) fear is augmented greatly by a SSoS-oriented fear that, for them, is always in the background and easily triggered. This constellation of anxiety easily adds up over time, and causes a stress level that is considerably higher than that in people with a healthy SoS. This much anxiety, ever present, can lead to exhaustion and deplete your body and mind of energy and health. I leave it up to the reader to imagine, for a moment, the numerous symptoms that this condition can lead to.

The SoS Method takes pride in shedding a different light on commonly accepted approaches to what are the causes of our problems and pains. More importantly, working with the principles for healing your SoS, you resolve your problems and pains on a fundamental level. And you do not need a doctor for it.

The red circle on the map is one to always keep in mind—if this picture applies to you. It represents the addictive path—the path of dependency that, at all times, should be replaced by a virtual green one: the path of your own life. To have an understanding of this map in mind when trying to escape from the claws of the addiction to a SSoS can be a life-saver. Recognizing at the right moment that, YES, you are walking on the red path and you need to

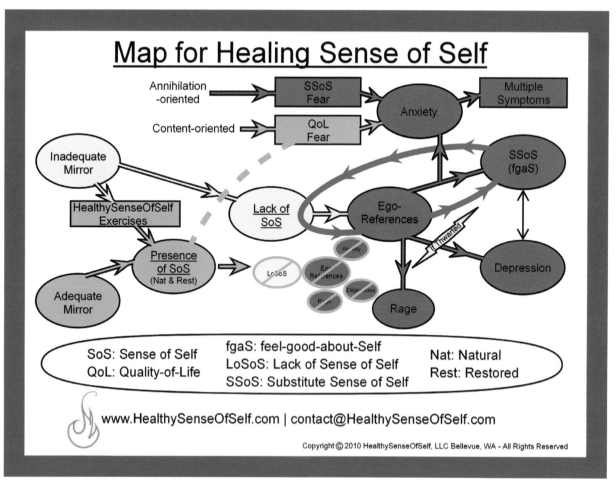

Figure 9.1: Full Map for Healing Sense of Self

step back toward the green path is a simple but powerful tool to have in your kit during your process of healing.

Now let us look at how this map has been crafted. What are the various elements in it? What follows is a detailed explanation with progressive illustrations that contain all of the basic concepts of the SoS Method.

This Map for Healing the Sense of Self is best used as a summary after studying the separate components of the SoS Method and having become familiar with the lingo used.

The full Map actually shows, in one view, two distinct pathways. The top part maps out the relationships between various concepts of the Substitute Sense of Self-oriented System and its cause. The bottom part shows what happens in the case of a healthy (Natural) Sense of Self. All the pathological results—that figure in the top part—are not present in this section. And in the case of a Restored Sense of Self, they have been eliminated. In the following, we will go into a detailed explanation.

EXPLANATION OF COLORS

The items in *red* refer to the key concepts of the SoS Method. Red is the color of emergency and represents the state of being dependent on a Substitute Sense of Self that comes down to being in an ongoing psycho-emotional state of emergency.

Blue fields refer to pathological aspects and elements in life, e.g., Substitute Sense of Self-related fear and anxiety, disease of all sorts, and dysfunctions on a variety of levels. (Blue as in "feeling blue," or as in having "high blood pressure.")

The items in *green* refer to roughly everything that has to do with the SoS Method's Motivation Theory. Green gives a sense of reassurance, of things being OK, of naturalness and authenticity.

The "balloon" of "Inadequate Mirroring" is *yellow*, as is the one of "Lack of Sense of Self." The color *yellow* is used to distinguish the fields from other sections and, more importantly, yellow indicates that the fields represent the root cause of the unhealthy results that are marked in red and blue.

Balloons outlined in green with *green diagonal lines* are meant to convey the message that the problems that result from an inadequate mirroring are *absent* in a person's life who has received adequate mirroring. There is no involvement of any yellow-colored field, when a person has been acknowledged through adequate mirroring by his or her caregiver. Consequently there is no Lack of Sense of Self, there are no Ego-References, there is no need for a SSoS, and therefore none of the unhealthy fields as marked in red and blue are there. That means no (SSoS-oriented) Rage, Depression, etc.

At first glance, the Map for Healing the Sense of Self looks quite crowded, so in the following series of illustrations we will isolate the various fields that form a unit, and give you a detailed explanation for each one of them. Here, you will find five different views of the map, and each one of them highlights a specific section. Then, we will end by showing the full map again, which by then should make more sense to you. Thoroughly understanding the flow of this Map greatly helps you to get the gist of the SoS Method.

Now let us look at the separate constellations.

STAGE 1

This part of the map shows only the root causes of human suffering according to the SoS Method: the Inadequate/Distorted Mirroring of the developing toddler/child by the caregiver and the immediate effects of this inadequate mirroring (read: lack of acknowledgment of the child as a "real" person). The result of Inadequate/Distorted Mirroring is the child's inability to develop a healthy Natural Sense of Self, which results in a Lack of Sense of Self (LoSoS). These concepts are represented by the yellow fields.

Where there is a LoSoS, there is an inner emptiness (Black Hole) that, subconsciously, forces the growing person to fill that void by way of developing a SSoS-oriented System. This structure provides the closest thing to a Self-experience that a person without a (Natural or Restored) Sense of Self can get. It is fully conditional: the Ego-References form the "conditions" the child subconsciously decides he or she needs to fulfill. Those conditions differ for each individual.

A Lack of SoS leads to the formation of Ego-References (the first red balloon) that, whenever successfully satisfied, enables the person to get to the fleeting moments of "Feel-good-about-Self," which functions as a Substitute Sense of Self (the second red balloon).

The arrows represent the force of nature: if Inadequate/Distorted Mirroring happens, then a flow automatically begins between the empty place inside the child's psyche and the next best thing to a healthy Sense of Self. It

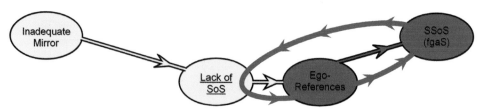

Figure 9.2: Map for Healing SoS, Stage 1—Sourced in Mirroring

is as if the child subconsciously thinks: *I am not being acknowledged as an independent and autonomous person (inadequate mirroring). I have no Sense of Self. I need some other sort of self-structure to be able to function (Substitute Sense of Self). The next best thing for me is to make my caregiver happy so, at least, I get some (temporary) positive feedback (Ego-References).*

So the child's ultimate goal becomes to get the real or virtual approval/acceptance of the caregiver through fulfilling the Ego-References (first red balloon), because it causes a "Feel-good-about-Self" that functions as a Substitute Sense of Self (second red balloon). Later in life, we will simply internalize our "parent" and continue to feel compelled to do as we did, when we were younger, and gain approval.

The red circle of arrows between the two red balloons refers to the endless repetition (compulsiveness) of this pattern, which is inevitable, because the SSoS is a very momentary experience and needs to be renewed repeatedly. It is this red circle that, in the Method, is referred to as "the red path of dependency on a SSoS" as opposed to the green path of living your own life.

STAGE 2

In this next illustration, we have added the component of the fear generated by the person's dependency on his Substitute Sense of Self-oriented System. At this point there are several anxiety-provoking situations going on that create an enormous amount of stress:

- First there is the (normal) everyday *Quality-of-Life level of fear* that even healthy people experience from time to time, as success in our endeavors is never assured or predictable (green rectangle).

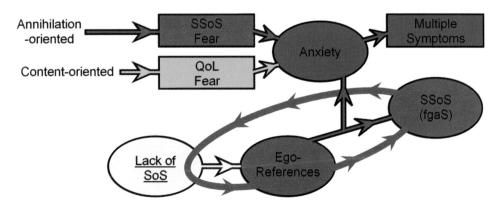

Figure 9.3: Map for Healing SoS, Stage 2—Healthy and Unhealthy Fear

- Then there is the unhealthy *Fear of Annihilation* that comes forth from "not being acknowledged as a separate person from the caregiver," and which lies at the root of the development of the SSoS-oriented System. (See the beginning of the red arrow leading toward the red rectangle.) This is the root fear underlying and leading to all the SSoS-related fears (red rectangle).

- There are the SSoS-related fears (red rectangle), and there are many (see page 112). Common *Fear of Failure* is one of them. Not succeeding in the endeavors of the Ego-References leads to great fear, for it means there will be no SSoS (FgaS), and without that "Feel-good-about-Self," a sense of Annihilation takes over.

- *Anxiety* is a form of fear that is vague, and its origin is not always identifiable. In my opinion, this anxiety is likely to be connected to the dependency on a SSoS for one's Self-experience as attaining the "Feel-good-about-Self" is a precarious endeavor.

Those fears generate untold types of stress, on top of the fundamental psycho-emotional stress of trying to function in life with a weak, pathological substitute for the real "spine" that should have been provided by a real Sense of Self. This compilation of stress is exactly the reason why a Lack of Sense of Self (LoSoS) is regarded as the root cause of so many seemingly-unrelated diseases and dysfunctional aspects of the lives of individuals, and thus, of society as a whole. Due to the extreme level of continuous stress, multiple pathological symptoms tend to develop sooner or later in a person's life (blue rectangle).

STAGE 3

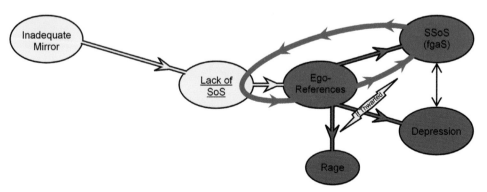

Figure 9.4: Map for Healing SoS, Stage 3—Results of Thwarted Attempts to Reach SSoS

This next figure shows what happens if an attempt to reach the SSoS is thwarted. The immediate result is RAGE (lower blue oval balloon). Sometimes, the person has, in that situation, given up (or is forced to give up) trying to realize her "Holy Grail" (SSoS, FgaS). Giving up or being thwarted is symbolized by the jagged yellow line between the red balloon of Ego-References and the blue oval of Depression.

When people have a Lack of SoS and are dependent on the outcome of their actions for their SSoS and are forced to give up their quest, one of which they aren't even aware of, depression is the result (lower blue oval balloon on the right). The person is de-activated; they lose inspiration; they "deflate," so to speak, if they feel unable to get done what they perceive matters most in their lives (which is to gain approval/virtual approval/Substitute Sense of Self).

STAGE 4

In this version of the Map, Stages 1, 2, and 3 are reflected in one composite illustration.

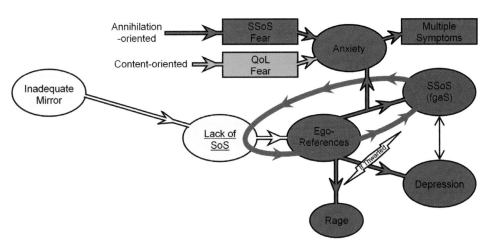

Figure 9.5: Map for Healing SoS, Stage 4—Stages 1, 2, and 3 combined

STAGE 5

Here we are looking at the map of a *Healthy Sense of Self* (second green oval balloon). The tiny balloons with diagonal lines through them indicate what fields are (fortunately) missing from a person's life who did receive adequate mirroring. To have a healthy (Natural or Restored) Sense of Self means that there is a gigantic reduction of stressors and stress-related symptoms compared to the amount of stress that plays a role in the lives of those of us who have a SSoS.

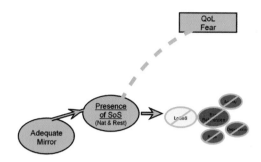

Figure 9.6: Map for Healing SoS, Stage 5—Healthy (Natural or Restored) SoS

The source of a Natural Sense of Self is adequate mirroring of the infant/child: acknowledgment for a child's independent and autonomous existence as a separate person (first/left-hand green oval balloon). In other words, by "not really seeing" your child, you can harm her for life.

The source of a Restored Sense of Self is to go through the Recovery process, as offered by the SoS Method, which on the map is represented by the green rectangle that says "HealthySenseOfSelf Exercises."

Of course, in both cases, (Natural and Restored Sense of Self) Quality-of-Life level stress is present; it is a normal part of life.

STAGE 6

Stage 6 shows again the complete map, only now you may have a better understanding of how the links between the separate fields with their

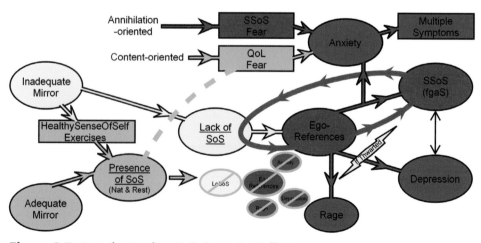

Figure 9.7: Map for Healing SoS, Stage 6—Full Map

sub-constellations form an explanation and a potential for healing of the many and great variety of ailments and dysfunction that you can recover from by restoring your SoS.

This is where Healthy Sense of Self's Tools and Healing Exercises (see Chapters 12 and 13) come in to help you heal your Sense of Self and eliminate many problems in your life. Healing/Restoring your SoS, when done with dedication and commitment, can bring tremendous improvement to your overall quality of life.

At various points in your journey through this book, refer back to this map and notice how much better you understand it!

DEPRESSION

Depression is a depressing topic. So many people have been diagnosed as depressed, yet its cause is still unknown. Many people cope on their own, others receive medication or are advised to use biofeedback techniques. These remedies seem to help some people; in other instances, the "remedies" can actually worsen depression. Medical and health professionals, across different fields, have not found a definite or universal cause of depression, thus a cure is impossible.

The SoS Method sheds new light on depression, revealing what could be an important key in the mystery. This key has become available because I was able to label certain patterns of behavior that, up till now, haven't been identified clearly enough because of the fact that they *manifest differently for each individual*. I have not come across any method that actively helps people to build a Sense of Self and describes the collection of aspects of what that comes down to. It is my sincere hope that this "how-to" part of the SoS Method may work as a portal to establishing a clear Sense of Self for many people so we all can enjoy "a good night's sleep" for as many reasons as there are out there among us.

Imagine that Janice is trying to get closer to her father (for acknowledgment) by becoming a doctor, Jake does it by becoming a good swimmer, and Gus does it by becoming a lead singer in a band. None of them is aware of their Hidden Goal but they highly depend on the outcome of their activities to FgaS so they feel anchored in themselves.

Most of us are well aware that children have a tendency to want to please their parents, and that parents have a crucial and powerful position in their children's lives. It is overlooked though, that this power becomes a dominant factor, a dictator in the lives of those children (and later adults), who then seem to be unable to develop in such a way that they learn to be in touch with, or to sense, who and what *they* are themselves. What people fail to recognize is that these children/people mistake the state of getting approval for self-realization. What a misleading concept! We need to understand that dependency on others is built based on this concept and with that the roots for depression!

But let us begin at the beginning, that is, with the thesis that the quality of your life is centrally determined by the quality of your SoS. I am confident in making the startling assertion that one major cause of depression lies, ultimately, in the lack of a healthy SoS. The connection between depression and SoS may not be immediately obvious so let us get into more detail.

Looking at the Map for Healing the Sense of Self (Figure 9.1), we can see how the jagged line indicates the onset of depression when a person realizes his or her Hidden Agenda is thwarted, which makes reaching the "Feeling-good-about-Self" (FgaS) state as a SSoS impossible. This is the moment: Depression occurs when an action or behavior perceived as crucial to achieving the (desperately needed) parental approval is blocked forever. Note that I do not say hindered or postponed; no, it is forever made impossible. Then the person feels that there is no hope for him or her to do what is perceived as necessary to avoid the feelings of Annihilation that are locked in the mind, and which he or she has learned to keep at a distance by working on getting approval. If the person who the approval is directed toward passes away, for example, it may happen that the child (most likely now an adult) becomes depressed, has suicidal thoughts, commits suicide, or even withers away.

My brother died at the age of 54, within six months of my father passing away. He had been struggling to get close to my father as well as to find himself during his whole life.

If, then, depression is an (in)direct result of not having been able to build up your healthy SoS, which I believe I made a case for, then the answer to overcoming depression is within reach for every one of us: Restoring your SoS. That makes you less dependent on the outcomes of your achievements, actions, or behavior, or on what others (including your parents) think of you. It means that you make your own goals in life as opposed to having the approval of your caregiver. That makes you not dependent (for feeling alive and allowed to be) on whatever happens to your caregiver, other than on a Quality-of-Life level. The moment you are truly independent of those, you are free and you will not get depressed!

There are other reasons leading to depression that are based on the same principle. Something might have happened to you, as the person who is in need of a score. You might have broken your arm when being a swimming champion was your Ego-Reference. Your father was a well-known sports-man, and he would be proud of you if you got a gold medal. In his self-centered existence, there was hardly room for you to be part of his life, and this is your only and best bet. Now you have injured your arm, and the doctor told you that it is never going to work properly so you had better start look-ing for another career. If you were a person with a healthy SoS, you would have been swimming because you liked it and were good at it. Losing that way of expressing yourself would certainly lead to feelings of grief, but you would cope with them. Soon enough you would adapt to your new situation and find something else you liked well enough to pursue as a career. However, if being an athlete was (also) the only way to get some sort of access to your father, whose approval you desperately need to feel good about yourself, hav-ing your arm become unusable has quite a different impact on you. Now the way to your father is cut off forever, and that may lead to depression or worse.

Resuming our view on depression, we can state that depression can de-velop if, over the long term, a person is unable to work on his or her Hidden Goal. This may be due to

- thwarted circumstances from outside yourself,
- a situation you have created yourself,
- simply because you are unable to for whatever reason, or
- when over a long period you have proven to be absolutely unsuccessful in reaching your Hidden Goal.

To anticipate feeling unable to reach that FgaS state would indeed be a *depressing* prospect, wouldn't it? There would be hopelessness about being able to feel like a person who really exists.

This scenario may seem far-fetched to you, but please make an effort to track, in your mind, the road an infant/child/young adult/adult travels. Start with the infant's unhealthy, unfortunate situation, which leads him or her to adopt unhealthy behavioral strategies for feeling like an autonomously exist-ing being. Then follow what that person goes through over time, the amount of effort he or she puts toward the cause to prove the parent wrong, the deceptions he or she endures due to not realizing that it isn't *his or her* fault but the parent's. Then follow the person all the way through the moment in which this person starts to feel hopeless about ever achieving a sense of exis-tence. I tend to think that this scenario is so common these days that we can consider it an epidemic. Just like depression.

The Way Out of Depression by Restoring Your SoS

The good news is that if the above scenario is an accurate description, then the way out of depression becomes clear. If the foundation of the problem lies in the way you experience your Self, then you need to work on getting a stronger and healthier SoS. You have to work on "restoring" it.

How do you restore your SoS? Well, you find ways to be deeply and constantly in touch with the awareness that your life is about you as an independent and autonomous person—not about getting the approval of others. You will have to learn these things to the point that they overrule your old ways. You will have to recondition yourself to a new program. Chapters 11 and 12 tell you how to do that, and on our website (www.healthysenseof self.com) you can find a lot of information on this as well as this is what we are all about. Restoring our SoS has become our lifestyle here at the HySoS Company.

With a Restored SoS, the behaviors you subconsciously used to identify with and that were required for your survival, or rather the survival of your SoS, are no longer needed or even desired. You no longer need them to generate a FgaS state to fill the inner sense of emptiness and invisibility because the void is no longer there. The Indirect Motivation loses its intensity, as ego-references and Hidden Agendas are no longer important for your survival. The Hidden Goal is obsolete as it is replaced by your Self.

Here is an example: I feel pulled to go to a performance by my child because I need to be a good mother. However, I have a conflict: a job that I perceive cannot wait to be done. If my motivation of either activity is indirect and rooted in achieving a Hidden Agenda, so I can get to feeling good about myself and satisfying my need for a SoS, I am in trouble. With a Restored SoS, I am better able to distinguish a priority between the activities, and I will not suffer or become upset if one of them doesn't get done. There is no agony, possibly just annoyance (a Quality of Life–level experience).

When we depended on a SSoS, we worked hard to be our best to avoid the ever-lurking (Fear of) Annihilation. Now with a Restored (or healthy Natural) SoS, we may still work on the same things, but we do them based on a different motivation. Indirect Motivation has become direct. The actions that we undertake have lost their emotional charge because now we (choose to) do them simply because we like doing them. We experience them as pleasant or enjoyable or because they need to be done. We have no Hidden Goal that keeps us spellbound, and therefore there is no experience of blocks on the road to a Hidden Goal. There is no longer any reason or cause for depression. We look at life with our own mind, through our own eyes, and with our own feet touching the ground. We know that our body is the home for our spirit and that our life is about us and what we *are* already and what we choose to *do* or *not to do*.

INSOMNIA

The inability to fall asleep or stay asleep is an occasional problem for some people and an ongoing problem for others. In the latter case, insomnia has a detrimental impact on our lives.

The cause of insomnia is often, as for depression, not clear. Why do problems sleeping arise in the first place? Doctors and researchers have not found an answer to this question. What we do know is that a lot of people suffer from lack of sleep, which affects society more than you think. It stifles a person's development and self-realization; it influences people's mood and social behavior, their productivity, their health, and even their safety. Yet for many people the problem remains unresolved and the bad consequences continue. I already mentioned my problems of getting a good night's sleep that lasted for some 25 to 30 years.

The medications most often used to treat insomnia are sedatives, antidepressants, and antianxiety pills. These can be harmful and addictive because they alter our brain's chemistry. More important, it seems clear that sleeplessness is a symptom of an underlying problem, and by eliminating this symptom, these medications merely mask the bigger issue. Then we not only become dependent on the medication, but we never get in touch with what causes the problem in the first place. Not knowing what is "off" with our perceptions or even with our concept of living means that we cannot work on correcting it. Thus we never truly address the underlying issue, and leave room for other ailments and dysfunctions to develop.

The Way Out of Insomnia by Restoring Your SoS

Although medical attention and medications might be necessary steps for some people, my contention is that insomnia can be resolved by changing our *un*healthy (SSoS-oriented) complex of motives and needs into healthy (direct) ones. Insomnia can be relieved if we can turn what used to be our life, but was only a performance, into being the "real thing" for us. Not keeping oneself dependent on the outcome of any action or behavior or the approval of others, but rather standing independently (and ultimately interdependently) in our lives, is the ultimate and real solution to many cases of insomnia.

Fear can lie at the bottom of the inability to sleep: fear of losing our hard-earned SSoS of the day. Fear of not being able to function so we won't be able to work our way up to a SSoS. Fear that others or circumstances will be in our way of doing so. Fear that we are screwing it up ourselves, and many other scenarios.

Most of these fears are related to our Ego-References and Hidden Agendas and to our perceived dependency from their outcomes, and they are all subconscious. If we decide to heal from being deprived as a child of healthy Mirroring by our caregiver, then we need to be prepared to do a lot of getting to know ourselves. We need to undergo introspection to learn to recognize patterns, and check out the nature of the way we experience our Self.

This book and the work of HEALTHYSENSEOFSELF LLC are aimed at assisting you with that. The reward is a lot more than sleeping better; it is a better life!

My Story of Insomnia

In my case, insomnia started after the birth of my first child when I was 39 years old. The underlying problem (a lack of SoS and dependency on a SSoS) also showed up in rage, fear, depression, gum problems, an aching face, and poor concentration. I resisted going to physicians because I did not want to be sedated or medicated. Insomnia ruled not only my life, but the lives of my loved ones as well. I could not hold a job and could not participate in society.

My parents and my siblings could not cope with my problem, and instead of finding support, I encountered rejection. They preferred to pretend all was well, let alone entertain the notion that they could have any part in causing my problem. At the time that I lived or visited home, there was no sight of the root of the problem. There were only the numerous and intense quarrels and wars, which nobody seemed to be able to avoid, that played out. We would start out with the best of intentions, but no matter what, our dialogues would escalate and end up in explosions. The use of alcohol played a role in this, no doubt. Visits to my parent's house were anticipated with fear and insomnia—I would not sleep when there—and it was even worse when the time to leave drew nearer. How could we manage to say good-bye and leave everyone, me included, feeling good about him- or herself? We had no idea of what was (perceived to be) at stake, but now I do. It sure felt like a battle of life and death. The FgaS state was the elephant in the room in my parents' house and we definitely had been taught to walk on eggshells around it. Every time somebody would accidentally cross the boundary of the elephant's territory it would result in heated arguments, insults, and tears. It is the one thing that we all tried so hard to prevent but that eventually would happen anyway as

Figure 9.8: The Elephant of "the need to FgaS" in the room

we were unable to label the actual cause of these arguments. People would be seriously in agony and defend themselves as if they were protecting their lives.

All that has become clear to me because I have been able to label things that made it possible to identify, analyze, and deal with them.

By now, I compassionately understand where I, as well as my parents and siblings, were coming from at the time. I only wish I would have known earlier.

Iᴛ ᴡᴀs ᴠᴇʀʏ difficult though, to be continuously sleep-deprived while trying to go through life as if nothing were wrong *and* honor my need to heal my condition at the same time.

Because I did not accept the typical treatments I had to develop my own, which led to my discovering the solution! I became aware that I was no more than a coping robot, a juggler trying to keep plates in the air. I studied and pondered what it takes to effectively be able to be yourself, and I found that the very first thing is Restoring your SoS.

The process turned out to be a lifelong endeavor as I am still learning every day, and it pays off. Besides, there was no other option. I *had* to—and still have to—take the time to put in the effort to restore my SoS. On my path, I have been exposed to a number of helpful therapies and I would like to mention one here: Sherry Buffington's work on redesigning your childhood experiences in order to heal core issues (www.quantumleap3.com). The philosophy here is that the oldest part of our brain has a hard time letting go of the images that have taken foothold in it since our earliest childhood can be reprogrammed by speaking the language it speaks: images. By overriding the traumatic experiences with positive ones we help effect the change we want. This can be a helpful tool in your reconditioning program.

ADDICTION

People are creatures of habit; we all know that. Some habits turn into addictions. Often, a very thin line separates positive dedication from negative addiction. For example, music students, at whatever age, are encouraged to practice and practice even more because they are made to believe that practice makes perfect. As you become more seasoned in practicing music, you find out that perfect practice may open the possibility to become perfect, that is, when it lies within your ability (because unfortunately we are not all equipped to practice perfectly, meaning do the right thing to become perfect in our skill). *We practice the way we are,* and if you have a healthy SoS, you practice with a healthy SoS. Unfortunately the opposite is true as well: If you have a lack of Sense of Self your practice strategy is based on that. By now we can imagine what happens in this case: music most likely is an Ego-Reference and the outcome of the activity becomes the degree to which we are able to feel safe from Annihilation.

This is how an addiction to practicing is created: My own practice habits at the time were pretty compulsive. In the year I started my long-term relationship as a bassoonist with the Amsterdam Philharmonic Orchestra I was going to go on my first major tour. During the tour, we had to give a number of concerts in different cities. Our instruments were transported in a climate-controlled truck, and so three days before leaving, the roadies would collect our instruments. I was used to practicing up to the very last minute before major events, and was very concerned with how to deal with the fact that I would not have an instrument available, so I asked to see the managing director. I explained my concern to him and that I wanted to be exempt from having to give up my instrument three days early, to which he replied, "Don't worry about it. You'll be all right!"

This was an example of addiction to an activity. To apply the example to yourself the activity can be replaced by any other activity that is relevant in your life, such as sports, fashion, or even being a mom or a dad. Many people battle addictions of a specific kind: substance, gambling, shopping, the Internet, and sex, among others. Depending on whether you do it from a point of Direct Motivation or not, you are more or less likely to become addicted to getting the desired outcome and overdo whatever you are supposed to do. There is no room for failure, right? Addiction to work can be explained in a similar way.

Research in the field of addiction has yielded incredible results during the last decade. Many new treatment centers have been built and we have a much deeper understanding of what substance abuse does to our brain chemistry. We know how our genetic makeup can be a decisive factor in the alcohol break-down process in the liver; some people lack certain enzymes. We now know how prolonged abuse of substances tears down the very protective walls in our cells, which immediately increases our need of substance use. Overall it is a pretty sad picture. But how do we become alcoholics in the first place? The disease model doesn't give an answer to that question. I think it is the most important question. For, once we know why something happens we can make a change so it does not happen anymore.

The Way Out of Addiction by Restoring Your SoS
The SoS Method claims that a Lack of Sense of Self is the root cause of every form of addiction.

Addiction is only possible when nobody is home. Overuse or abuse of substances and/or the use of one's resources may be used to stimulate us to feeling alive (gambling, shopping), or to avoid having to face the reality of one's life by filling the lurking emptiness inside (and outside sometimes). The immediate effects of addiction are destructive for our health and well-being and for that of our loved ones. Therefore, I state that only those of us who are not really in contact with what there is they might lose—their Selves—fall victim to long-term addiction.

Addiction can only take place when the house is empty! This occurs when you are not really occupying your own life and your own body and when you perceive little is at stake in the destruction process.

Alcoholics are like suicide bombers who give up their lives for a political cause or a religious belief. They can only do that when they do not have a sense of what is at stake: the gift of life they have been bestowed with. That gift, life, makes us all equal and therefore similar in our needs and wants. If you have never learned to connect with it, you do not know you have it in the first place. You are not even really aware that you can lose it forever! *When you are never home, you won't miss it!*

Now, being dependent on a SSoS for experiencing your Self in itself is an addiction, and it follows the same rules as all the other addictions. It can only happen when *you are not there* with *yourself.* When you have never had the chance to take into possession your life and your body.

A third cause of addiction is also related to the dependency of a SSoS. It comes forth from the need for a reward, in absence of the parental approval. This process has been described in Chapter 6, page 77 (Indirect Motivation— Rewards and "Highs").

There is a hardship in living addicted to the SSoS that we generally do not recognize: It requires a huge amount of effort by the person. Thus, the need often arises to reward ourselves for the hard work and the occasional successes, especially because, due to the nature of the issue, the nature of the real Hidden Goal is fictional and will never be realized. Now guess what the handiest form of reward is—engaging in one of the many possibilities in our society that provides a high that fills the Black Hole, be it overeating, drinking too much and/or too often, gambling, or shopping, among others.

Another factor operating in those with addictions (and a lack of SoS) is a stronger than average need "to belong," which is easily filled by hooking up (pun intended) with other people in the same condition. Needless to say, we all know how that reinforces addictions.

People with a lack of SoS find it is challenging, if not impossible, to listen to themselves because they have no SoS. They do not sense themselves. They don't own their own lives and are, therefore, not in touch with their own bodies. In effect, they have no Self to listen to, which in turn, gives them no Self that is invested to sense what's going on in their bodies. They think that they do not have the willpower to stop and end up feeling weak and inadequate. Lacking complete understanding of their predicament, instead, they divert their attention from themselves through these dangerous behaviors: an unhealthy reliance on "belonging" or being/looking cool that functions as a sort of semblance of approval. They try to fill the Black Hole and avoid the Fear of Annihilation, while remaining unaware of their true problems. In the process they risk becoming more and more addicted to the behaviors, actions, or substances that fuel their SSoS.

I am a strong advocate of implementing in our treatment centers and techniques a SoS assessment, as well as a program that offers help to people in restoring their SoS. It seems to me that many relapses could be prevented if people were encouraged and educated to own their own lives and bodies by sensing themselves in healthy ways. A lot of money and effort is wasted when relapse programs are offered without this explicit item to recover from: a SSoS. In that case all the therapist can do is teach the person a trick that will hopefully be remembered at the moment needed. What needs to change, though, for a person to be effective in the recovery of substance abuse is the motivation. The person needs to have something to lose when engaging in drug use. That something is his or her *Self*.

Resources

For strong and effective guidelines to recovery from addictions, in general, I recommend the literature available from the Washington State Alcohol and Drug Clearing House (www.adaiclearinghouse.org), or from your local authority on this subject. I recommend the following for learning more about the addictive nature of substance abuse and its effects on the brain and lifestyle:

> *Staying Sober: A Guide for Relapse Prevention* by Terence T. Gorski and Merlene Miller (Thorofare, NJ: Independence Press, 1986)
>
> *Under the Influence* by James Robert Milam and Katherine Ketcham (New York: Bantam Books, 1984)
>
> *Beyond the Influence: Understanding and Defeating Alcoholism* by Katherine Ketcham and William F. Asbury (New York: Bantam Books, 2000)

There are many good resources out there about recovery. For substance abuse, which this Method considers a complication of the addiction to a Substitute Sense of Self, you might also consider treatment in any of the better addiction-treatment programs in the various treatment agencies listed on the Internet.

LOOKING AHEAD

The SoS Method claims that for true and complete recovery from *any* addiction a necessary shift from experiencing the Self based on feeling-good-about-yourself when things are going well for you to a real, adequate, and healthy sense and awareness of what your Self really is and how easily you can abuse it, which leads to self-destruction. In the next chapter, we will discuss the benefits and challenges of the Restored SoS.

10 | The Restored Sense of Self (Rest SoS)

WHAT IS A RESTORED SENSE OF SELF?

A Substitute Sense of Self (SSoS) cannot be replaced directly by a Natural Sense of Self (SoS); that opportunity is gone forever if a Natural SoS was not developed at the appropriate time. However, the good news is that if you have been living for decades with a lack of SoS, which results automatically in a dependency on a SSoS, it *is* possible to move to the situation of having a healthy SoS—even if you have no memory of feeling you really lived in such a way that you "owned" your life. What we can achieve through awareness, training, and exercise is a **Restored SoS™**. This (re)learned SoS then fills in where once there was an inner emptiness.

Restored Sense of Self

As a result of effort to recover or heal from a Substitute Sense of Self, this is a steady awareness of being an entity not dependent on the outcome of fulfilling conditions. Restored Sense of Self functions as an inner home of freedom and self-love. After healing, this fills a previous inner emptiness.

I speak about *restoring* the SoS, which implies it has already been there and is gone. That implication is not really true, but I believe that having a Sense of one's Self is an intrinsic part of a human being and that the seed for being connected to one's self is always there. The process naturally initiated itself but was aborted at an early stage depending on how we were nurtured by caregivers. So the Natural SoS never had a chance to develop properly, and fully. Through awareness and training—reconditioning—we can create and implement in our "being" healthy and appropriate boundaries to the outside world, as well as cultivate within our "being" a sense of being at home and at peace with and for ourselves.

A Restored SoS is the experience of finding a home in your Self, where it is a duty to take care of yourself. It is only natural to put yourself first in your own life; this has nothing to do with being egocentric or egoistic. I believe that we are given a body to be able to manifest our soul's intentions, and it is up to us to manage that body and our life to make that possible. We were not meant to be ruled by others, consciously or subconsciously. (Here, I am not referring to organizations that serve society such as governments and the like, that is, if they truly function in such a way that they do serve the people.) What is needed from you is that you spend active time on reconditioning yourself. Ultimately, your Restored SoS will function like a Natural SoS for you with all the benefits that come with it.

A RESTORED SOS VERSUS A NATURAL SOS

We can state that a Restored SoS will, in the long run, work for us in the same ways a Natural SoS would have, if developed at the right time. That they are not totally the same needs for clarification. Let us take a moment to compare the Restored SoS with the Natural SoS.

A Natural SoS develops in childhood in a natural way, and a Restored SoS is developed by ourselves, because we want it to develop. So it is man-made, if you will. And because it is a relatively new habit it might be more vulnerable to life circumstances than is a Natural SoS. On the other hand, it might be stronger since we have created so much more awareness that is conscious around our SoS.

Let us take the time to think back to the layers of Self as explained in Chapter 2.

The picture shows how, in the Substitute Sense of Self, there is a split in the third layer. During the healing process, the third layer of Self (the conscious thought-form) reconnects where it once was separated from the psycho-emotional layer of the mother (Step 1). It is healed when it becomes a solid layer of Self as a conscious thought-form (separate from the caregiver). Now, both the fourth and fifth layers of Self (the Psycho-Emotional and

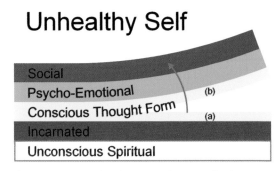

Figure 10.1: The damage done to the layers of Self of a person with a SSoS

Social layers, respectively) are well supported and have a chance to become healthy as well. In other words, when the third layer of Self has healed from perceiving itself as part of someone else, to keenly seeing a person as being an independent autonomous human being, the health of the Psycho-Emotional and Social layers falls into place. At this moment, the root cause of the previous addiction to a SSoS and dependencies on approval will be eliminated, and your life will be truly your life!

With time, the Restored SoS does become "natural" in the sense that it becomes fully adopted, integrated, automatic, and normal.

THE BENEFITS OF A RESTORED SOS

If you are as I was, your life is a struggle; you are most likely having all sorts of problems at this very moment. These problems might be caused, without your knowing it, by letting a SSoS-oriented System be the ruler of your life. Becoming aware of how you function, or rather cope, and what you can do to become the captain on the ship of your own life are crucial for you.

By becoming your own boss in your own life, I claim that your quality of life will be greatly enhanced. By replacing a SSoS by an intrinsic awareness of your own value and right to exist you will automatically succeed in dealing with many of the issues in your life. With this new conviction that you are OK just as you are and that just by being born you have a right to exist, which is equal to the same right other people have, you feel calmer and more balanced. It will be much easier for you to get a grip on or get clear about what you really want and what needs to be done. With a Restored SoS, you have a direct relationship with yourself and with the things in your life. Your motivation will be direct and straightforward. The need to obtain the feel-good-about-Self (FgaS) state will have disappeared. You will be able to get a real sense of who you are and make decisions and choices geared toward your well-being and the expression of your real, authentic Self based on your SoS.

Restoring your SoS will allow you to know your own preferences, tastes, and inclinations. You will be able to make clear choices that are based on your own opinion. You do not have to worry anymore about giving all your time and energy to keeping up with the maintenance of the SSoS-oriented System: fulfilling your (former!) Ego-References, reaching your (former!) Hidden Goals, working on refuting these negative (parental) beliefs about yourself. No further need exists to experience the FgaS state that functions as your SSoS.

With a Restored SoS, you experience the freedom that is the birthright of every human being, but now you know that for you, it wasn't given freely.

You had to work hard for it because of the abnormal, deprived situation in your early childhood, which resulted in your need to develop a SSoS. Now you can pass it on to your children—as they will to their children. By then we will truly have contributed to the world becoming a better place.

One benefit of Restoring a SoS is that the Ego-References turn into simple Quality-of-Life matters, and this change alone removes a great deal of stress. Those who have had a chance to develop a Natural SoS or restore their SoS have the ability to select people for who and what they are because they are guided by their true and honest motives and have no Hidden Agenda. They are more likely to marry the person they really like or love, and to decide to start a family because they would love to have children and be a parent. People with a Natural or Restored SoS are likely to find the job they truly enjoy and are skillful at or commit to a hobby or a volunteer job. This as opposed to those of us with a lack of SoS who might end up marrying the person your parents want you to, choosing a job that makes good money to satisfy your father's view on life, and having kids because you perceive your mother wants you to have them. In short, it is safe to say that a Restored SoS leads to a tremendous change for the better in your quality of life.

With the SSoS, you experience numerous dependencies based on the outcome of your actions and behavior, and you are always hankering to get a sense of satisfaction that will deeply fill you with relief. When you have achieved a Restored Sense of Self, all this vanishes because you know that you are—and forever are meant to be—an independent, autonomous being. You now are the master of your life (next to God, or the Universe, if you will). With a Restored SoS, the many harmful effects of the SSoS-oriented System mentioned throughout this book will be gone, and the reverse of them in-cludes many beneficial effects (see the List of Benefits on page xxv).

Because this approach and the SoS Method are absolutely new (date of birth: 2010!), there is not much information on how a Restored SoS is going to keep up. It is realistic to expect that most likely there will always be some residue of a SSoS-oriented System in your psyche (and emotional body) and that you, unless you are a person with a Natural SoS, might want to do some maintenance work on yourself. What *is* clear, though, is that with a Restored SoS, an endless road of improvement and growth has opened for you.

HOW A RESTORED SOS FEELS

When you have restored your SoS, you feel much more balanced compared to the former state you were in; you are able to look at things through your own eyes and to make sensible conclusions and decisions. Common sense kicks in! You feel as if your body gets more oxygen; your muscles do not tense up so easily; your nervous system comes to rest. And what's more, all this gets better every day!

There are numerous processes in your life that go much more smoothly: You sleep better; you don't quarrel as much; your anxiety is gone. Emotionally you are balanced and not afraid of your own behavior! You have no desperate need for a high. Your calm inner knowing that you are OK makes you more approachable to others. You might have more friends, if that is what you fancy, but now without dependence on their approval. Your relationships stand a much better chance of being great and lasting. You have better focus and energy. You no longer have compulsive and/or obsessive behaviors. Panic attacks and suicidal thoughts are gone. Excessive muscle tension has decreased or disappeared, and you are smarter with your money. You are not so defensive and overly sensitive, as you used to be, and being criticized is not the end of the world. You have a life, and nobody can take it from you!

It is important to know that sensing your Self as in a Restored SoS, especially in the beginning, is a subtle experience. In the modern world, our senses are continuously exposed to loud and intense stimuli: The quality and frequency of input from television, movies, computers, cell phones, and loud music and urban noise of all kinds in our lives have made us less sensitive to the subtleties of the signals of our own bodies. In addition, the intensity of traffic and the 100 percent attention required to navigate it, as well as the continuous hurry that we are in—these are types of experiences that are totally different from the subtle experiences we sense and can easily overlook when we finally decide to turn our attention inwards to our Sense our Self. Thus, if you want to know more quickly and easily how a Restored SoS *feels*, you will need to arrange your life to be quieter.

QUALITY-OF-LIFE EXPERIENCE

In addition to unhealthy SSoS-oriented stress, we certainly also have *normal stress* associated with everyday life. Every action that requires some sort of a special attention or skill brings forth a sort of mental tension geared toward the outcome: "Will it go well?" There might be unexpected situations that interfere, which increases the stress about bringing the action to a good ending. This is what I call Quality-of-Life stress; it affects us but only on the surface, as opposed to the SSoS-related fears that are based on the perceived life and death threat of Annihilation.

When we are working to achieve a particular goal, we might experience some stress depending on what is at stake. If we take a good hard look at how much stress we are experiencing and discover that the degree of stress is not really justified by the nature or the apparent goal of the activity, then something else is probably going on: a SSoS is probably at stake and depending on the outcome of our activity. In the process of fulfilling Ego-References there is always an excessive amount of stress involved because the action is based on Fear of Annihilation. So there is a degree of a flight-or-fight aspect to it. This excess of stress can help us to identify whether we are coming from a healthy SoS or from a SSoS. In other words, measuring the amount of stress associated with the event or action, and comparing it to what would be a normal amount of stress related to such an event or activity, can help us identify whether our motivations are direct or indirect.

With introspection and by noticing the *degree* of stress we feel when working toward certain goals, we can distinguish whether we experience the impact of the potential outcome of these efforts with the intensity of a life-or-death threat or of a normal Quality-of-Life level of stress.

In the healthy versions of our SoS, we do not experience the life-or-death Fear of Annihilation. Here are some more examples of ways in which our quality of life changes when we can experience feeling good about ourselves when our motivations are direct:

- Independence from other people's opinions, tastes, and choices
- Independence from what other people mirror back to us about ourselves
- Independence from our achievements
- Feeling acknowledged and accepted unconditionally
- Bonding with others
- Feeling included
- Being able to fully be yourself and live up to your potential
- Sensing that "I" is my "**Real Self**"
- Being realistic about your potential and possibilities
- Using given opportunities to speak freely, when appropriate
- Having a voice in a group
- Sharing freely things about your life (when appropriate and according to your nature)
- Feeling balanced and not overly intense when experiencing emotions like joy, grief, sadness, and anger

Real Self/Authentic Self

One's Self is experienced in the healthiest, most integrated way as an independent and autonomous Being; actions and awareness are based on living experience not contaminated by pathological motives. See Natural Sense of Self.

- Being able to judge situations fairly
- Knowing fully on every level of awareness that you have a right to exist

A person with a healthy SoS still might experience moments of apprehension and/or fear on a daily basis. The difference is that for this person there is no SSoS at stake, so he or she reacts differently to it. Arriving late to work, having a disagreement with someone, needing to do a lot of work in little time, and many other things, of course, are things that can cause stress and uncomfortable feelings in all of us. However, other than the result of being late, missing the beginning of the event, or having to cram in extra hours at work, there is nothing at stake. So the stress is relatively small but it doesn't have to be small either. It is the normal amount or intensity of emotion that is to be expected of facts and situations in our everyday living. Note that being run over by a car can be a near-death experience that provokes a fair amount of fear and stress, even for a person with a Healthy SoS. Note that in this situation, people dependent on a SSoS will be less inclined to worry about their own well-being and survival. They will be devastated, however, when they will feel deprived of the ability to work on their SSoS when ending up in the hospital.

Thus, Quality-of-Life related fear has an entirely different basis from a SSoS-related fear. The former refers to a healthy, temporary, everyday type of apprehension; the latter is a deeply rooted psychological, existential type of fear. Identifying these two aspects within ourselves is important, because our goals and objectives always have a Quality-of-Life (logistical) side to them.

So the stress caused by the underlying Fear of Annihilation involved in fulfilling Ego-References adds to and considerably raises the level of the normal (QoL-level) fear. The normal and generally expected Quality-of-Life stress present in most of our actions and activities is now entangled with the SSoS-oriented fear. It is a complex fear that is hard to identify. People might be inclined to think that "fear is fear." But now we know that the fear a SSoS-oriented person experiences is a complex fear that is always present and running in the background. And that is why the stress levels are so much higher. It is a level of fear that is out of proportion compared to the action or activity performed, thus we can spot the problem of dependency!

Let me explain that in a bit different wording: All Ego-References have both a Quality-of-Life aspect and a SSoS-oriented aspect (see Figure 10.2). The green half of the leaf represents the normal behavior (e.g., to be on time); it is very common to have a bit of fear of being late. The red part of the leaf, though, represents the SSoS-oriented part, which is brought on because

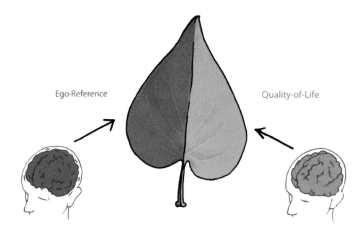

Figure 10.2: The dual aspects of stress in Ego-References

of the activity being an Ego-Reference. There is a life/death fear associated with the activity now, which is abnormal. This dual-aspect complexity makes identifying the dependency (and thus the pathology) involved in any ego-reference behavior almost impossible. So far how people would explain an excess of stress or fear is by saying something like: "Looking at what is happening to that person everything looks normal to me, right. Some people are just more fearful than others." And that would be that. It would have been a fact that has to be accepted. With a Restored SoS, the red part of the leaf vanishes: the leaf would be entirely green. Imagine the relief that would give to the person it concerns.

THE CHALLENGES TO RESTORING OUR SOS

If we want a better life compared to the hardship of being dependent on a Substitute SoS for our self-experience, we don't have a choice other than to restore our SoS. True, you could choose not to go this route because creating a Restored SoS is intensive; there is *no quick fix*, and doing the work needed requires great persistence and endurance.

Denial

At times, whatever you are doing to keep scoring with the SSoS-oriented goal seems more important to you. At those moments you convince yourself that you are making much better use of your time, dedicating yourself to achieving good outcomes in your activities, getting good Mirroring back from other people—in short, working hard to get your Ego-References taken care of. Tackling the healing work involves all the challenges described. Many moments of discomfort and even anxiety are to be expected as you move through the healing process, but it is all worth it.

Imagine that you have a piece of machinery that works in a stumbling but predictable way. For it to function more effectively and productively, a specific part that so far has been missing needs to be inserted. Now first you must find out what is missing. But that is not the only challenge because the part is not for sale and if you want it, you will have to build it yourself. So you have to build that missing part yourself and implement it in the machinery, which is just as hard if not harder than figuring out what it was. Therefore, I urge you to be prepared to observe yourself intently. Pretend *you* are the machinery. Your machinery works but it could work a whole lot better and you know it. Obviously a part is missing. Figure out what is missing. That is not easy but it is the only way! Then try and insert it in your machinery. Study how other people's machineries function and learn from it. Little by little your machinery will work more smoothly, use less oil, and be more productive. Aren't you glad you went through that trouble?

The Pull of the Black Hole

During the process of healing and change there will be a gigantic psycho-emotional pull for us to return to the SSoS-oriented System. With the power and intensity of a force of nature, the SSoS-oriented System that used to function as our survival system will push its way through your desire to change and do its job: suck up whatever goes well to fill in the Black Hole. After all, we are talking about a survival system that needs to keep functioning at all costs.

The absence of a Natural SoS has generated a psycho-emotional Black Hole that absorbs a lot of our effort and energy to create and maintain a Substitute Sense of Self. We use it to create a surrogate backbone for our spineless Self, and our old (childhood) survival system makes us subconsciously believe we do not have the option of living differently. That would be perceived as a real threat to our being taken into account as a real and present person.

Only by *immediately replacing* "whatever we have been using so far to fill that hole" with the "real-life experience of our (real) selves" can we be successful in patching that hole and stop its pull. What we need is a deep understanding that the only way we can reach our goal of restoring our SoS is with gentle perseverance, frequent exercises, mental rehearsal, continual awareness, and complete honesty toward ourselves.

A man is walking mile after mile on this long and dusty road to the next village, while heavily leaning on an old red cane. Suddenly he sees, leaning against a tree, a bright green cane with a golden knob for a handle. He scurries toward the desired object and grabs it with his left hand. He is puzzled by figuring out how to get that beautiful green cane with the golden handle into his right hand. He has no time to lose but he knows he is unable to walk without a cane for any moment at all. He would immediately collapse on the floor. Without pausing he moves the new green cane next to his old red one and holds both canes in the same hand as he continues on his path with a grin. He sees what needs to happen. He rids himself of his old cane by letting go of it while still walking and leaning on the new cane. This cane, he knows, is going to dissolve over time and on that day he will be able to walk all by himself.

The SSoS-oriented System can be considered a crutch you have leaned on your whole life. Make sure you have parts of your Restored SoS in place when you try to drop your old cane!

Habits and Slipping Back

Let us get a clear understanding of the hurdles you have to be prepared to jump. Throughout your life, to this point, you have lived based on the habit of depending on a SSoS. Humans are creatures of habit, and therefore it is safe to say that you can and will slip back into the SSoS-oriented System because it is a habit. You should have no judgments about that; it is just a fact of life. Beating up on yourself for any slips will only cause suffering and slow your progress, so refrain from that!

Recovering from a SSoS requires continuous effort to install the new Restored SoS and prevent falling back into the habit of the SSoS-oriented System. There is no way around it: You have to persuade yourself that what originally was your survival system needs to make way for your Self as a reality. With time and persistence, you win.

Figure 10.3 presents a diagram of this stress in our brain. Similar to the representation of the two types of stressors at work in Ego-References, we have represented what the challenges are for a person who is recovering from a SSoS addiction. There is the continuous threat of relapse. With a Restored SoS the person walks the green path of his (own) life; what happens when relapse occurs is that a trigger in the person's life makes that person switch from the green path of motivation to the red path of motivation. (As a reminder on how things work, please look up the Map for Healing the Sense of Self in Chapter 9 [Figure 9.1]. Here we see that the red path is the circle of addiction.) That person switches from being motivated by his or her own well-being to the well-being of the caregiver, virtual or real. The moment our thought/feel processes start to change color, we are on our way back into the unhealthy SSoS-oriented System.

So the Quality-of-Life side of an action or a behavior comes from a "green brain" (to the right), reflecting the functioning of a brain that belongs to a person who is on the life path of being connected (naturally or through healing) to the Self. The SSoS-oriented aspect of the activity or behavior comes from a "red brain" (to the left), which belongs to the person who is on the life path of addiction to the SSoS. Yet these two aspects coexist in a person with any particular Ego-Reference behavior that allows a person to stay in denial of his or her problematic psycho-emotional makeup. It goes without saying that the preferred status for us is to have a totally "green" brain, in reference to the image in Figure 10.3.

It takes a lot of convincing/reconditioning to have new feelings, thoughts, and actions override the memories of your old behavior that you have been holding for so many years that they have become hard-wired in your brain. Yet it can be done. Taking the quantum field approach described by Dr. Joe Dispenza in his "Guide to Changing Your Reality from the Inside Out: The

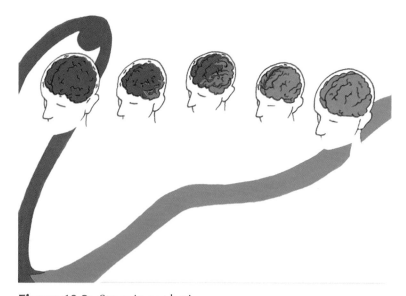

Figure 10.3: Stress in our brain

Reinvention of Self"[9] can be a tremendous help. You can find out more about this product at www.drjoedispenza.mybigcommerce.com/.

To guarantee a successful implementation of a Restored SoS, it is absolutely necessary that the exercises of awareness presented in Chapter 12 have a permanent place in your life to keep you from slipping back into the habit of a pathological SSoS-oriented System. Encourage yourself by noticing how your problems and pains are diminishing.

Addiction

A SSoS is to be considered an addiction because it is a habit that has to be performed at all costs since it is experienced as *a life-or-death matter*. That said, we can deal with it in a similar way as with any other addiction. So to make things easier, compare yourself to a drug addict, nothing more and nothing less. Just like a junkie, you are continuously falling prey to the numerous triggers that lie in yourself and your environment. Only with the strongest will and most determined intention, as well as time, are we able to choose another path, the path of healing that leads to a Restored SoS.

Think back to the images of the branches of trees as presented in Chapter 2. Look at those branches and pretend they represent your addiction to the elements of the SSoS-oriented System in a physical way: the branches are your brain neuronal wiring. It leaves no doubt at all that they are physically there. Now, to get rid of branches you can pick up a saw and cut them off; with brain wiring it is clear that this can't be done. So a different strategy is needed to get rid of unwanted neuro pathways. What you need to do here is called re-conditioning and comes down to learning new ways of looking at your Self, sensing your Self and thinking about what your findings are.

Please be patient with yourself, though. What you need to do mentally and emotionally is to step away from those already carved pathways. Leave them behind and consciously and actively choose to create other neuronal pathways from scratch. These newly formed pathways then are like a freshly cut path in a jungle: The moment you stop cutting the bushes and plants that are on your path, they grow back—and they grow back fast! Before you know it, the new path toward a Restored Sense of Self that you created just a few hours ago looks completely overgrown, with seemingly no trace of it remaining! (In truth, the new neuronal "grooves" are still accumulating, thank goodness!)

---

[9] Joe Dipenza, *The Reinvention of Self*, vol. 2 [audio CD]. Produced by Armenus Productions LLC, 2011.

Figure 10.4: The branches of the tree representing your brain wiring

For you, just like for alcoholics or drug addicts, there *is* hope for complete recovery. It is a great advantage if we have not reached the point of overly using or even abusing alcohol and/or other drugs. People who are dependent on a SSoS for experiencing their Self are more likely to use drugs or alcohol, though. It is so much better if, next to the addiction to a SSoS, there is no additional physical addiction, no substance involved that we have to deal with first.

Not only that, but being able to think clearly and be committed is a must for this process to be successful. During the beginning of the recovery process, you will have moments in which you are like a dry drunk: explicitly avoiding working on the Ego-References but mentally focused on them all the time. The problem is that you have to pay attention to them in order to single them out. How else are you going to become aware and remember what it is you do not want to do?

In my own recovery process, I would start out by learning my list of Ego-References by heart. Some people might suggest that it is better to be busy with the positive than with the negative. My truth was that I needed to be aware of what the negative was so I could turn it into its positive. For example, if your Ego-Reference is being on time, you have to be aware that you are always late and that you really do not want that to happen. Yet you are. Just by stating I want to be on time is not going to do the trick. So I explain to myself as often as needed (and that is very often): "I do not have to worry about being on time because I know it isn't for the sake of the event or activity. It is only for fear that I won't get my VIPV's approval. How silly of me to still worry about that. But I do not blame myself for it. It is not that I am silly. I have conditioned myself that way because I perceived it to be the only way to get closer to my caregiver's approval, which I took for acknowledgment. And all I wanted was to be seen and heard as a real person. Not being late is not going to do that trick for me. So I might as well not worry about it."

In a later section we will get back to the similarities between healing from the addiction to a SSoS and recovering from drug and alcohol abuse.

Fear and Blame

Remember also that you developed a SSoS-oriented System, because during your childhood, you were deprived of appropriate regard by your parent/caregiver. This resulted in emptiness inside of you. There was the constant threat of feeling the Fear of Annihilation, and all you were about was trying to avoid that feeling. This is heavy stuff. We are talking serious existential terror. So cut yourself some slack while not letting up on your will to heal. Expect those fears to come closer to your conscious awareness, and just have compassion for them.

There is no blame to be had; your mind when you were a child did the best it was capable of in the unhealthy situation you were in. Do not impede your healing with the nonsense of blaming yourself for anything, including having "wasted" years of your life. You might also need, as part of your recovery process, to learn some forgiveness techniques that work for you regarding your parent(s) or other caregivers to diminish your inevitable blame of them. This works wonders on your own ability to live in the present.[10]

Special Challenges of Recovering from Ego-References

Recovering from being slaves to our Ego-References presents some special challenges because we perceive so much is at stake. Separating ourselves from our Ego-References equates to losing our sporadic and tenuous grip

---

[10] For help with this process, I recommend *Radical Forgiveness* by Colin Tipping (Louisville, CO: Sounds True, Inc., 2009).

on *any* experience of identity. Thus, separating ourselves from our ego-references—recovering from having a SSoS—is hardly an option until and unless we become utterly aware of our slavery to them, and we powerfully determine to carve our path to freedom. This Method envisions all that, and hopes and endeavors to facilitate it for you.

In trying to fulfill our Ego-References, we are like Don Quixote battling against windmills, but we cannot afford to realize that. We are striving for a fictitious, unattainable goal, but we cannot allow ourselves to see that. We are skipping our own life altogether by being the slave of the Ego-References instead of being the masters of our lives, but we are oblivious to that.

How deeply can we be trapped in this pattern? Consider this: At some point in my own healing process, when I was breaking through my dependency on the fulfillment of my Ego-References, I experienced moments of terror, or anxiety attacks. This terror came up despite the fact that I was the one who had consciously made the decision to counter my compulsions!

When I was healing myself and opening my own path to freedom, I would resist trying to fulfill my Ego-References, such as compulsively practicing piano or violin, working on my website, or cleaning the house. I would deliberately not do those things and would do other things or nothing instead. It was almost impossible to resist the pull of the Black Hole and not fill that emptiness inside, where a Natural Sense was meant to reside with a SSoS, and this led to anxiety and undefined frenzy feelings. When our only way (the Substitute way) of experiencing our Self is not allowed to take place, we get a frantic fear that may result in rage and possibly violence as well as in physical symptoms like insomnia and depression.

So very much seems to be at stake. We feel threatened with the collapsing of our inner structure, the backbone of our psyche. Our Early Childhood Survival System (ECSS) simply will not tolerate that. Our subconscious reflects what we have been programmed to do since early childhood and is (misguidedly but sincerely) trying to warn us we are doing something dangerous to our very sense of existing! That is why we cannot throw away the crutch we are leaning on, our SSoS, without first putting in place a more positive healthy beginning of a Restored SoS. (Remember the story of the red and green cane on page 157.)

The SSoS-oriented System is very tricky. You can allow it to co-opt your healing process. Do not let your new experiences become your SSoS in disguise. Inspect your intentions conscientiously, and honestly assess whether you might be letting your problems be a way that you sense and relate to your Self, or whether you are allowing yourself to feel alive through your problems.

Step into the world of being in touch with your own person using your own criteria in your thinking as opposed to blindly and habitually being led by memories of what made you feel (close to) accepted by your parent or caregiver. Your current life might feel gray and undifferentiated simply because you no longer experience the emotional extremes. You have become used to those and have known nothing different. Most likely, you will at first miss the great highs and lows you are giving up; until now, these have been your sense of being: the drama in your life that gave you a sense of being alive. Your new life will color up beautifully, trust me on that!

Stress

Recognizing exactly which specific stressors are at play in our lives now is needed in order to free ourselves from them. We have to see the connections in our lives between our past and the missing acknowledgment in that past. We have to become consciously aware of what our observations were as children, the adjustments we made, and what we hoped to achieve with those adaptations to our caregivers. That will not be easy as most of these processes took place entirely on a subconscious level. But we have to work with what we can trace back to and then connect the dots. You could call this creating a map of your stressors as they manifest in your current life and of what the initial reasons for these were. We then can play with all the elements in that chain and become familiar with them so we can learn to draw different conclusions that overrule the old ones (a process called reconditioning ourselves).

Here are a few examples of how you can play with these concepts with the purpose to ultimately free yourself from, and eliminate, the addictive need for unhealthy substitutes, and replace them with true, healthy acknowledgment. Each of us needs to

- connect to our body.
- realize that "Yes, I already *am*; I already exist. I do not need any approval (or virtual internal parent voice [VIPV] approval); I do not need to FgaS."
- realize that "I don't have to continuously improve my Ego-References anymore. All I used to focus on was having more chances to realize my Hidden Goal, or my Substitute Sense of Self through feeling-good-about-Self. I now know where that comes from, and there is no need for me to comply with these Early Childhood Survival observations as I now sense my Self with a Restored Sense of Self. I know I *already AM*."

- realize that "I don't have to use my daily activities and behavior as Vehicles anymore. I can do the action or activity for its own sake. All
this was based on the hope and compulsion to improve on my Ego-
References, which then was meant to ultimately give me a better chance
to realize my Hidden Goal to convince my parents that I am a better
person than they think so they will take me into account. I do not need
to do that anymore just as I do not need a Substitute Sense of Self. I
already *am*, and I have a Restored Sense of Self."

Whenever we notice that we are stressed, we need to *stop*, draw strength
from the depths of our being (our real Self), and wonder, "What do I
authentically—my Self—think of this situation?" By asking ourselves what
we are actually after and actively making it a point to think with our own
mind, we might discover we are actually after approval from our parent or
proving ourselves because through that approval we hope to get a sense of acknowledgment we missed out on when growing up. All those questions, and
our seeking and finding the answers, will have a healing effect on our lives.

TOOLS AND TIME ARE NEEDED

To be able to get that Restored SoS, you need many tools to support you:
imagery and visualization; body work; creative expression through crafts, arts,
music; and the like. Later chapters in this book, and resources on our website,
offer additional tools you might find useful. Please be fully aware that this
recovery work is hardly something you can do "on the side." If you want to
succeed, you must give it a lot of attention and action. You have to make
becoming yourself the master plan for your life, for the time being.

I should let you know that a halfhearted recovery attempt might cause
more suffering than it alleviates because the fears and blame mentioned previously will emerge in a big way, and you might feel like a failure as your habits
and addictions keep reemerging. As you proceed on the path of implementing
the Restored SoS, you are entering a new world, a world where it is about *you*.

ACHIEVING A RESTORED SOS IS POSSIBLE

Come and step into the world of the "reality" where you are less attached to
what happens in and around you because for you nothing is at stake on an
"existential" level. There will come a time when the Restored SoS is strong
enough to change your motivations in life from indirect to direct. Then the

Hidden Agendas will cease to pull, and the Ego-References and the SSoS will have lost their appeal to—and their hold on—your subconscious mind.

At this point, you will Sense your Self in a direct way, which by then will have become more natural and more automatic to you. *This is what, through my work in the world, I hope to help you establish.* Then, instead of being the slave of your Ego-References, you have become the master of your life.

I myself am just over the threshold of having successfully implemented this Restored SoS in myself. It is my hope and reasonable expectation that this SoS will grow stronger through the accumulation of experiences based on it. But that implies I actively maintain a strict and never-lessening awareness of the "I" in everything I do or feel.

Putting a SoS in place where there was never one experienced before is quite a challenge. This Method encourages you to spend time and effort observing your own thoughts and behavior and introspecting on what lies behind it, followed by an analysis of your findings done with the utmost honesty.

The Comparison Chart in the Appendix can be used as a checklist and is very helpful for self-assessment. It helps us to recognize whether our lives are ruled by a SSoS-oriented System instead of by us in our right mind. Fearlessly scrutinizing our motivations (perhaps using the Comparison Chart in the Appendix) might reveal to us that we are pursuing a SSoS-oriented goal and that deep down we are after the Hidden Agenda. We might get in touch with the inner causes of our emotional states, our addictions, and our compulsions and through this find the proof of our lack of a Natural SoS. We will want to take action to replace our SSoS with a healthier self-awareness, which will help us lead happier and more productive lives. Then we will finally establish a true, direct connection with our Self, our truly own individual being, and truly lead our own lives.

LOOKING INWARD

I had to dig deep into my psyche and figure out how I got that big hidden-agenda motivation! The answer was found in what happened in my early childhood—or, rather, in what did *not* happen in that childhood.

In order to take advantage of the Method presented so far, you will need to apply it to yourself. That will require some serious exploration of what is going on inside your head—and body. Knowing ourselves more fully will enable us to make smarter decisions from which others also benefit. Self-knowledge is power!

In my own journey, I found that the most useful and fastest route to understanding myself was to get to know my motivations: Why was I doing what I was doing? Why did I avoid doing some things? What was I after? What did I seek or wish to avoid? What were my goals, my agendas, for doing things? Questioning my motivations and coming up with true, sincere answers was the key to getting the insights I needed while working through my own self-knowledge toward my healing. "What exactly is driving me to do what I am doing and to get to a certain outcome at all costs, or to be so strongly intended to avoid another thing with all my might? What are the *real* reasons for my particular choices and behaviors?" Once the insights were there, the potential for healing was created.

Unless we can answer these questions about ourselves, know ourselves thoroughly and learn what we are all about, it is no use to attempt to make a behavioral change and take that seriously. Without knowing what we are/ were all about, that change will be impossible. Until we have understanding, we are like monkeys learning a new trick. We do not want to be a monkey!

In this Method, we do not focus on the obvious universal motives of securing food, shelter, warmth, and so on. Instead, we are looking at other kinds of motives. We are looking deeply, beyond the surface: "Are my choices in life *really* motivated by what I *believe* my motives are? What is the *real* relationship between my goals and my motives? Am I really in touch with what drives me? Are the choices I make in daily life indeed directly linked to what seems, on the surface, to be my goal?"

For example, ask yourself the following: "Why do I want to dress a certain way and how important is that to me? Is it to express myself, to manifest my own identity? Am I flexible about it and can I make minor/ major compromises depending on availability and/or budget? Or is there more at stake? Is it more of a statement, maybe? Has it to do with wanting to belong, giving impressions, performing a behavior I don't trust I have?" Many more questions could be relevant to inspect such a trivial decision of what to wear.

You might assume that everything you want or do not want is based on free choice, but upon looking more deeply, you might discover your choices are not that easily changed and not as freely optional as you might have believed they were. Do you sometimes feel as if you're being driven by an invisible power? That is one clue that your choices are somewhat addiction-based; all motives in the SSoS-oriented System are addictive, be it approval or rebelling in order to establish your own identity at all costs (see the discussion about reactionary Ego-References in Chapter 4).

This book helps you look into what might be the invisible power behind your motives, and where, in many people, that power might come from. *Knowing our true motives is important* because our health and well-being depend on *which* motives are operating in us. When you know your *true* motives, you can use this Method to help develop strategies for improving your quality of life.

Willingness to Be Honest with Yourself

Discovering our motivations is key to recovering from an unhealthy (Substitute, or fake) SoS. However, it requires total honesty with ourselves. That might seem easy enough. It isn't. Finding out the truth about our deepest motivations is not obvious, nor simple, nor easy.

It is a challenge because we human beings are masters of denial. We might be ready to admit that we sometimes deceive others by pretending we are closer to our ideal self than we are. Try on the shocking admission that you might be going out of your way to deceive yourself, even for a whole lifetime! Yet that is what many of us are doing!

This Method offers a variety of ways to help you dig down and get clear about your own motives—including motives for wanting to deceive yourself about your motives! That getting clear is a huge part of the healing process and the way to become healthier, happier, and more successful—in other words, free from the addiction of approval, and free to be your own true, real Self.

Admitting to yourself that you depend on the outcome of your ego-references is a big step in overcoming what is in fact an "unreal" way of living, based on a fictional Self. Being totally honest with yourself is an absolute requirement for investigating—via introspection—which of your current thoughts and feelings are actually rooted in and part of a SSoS-oriented System at work: your SSoS-oriented System. For the sake of recovery, each of us has to be willing to get to the bottom of every thought and feeling, to find the truth *hidden* underneath—*actively* hidden by ourselves from ourselves!

I Thought I Knew My Own Motivations

During the 25 years of introspection and discovering and thinking about my motivations, I realized that my mind was full of agendas and motives that were hidden from myself and others for many decades. And when I first started to get to know myself and got some insight into what was at the bottom of my drives, I was very surprised to discover that until that point, I had been very skillful at coming up with excuses and justifications for doing what I was doing, without ever having to look at my real motive. There always was a real good reason that served as the conscious excuse and justification for my motives, hiding the true motives from myself. That way the continuation of the pursuit of the Hidden Agenda was guaranteed. You can say that there is an addiction operating! It is funny how there always is a good, acceptable excuse to get ourselves to work on our Hidden Goal using Vehicles for our Ego-Reference to attain the goal of getting the "Feel-good-about-Self-" state from approval *without ever having to face it.*

Here is an example from my own life: Even though I had a good job as a bassoonist for years, I was dissatisfied with what I accomplished. I was unable to live up to that level of mastery that I had aimed at and worked for throughout a good part of my life. I strongly felt I would have been a better violinist than a bassoonist, so when my kids were little and went to Suzuki music education I benefitted from the opportunity to start my violin lessons. For about 3 years I practiced like mad—rather a victim of the SSoS-oriented drive to become that great musician after all. Then we moved away to a different city and a different setting: it wasn't meant to be. From then on I started working on this Method, which took up all my time and later, helped me to accept, that I WAS already. That the Black Hole in me would forever push me to become that "great" musician and (finally) gain my parent's (virtual) respect, but that I would be smarter countering that pull and learn to be present to my self and really enjoy music, in whatever way or shape. Then, maybe then, I could consider playing some.

THE CHALLENGE OF BEING HONEST

How can the existence of this unhealthy phenomenon of Indirect Motivation not be common knowledge? Because it isn't visible to those of us living with a SSoS because we are fooling ourselves and living a continuous lie. Remember, when we live with a SSoS, nothing is really as it seems as we are continually trying to overcome barriers from our childhood. The only way to discover Indirect Motivations is by being completely honest with yourself—and there is, as mentioned earlier, subconscious motivation to choose to deny your Indirect Motivation and your Hidden Goal altogether.

To gain a Restored SoS means healing yourself from the addictive behaviors induced by Ego-References. This means recognizing and dismantling the SSoS we have become reliant on. To the part of your inner child who is in survival mode, blowing the whistle on that game could result in your Annihilation as a Being, so maintaining the SSoS has become a matter of life or death to that inner child. This is nothing to mess with, even for the sake of healing, which that part of us is ignorant or skeptical about, and resistant to. Too much is at stake to go trying something new! Thus denial is in the "self"-interest of the System.

Here is another example of how an everyday trivial thing—a kiss—can carry the deep emotional charge of an Ego-Reference that has to be satisfied at all costs. In this example, a kiss functions as a Vehicle for the Ego-Reference: I have to make sure my significant other won't abandon me. If you were a person with a SSoS whose parents told you repeatedly, "No wonder every man leaves you; you are so . . . ," a kiss from a significant other is no longer a kiss for the sake of its lovely experience. Nope, it becomes a signal of "all is well; I am safe." If, to attain your parents' approval, you have an underlying drive to keep this significant other at all costs, upon receiving the kiss, you may subconsciously think, "I don't really want to admit it but this kiss carries the emotional charge of feeding my Substitute Sense of Self. It is not my spouse's love or appreciation I experience but a confirmation that he or she is not planning to leave me. All is well." Thus, you can feel that parental approval in the back of your mind and "Feel-good-about-Yourself"—rather than being judged for being too whatever—and that feeling/state *functions as* your SSoS.

Now, why would you not want to admit all that to yourself? Well, we prefer to stay in denial so that we can live up to our Ego-References. Until we are ready to assess our motives honestly, introspection is impossible. It requires a great deal of courage to face our Fear of Annihilation, the causes of our stresses and discontent in life, and our true Hidden Agenda.

LOOKING AHEAD

Attaining a Restored SoS is being able to sense our Self using the right criteria instead of performance-based ones. It comprises a reconditioning of ourselves to a new inner reality: We now are fully in touch with and connected to the physical, emotional, and psychological aspects of our own being instead of being enslaved to circumstances and to other people.

All along in this book, I have been referring to the possibility and the process of replacing the SSoS. Now that you know more about what a Restored SoS might be and might feel like, it is time to look more deeply at the process of gaining one—the topic of the next chapter.

11 | Tips and Tools for Restoring Your Sense of Self

In my own life, I had to find, invent, and test out what seemed to work to help me feel less dependent on, less of a slave to, less swallowed by, less identified with, and less harmed by my Substitute Sense of Self (SSoS)–oriented System. In this chapter, I share some of what has helped me, and I hope it will help you, too. This recovery-aspect of the work of Healthy Sense of Self is still in development, and a great deal more will become available within the coming months, in other publications and via our website, www.healthysenseofself.com.

One particular program has been supportive in actively getting me started with my own recovery process. This program is called the Silva Mind-Body Healing Method (see www.silvamindbodyhealing.com). It is based on 50 years of teaching various techniques of relaxation and visualization, yet it has stayed up-to-date and in touch with the latest research on mind–body interaction. The many audio CDs and other material the Silva Method offers are a great way to get started on an inner journey. Remember, it is not enough to just buy the CDs and have them on the shelf at home. If you are serious about making certain changes, you need to be effective in developing the habit of listening to them and doing the exercises. It helped me to decide to set time aside to focus on the process of laying a foundation for implementing in myself a healthy Sense of my Self. It taught me, among other things, to implement a routine, and take this reconditioning task as a job that needed to be done. The Silva Method encouraged me to turn a vague notion that something had to change into a scheduled commitment. Like most people, I was very reluctant to take time off from my busy schedule. Interesting note: that schedule was full of tasks and plans that were there to feed the need of the SSoS, but I wasn't quite well aware enough of that to comfortably focus on my healing and real well-being!

So be prepared, those of you who do want to make the change. You have to make it a priority in your life when you want to shift habits that you perceive your (well-)being depends on.

THE STAGES TO RESTORING YOUR SENSE OF SELF

As has been discussed in previous chapters, having a SSoS is an addiction in itself. The reason it may not look like it, or even feel like being an addiction, is because the harmful effects are not obvious to the eye, and occur spread over a whole lifetime. I have found it very helpful in my recovery from a SSoS to look at and compare it with the recovery of substance abuse. To replace any unhealthy behavior by a healthy one we need to go through various stages of change.

In my education as a Chemical Dependency Professional (CDP) at Bellevue College, I was introduced to a model of the stages of change.[11] It helps (addiction-) counselors to get a better overview of the various processes that a person goes through when recovering from alcohol and/or drug abuse and it can help you too. You can use it as a compass as it tells you where you are in the process of change. And it shows you that *there is* a shore on the other side of the ocean that you are trying to cross in your little ship. You are unable to spot it while you are in the turmoil of trying to survive a storm but it is there!

The model distinguishes five stages of change:

Stage 1: Pre-contemplation

Stage 2: Contemplation

Stage 3: Preparation

Stage 4: Action

Stage 5: Maintenance

You can find information on this subject in any good book about addiction and/or recovery. Please note though that this sequence is also valid for recovering from dependency on a SSoS.

---

[11] James Prochaska and Carlo di Clemente, *Changing for Good* (University of Rhode Island; Transtheoretical Model (TTM) 1977-1983).

Stage 1: Pre-contemplation

This is the first stage of change. We seriously consider whether we are actually addicted to a Substitute Sense of Self. Does it apply to us? Do we have the symptoms of the addiction? Take this opportunity to review the Comparison Chart in the Appendix.

For those of us with "symptoms" of being ruled by a SSoS there comes this moment that lasts only a split second that functions as the "tipping point" in our awareness. In this brief moment the notion flares up that yes, we would be wise to look into what it is that causes our unhappiness, stress, addiction, or anything else. It is a crucial moment, even though at the time it seems minor. After that moment, we need time to effectively let the motivation for recovery grow before we implement the rest of the process.

Stage 2: Contemplation

If we find we are addicted to a SSoS, we are likely to ask questions such as "What does this actually mean for me in my life? What benefits would recovery get me, and what does it take to get there?"

By now we know that we have to dig deep into our conscious mind and find out things about our subconscious as well. Well, that is where we eventually end up. Where we can start is with posing the obvious questions: "What am I all about? What is motivating me to do what I do? What is my ultimate goal with this or that action, activity, or behavior?" Now that we know that motivation can be direct or indirect we can ask ourselves which type of motivation we are dealing with, and especially in specific cases that seem to be important in our lives.

There is a very efficient way of asking questions that I learned from Wendy Lipton Dibner. Here is an example of how that goes:

> *"I want to become a medical doctor."*
>   *"Why? What would that get me?"*
> *"I would be able to help people."*
>   *"Why? What would that get me?"*
> *"I would be able to establish myself in a little village and be part of a nice community."*
>   *"Why? What would that get me?"*
> *"It would be like having friends and family for life."*
>   *"Why? What would that get me?"*
> *"I would feel safe."*

This sequence of questions and answers does not come out so negative, fortunately. Feeling safe seems like a legitimate motivation to do or avoid things. But this sequence could also lead to quite unexpected, less healthy goals in our lives:

"I want to become a medical doctor."

    "Why? What would that get me?"

"I have been interested in helping people since I was a kid."

    "Why? What would that get me?"

"I would have found a way to do what I seem to be good at and make money as well."

    "Why? What would that get me?"

"I would be respected by my dad and do something he really likes."

    "Why? What would that get me?"

"I finally would know that I please him!"[12]

Go ahead and try to ask yourself the questions that apply in your situation. Knowing the ultimate answers to your questions is key to assessing what your ulterior motivation is—in other words, to finding out what you are all about.

Stage 3: Preparation

Once we know what our deepest issues are we can get a clearer view on how that affects our lives and our choices. Based on how much impact they actually have on our lives and that of our loved ones we might choose to study the SoS Method more thoroughly and get a clear overview of what is needed to move away from our unhealthy motivations.

Once we have an overview we can proceed to list the order of things we need to work on to recover from the dependency of a SSoS. Now we can make decisions about which practical and emotional steps we are going to take in order to implement change in our lives.

Another tool you can use in this stage is the Motivation Check as described in Chapter 12. That, next to comparing and applying the SoS Method with the reality of your own life, will give you a good sense of what needs to happen in order to be able to change.

---

[12] Reprinted with permission from the best-selling book, *Shatter Your Speed Limits: Fast-Track Your Success and Get What You Truly Want in Business and in Life,* by Wendy Lipton-Dibner (Wilton, CT: Professional Impact, Inc., 2010), www.ShatterYourSpeedLimits.com.

Stage 4: Action

In this phase, we are actively involved with various exercises and steps as we can find them in the next chapter. We do frequent Motivation Checks (see Chapter 12) and continuously question the motivations for our behavior. In this stage, we are absolutely honest with ourselves and ready to admit our Indirect Motivations. We are starting to see that we actually *are already* and we now are actively addressing our need to cultivate a deep, abiding Sense of that "be-ing." We are learning to connect to our body, which forms a big part of our being. We act, in this stage, with the ultimate goal of redirecting our energy, attention, and focus away from fulfilling Ego-References toward actively and consciously noticing, re-cording, and remembering that all of the parts of ourselves are ours. We own them, they are us, and consequently we do not have to exert any effort to "earn" them.

Exercise and meditation, several of which are detailed in the following chap-ter, are our daily companions. The meditations included in this volume are for exploring the territory of Self and for mapping the Self by finding landmarks and road signs on our paths to a healthy SoS. It is important that you have an open mind here and that you do not set expectations of worlds in meditation to be similar to worlds outside meditation . . . it is another reality. Be ready to explore.

Stage 5: Maintenance

This is a very important phase in becoming and staying successful in your recovery to a healthy Restored SoS. We need to actively and consistently main-tain awareness of our deep, abiding SoS because the old system is so easy to return to. The Black Hole of the (former) lack of SoS keeps sucking us in with its re-lentless hunger for everything it used to suck in, making us susceptible to relapse. Also, now that we are improving our quality of life, everything starts to work out better in our lives than before, and even that tends to lead to many a relapse. You have to hang in there, there is no option. Never give up! There is everything to gain! Brush up on the use of the tools that are offered to you in this method and on those you develop yourself over time as well. Persist in your awareness of self-exercises and you will find your way to a Restored SoS. It is true, you will need a significant amount of determination in motivation (keep it "direct" at all times) and gentle understanding of your own situation to work your way through the minefield of potential fallbacks that is part of the change process.

Figure 11.1 represents the process of change and speaks pretty much for itself.[13] Imagine the line being a path and you are walking on it. It is the

---

[13] Illustration based on an original piece by Virginia Satir (1916-1988) American (family-) psychotherapist.

second stage of change. You have decided you are going to do it. You are going to take that leap into a better future. The jagged line marks the place where you start to actively implement different behavior. With your list of what needs to be done in front of you, you start to undertake more and more decisions based on what is good for yourself. As you go you leave your old habits behind, and at some point there will be confusion and chaos. You have to remember the rules for your new behavior and keep yourself far from old habits. Your body and mind start to object and display symptoms of stress because of being deprived of the old input that was perceived as the only way to survive. People around you act differently because you are changing—some of them might support you and reinforce your change; others might resent it, because it threatens their status quo.

Figure 11.1 is a helpful image. You can look at it over and over again and be comforted that there is going to be a moment that the chaos and confusion lessens. Once you get through the jungle the path becomes easier to follow and your efforts will be rewarded. You are better able to keep up the new behavior. You have made the foundation for a healthy (Restored) SoS. Now you have to stay alert to prevent the Black Hole from using your achievements to score with, but over time the new SoS stays with you and becomes more natural—until you can't imagine anymore how it used to be for you.

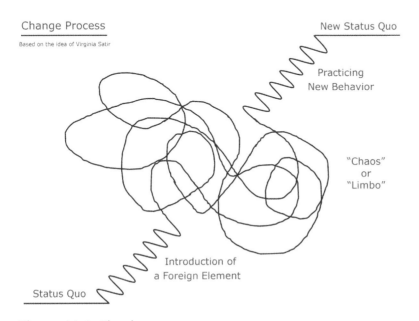

Figure 11.1: The change process

RECOVERY FROM THE ADDICTION TO A SSOS

Note that by "recovery" I mean restoring and/or strengthening your SoS. I talk of strengthening because maybe you are not totally missing the healthy way of sensing your Self, but it is just not so strong and you are inclined to give in to other people's demands too easily.

What we are recovering from is the *addiction* to experiencing the Self in an inadequate, incorrect way, through the SSoS, for which we have to expend a lot of effort. What we replace it with is learning to become aware of the collection of characteristics we are and have as a human being, and specifically as ourselves and that we do not have to do anything for. I am referring to such characteristics as our body, our mind, and the ability to use intention and our energy, inclinations, strengths, and weaknesses. Remember, we are recovering from a set of subconsciously operating behaviors that used to function as a way of connecting to what we thought was our Self. Now we are shifting toward sensing our Self the right way so we become in touch with who we really are.

Once we have the beginning of a healthy Restored SoS, we find that some of the changes we need to make to recover from self-destructive habits take place almost automatically. These changes then are here to stay, because we have changed ourselves. So, if we begin with only one behavior, after beginning to implement a healthy Restored SoS, we can begin to hope that we will be successful in recovering from *other* self-destructive behaviors, such as other addictions.

A WORD OF CAUTION

A short warning is needed (once more) as I do not want people to think that there is a quick fix for any of the problems that result from the dependency on a SSoS. Rather, consider tackling this issue as a thorough lifestyle change as it is a big thing: The foundation of your concept of living needs to be replaced by a healthy one. On the surface, you cannot expect everything to go on as if life is normal.

Restoring your SoS is a reconditioning process that may take from a few months to several years; it doesn't happen overnight, although at given moments in time you will get inspired thoughts and insights that change you forever in the direction of a Restored SoS. It takes time and dedication, but this time your dedication is geared toward yourself, toward your own life. This process is absolutely necessary to be successful in freeing yourself from the unwanted and self-destructive behaviors as well as in ridding yourself of the excess stress and its related result: disease and dysfunction.

Do not be discouraged either, though! You can work on changing the way you sense your Self at any moment and in most any situation. If you do not tell anybody people only will notice a shift in you for the better. After all, this change comes down to a shift within yourself. Your family and friends will only wonder how, on earth, you have gotten so balanced and patient. They will register a change in you that might make them curious. Then it'll be up to you to step up and take your chance to pay it forward and contribute your part to make the world a better place.

In the Recovery process, the order in which you tackle things is important. To eliminate the unhealthy behavior of being dependent on a SSoS for your self-experience, you first need to have a healthy replacement operating. In other words, in order to be able to outgrow/replace the compulsion to "Feel-good-about-Self" that functions as a SSoS, you need to have in place—at least partially—a healthier way of experiencing the Self.

As you are eager to replace your bad habit with a good habit I need to give another short warning, which is best worded as follows:

"It is impossible to live in a vacuum." In other words, even though you want nothing more than to be living from your own core of being, so far you have been filling that void of where the true and real Sense of Self needs to be by conditions and achievements you thought you had a grip on. These conditions and achievements need a lot of attention and input from you, which has become a very predominant habit: we call it a compulsion. Just stopping the compulsion is not going to work, as a sort of vacuum would arise. And since your self-experience depends on what, for now, is in that vacuum, you can't just take it out. Remember, the SSoS functions as the backbone for the psyche. It would be highly anxiety-provoking and you would (virtually) fall apart, because the real backbone is not in place yet. Of course this is just a metaphor, a visual aid I use to help you understand the importance of holding on to the old crutch while in the process of exchanging it for the new one (compare the story of the old man and the cane (page 157).

So the first thing to do is to make sure to have a few tools available that enable you to begin to build a genuine, lasting Sense of Self.

If you work your way through the steps and exercises described in the next chapter systematically you will build up your self-experience from scratch. Your first step is body awareness. Gaining a solid awareness of your body is the part where the man walks with two canes. When that awareness is well in place, you can increasingly start to stop living up to your ego-references and throw away the crutch that requires having to gain a FgaS for your self-experience.

LOOKING AHEAD

Now that you are aware of the wonderful benefits that are awaiting you when you take the time and invest your best effort to restore your SoS, you might want to know how to proceed. In the next chapter, you will find several detailed exercises and affirmations that will help you implement and maintain your recovery.

12 | Exercises and Affirmations

This above all: to thine own self be true,
And it must follow, as the night the day,
Thou canst not then be false to any man.

—Shakespeare, *Hamlet* (Act I, scene 3)

THE PROCESS OF RECONDITIONING ONESELF IS BECOMING MORE COMMON THAN it used to be. Dr. Joe Dispenza calls it mental rehearsal. What we need to achieve with it is to convince our memory that the conclusions we drew as a child need to be overwritten by new ones, ones we have come to conclude at a later age, and that will serve us better. Whatever way we can do that is fine. In this chapter we describe awareness exercises and invite you to train your mind to replace your old strategies. We could call this a reconditioning program as it is a reprogramming of our mind. Anyway, I find it difficult to capture what I have to offer to the purpose of helping you to "reset" your approach to life in one or two words. And that doesn't really matter; the most important thing is that the text does what it needs to do: get you to decide to take action and accompany you on your way to reprogram yourself to live to make yourself (and with that, others) as happy and as productive and successful as you can possibly be.

We know the proverb: The way to hell is paved with good intentions. Well, that proverb is especially true here. I have found that it takes a lot more than good intentions to stick to the plan of reconditioning yourself. A lot of discipline is needed before you have your focus and energy directed to actually

Figure 12.1: At times, you may feel you are like Sisyphus . . .

sensing your Self, and to let go of your old patterns of behavior before you trust yourself to actively listen to and obey your authentic Self.

Reconditioning ourselves means leaving our SSoS-oriented ways behind, and looking at ourselves and our lives in a new way. In this new way we are the heart of our existence, where our purpose is our own well-being, based on our own criteria.

As with all new behaviors, a learning curve is involved and at the same time relapse is always lurking. Imagine two opposing energies, the old and the new. The old one is strong because it has been reinforced over and over for a long time. It has established a clear path in your brain wiring (compare Figure 10.3, page 158): you can say it has become hard-wired, and is therefore difficult to get rid of. The new one is full of good intentions, maybe even based on desperation because you cannot go on any longer in the old way. At times, you may feel as though you are Sisyphus from Greek mythology, eternally pushing a huge boulder up a steep hill and, just before reaching the top of the hill, having the boulder roll back to the bottom.

OVERVIEW

That being said, here is an overview of what you can expect to find in this chapter. First, you will find 12 very important key phrases to re-program your mind. I give those to you right away because they are utterly important in the process.

Then we go back to assessing where you are in the process of being dependent on a SSoS. I will explain to you all about the Motivation Check and how to do it.

Next we do a preparatory exercise for creating your own 12-step program: We write up a portrait of a SSoS-oriented person that has your characteristics. You will find an example based on my own findings about myself.

Finally you make a list of what you have found out about yourself while putting this portrait of yourself together. This is going to be a list of the things that make your life harder instead of easier.

Now that you know your negatives, you can turn them into positives. In other words, you now are able to create your own 12-step program that will help you find your way to a healthy Sense of Self.

FOLLOWING ARE THE 12 Healing Statements. This is the heart of the reconditioning program used in the SoS Method.

1. My life and my body are mine.
2. I experience myself directly.
3. I think for myself.
4. I am present to the Here and Now.
5. I see other people for who they are.
6. My conversations occur to transfer information or just for the heck of it.
7. My work/doing is to get from A–B or Z.
8. I have access to my own preferences, opinions, and feelings.
9. I am consciously aware of my five/six senses.
10. Relapse is always lurking.
11. I am ready to share my life with others.
12. I am ready to be part of a healthy community.

MOTIVATION CHECK

Earlier we saw that there are two types of motivation—direct or indirect—and also how they are indicative of the type of Sense of Self we have: a Natural Sense of Self or a Substitute Sense of Self, respectively. Learning to become aware of our motivation is therefore an important part in the process of Restoring our Sense of Self (SoS).

The only effective way to break the various unhealthy emotional and motivational patterns described in this book is to actively work on getting a Restored SoS. Once this is in place, your motivation automatically has cleared up. *There is no need for a SSoS if we can learn to sense and truly connect to what is really ourselves!* Then, there is no need for us to bring the Ego-References to a good ending, in every instance, because the Hidden Goal no longer exists. We no longer have to generate a SSoS. Automatically, our Vehicles lose their function as Vehicles, and finally our motivations turn into straightforward (direct) ones.

The Hidden Agenda of getting approval, shows up in our lives with many faces, as many different Vehicles cover it up. These Vehicles are therefore not always easily recognized but the Hidden Agenda is *ultimately* about the *same* thing: finding ways to being seen, heard, and acknowledged.

The need for *approval* shows up with many faces. It all depends on what our trial and error got for us as children. How did we get closest to feeling acknowledged? Was it through getting a compliment, getting attention, being taken seriously, being smiled at, being hugged, being asked for advice, a certain look in the eyes of someone else, *not* being frowned at, getting a certain tone of voice from someone else, or being allowed to participate in certain family activities—or maybe any of a thousand other faces?

The *feelings/thoughts/self-judgments* (lumped together as "Feeling-good-about-Self") that result from successful achievement of the Hidden Agenda to get approval also have many faces:

Motivation Check

A crucial tool in getting clear about the crooked nature of our (Indirect) Motivation that serves to (a) detect Indirect Motivations and Hidden Agendas in your Self and (b) to record and become familiar with what your Ego-References, Hidden Agendas, and Hidden Goal are.

feeling acknowledged,

feeling taken into account,

feeling admired,

having a sense of belonging,

feeling safe,

feeling alive,

having a voice,

not experiencing ridicule or humiliation,

feeling valued,

feeling a sense of relief,

and so on.

The **Motivation Check** serves to (a) detect Indirect Motivations and Hidden Agendas in your Self and (b) to record and become familiar with what your Ego-References, Hidden Agendas, and Hidden Goal are. It is to become consciously aware of what actions, activities, or behavior you chose as Vehicles for these Ego-References with their Hidden Agendas.

Figure 12.2 indicates each of *the concepts* in Indirect Motivation and describes more detail about their actual content. This overview shows the relationship from the Vehicle to the Ego-Reference, and from the Ego-Reference to the Hidden Agenda and ultimately to the Hidden Goal or its substitute.

Figure 12.3 contains real-life examples of each of the concepts listed in Figure 12.1. In case of a Direct Motivation, the Vehicle in this picture would be the honest goal for which an action or behavior would be performed; in the case of an Indirect Motivation, it is merely a cover-up for the performance of an Ego-Reference.

The design of these lists gives a clear outline of how, through Indirect Motivation, we use a Vehicle to work on improving ourselves with respect to those conditions that form our Ego-References, with the ultimate goal of accomplishing our Hidden Agenda.

Here is what you can do to make your own lists: copy (or download from our websiteathttp://healthysenseofself.com/store/items/motivation-check-forms/or

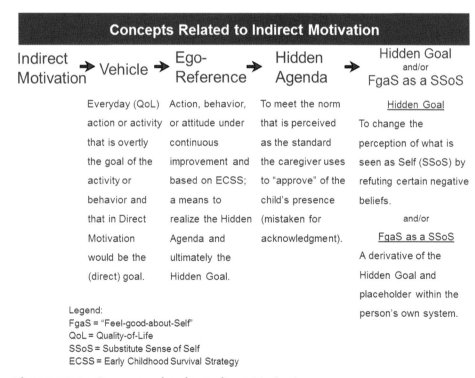

Figure 12.2: Concepts related to Indirect Motivation

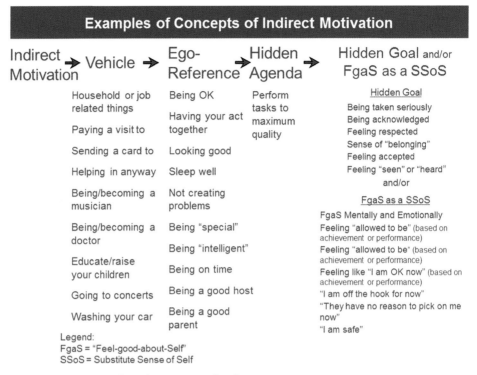

Figure 12.3: Examples of concepts of Indirect Motivation

http://bit.ly/SoSMotivationCheck) the two forms that follow (Figures 12.4 and 12.5) and fill them in with your own information.

Figure 12.4 shows the difference between both types of motivation. In case the motivation is direct, "you get what you see": a behavior and/or action is performed for the sake of a simple, relatively obvious goal. There is a healthy congruency between the means and the goal. The feelings involved in this process are regular and healthy Quality-of-Life level feelings.

In case of Indirect Motivation, what would normally be the actual goal of the action becomes a Vehicle to perform a certain act or behavior that is meant to show a specific quality or a characteristic of the person that, she perceives, her parent has doubted. This activity or behavior, called an ego-reference, has the Hidden Agenda of proving that the person can do better than (he perceives) the parent thinks. The ultimate Hidden Goal of this subconsciously motivated activity is to be valued and acknowledged by that parent. So, the Ego-Reference and its Hidden Agenda are the means to get to the Hidden Goal and/or Substitute Sense of Self.

Overexcitement, or "butterflies in stomach," apprehension, and excessive stress, possibly accompanied by insomnia, are some of the feelings (see

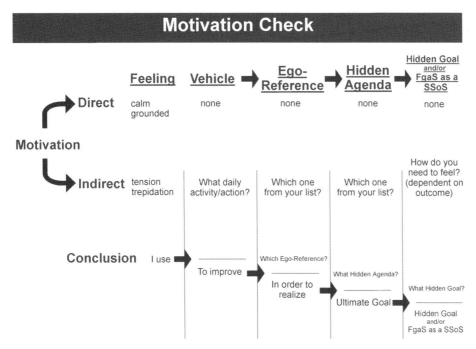

Figure 12.4: Motivation Check questions

the Feeling column) that may show up during Indirect Motivation. Another strong characteristic of Indirect Motivation is experiencing the compulsion of having to go on doing something until there is a "Feeling-good-about-Self" state reached.

The Motivation Check is a crucial tool in getting clear about the crooked nature of our (Indirect) Motivation. I urge people who take their recovery seriously to work with these forms. In Figure 12.5, you write down your Vehicles, your Ego-References, your Hidden Agendas, and your ultimate Hidden Goal, and in the process discover the truth about yourself. I highly encourage you to do this because it is a great help in learning to identify your motivation pattern, which is necessary to find out what your ultimate drive is and what that means in your life. You might want to make more than one copy of this figure because, as you study this Method and learn more about yourself through introspection, you will become increasingly clear about what to write on it! So filling out a new copy of the chart every few weeks is a good idea.

On this form, you can line up what you have found out about your patterns of motivation. By creating this overview, you are becoming aware of and therefore are on your way to taking a step back from these patterns already. Just paying attention to yourself doing these things and being aware of

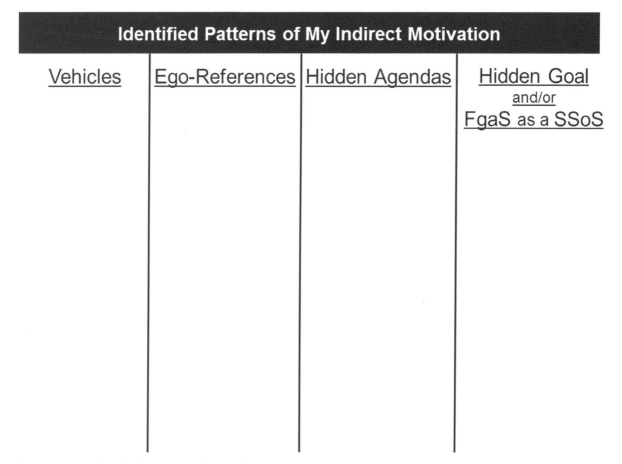

Figure 12.5: Identified patterns of my Indirect Motivation

why you would do certain things lowers the acuteness of the need to actually do them, a first step on the path of healing yourself and toward truly being yourself.

Preparatory Exercise: A Portrait

Our goal in this section is to have you create your own 12-step program. It will be built on whatever you have discovered during your Motivation Check about yourself. It will be based on the Ego-References you have found that motivate you during the course of your day—your Hidden Agendas and your ultimate Hidden Goal.

What most likely will be identical with what you find in the steps in this chapter is the element of compulsion and the result of the single-minded focus on these agendas and goals that lead to the specific behaviors you now want to change.

Each of following statements is meant to label aspects of your behavior where you might have developed a wrong concept of, or that is the direct result of your thwarted development of a healthy way of, experiencing yourself. This has led you to become dependent on outcomes that you had to work hard for, get exhausted from, and feel good or bad about—in short, that totally occupied every aspect of your being.

To single out these strategies of behavior and/or the mental-emotional or even physical results from those strategies and dependencies, will help you to get a global overview of what aspect of your behavior needs change. A list of all the things that are in need of change also gives you a good overview of your whole reconditioning program and it serves as a progress check: You can look back on it later and say: "Hey, it is not that way anymore for me. I have changed quite a bit!"

To get started on this endeavor pretend you have to write a portrait of a person with the traits you would like to get rid of in yourself. List the characteristics of that person, who is addicted to the "Feeling-good-about-Self" state of the Substitute Sense of Self, just like your (former) self. For me, this would read as follows:

1. *Lack of presence:* My person is a sort of body-less *floating brain* who (that) is thinking and rationalizing its way to the much-desired effect of "Feeling-good-about-Herself." She feels it as the only way to have the right to exist. It's the only way she feels a sort of alive. She does not really experience herself the same way others seem to. Something is *off* with her, and she is unable to put her finger on it. Others seem to know what they are doing and where they are heading. Her peers all seem to know what they like or do not like. My person here cannot even figure out what she should wear. She has the hardest time making any decision.

2. My person has an Indirect relationship with her Self. The degree to which she experiences her "self" depends on the outcome of her achievements or on what others make her feel about herself.

3. She is merely functioning on automatic pilot. She is not really present to herself and therefore unable to use her own mind. She does not have clear personal criteria, opinions, or tastes. Everything is of service to the FgaS state as a SSoS, to get her caregiver's approval or the approval of her VIPV. She is not truly present as herself and functions as a robot, and of course she is not aware of it.

4. The person is not "present" in the present but living in the past. The person lives in the unreal memory state of the past and transposes all she encounters in the present automatically to this state *in the past*. She lives in a continuous state of "trance." She cannot move out of the past because something is in need of repair: my person has a big need to feel acknowledged as a visible and respected "other" human being.

5. My person sees other people only insofar as they have relevance in the light of their Hidden Agenda or goal. She is only drawn to another person if she can use them for SSoS-oriented purposes. To see the personal nature, history, present, and future of another person is not within the scope of my person who looks at things in a SSoS-oriented way.

6. Every interaction that takes place, every bit of communication, is evaluated in the light of its use to get to the Hidden Goal. Things that do not fit in the plan are at the most "tolerated' with impatience or rejected. In every conversation there is the Hidden Agenda to end it with a FgaS.

7. Any work or task that is undertaken should also ultimately be useful in the process of gaining a SSoS; if not, there is no interest or there may even be resentment.

8. The moment my person has left the green path of leading her life with her own well-being in mind is the moment she is after the FgaS state (on that SSoS-oriented level) again. She walks on the treadmill of the SSoS-oriented system, which keeps itself going in circles as there is no way out. The Hidden Goal is never reached and a Sense of Self is not really there. My person stays a victim of the compulsion to get it right "this time around."

9. Because she is not really interested in what happens outside herself she does not really use her senses. My person does not sharpen her senses by using them; they become dull instead. My person's eyesight blurs; she loses the edge of her hearing; her ability to taste and smell diminishes and her touch becomes compromised. She does not really feel the surface of things anymore when she touches them. Does she really feel or sense the person next to her?

10. *Grandiosity:* She is so focused on becoming great that she is hardly aware where she is on this planet or how many years have passed. All she wants is to "Feel-good-about-Herself" and have a peaceful environment in which she can do her thing. You know, she *needs* to be good at something, but she still has not reached her goal and time is pressing now that she gets older. What if she would die and never really lived up to her own expectations? What if she would die and never really lived? What if she would die and never had fun? What if she won't be able to make a difference in the world? Her life would have been so trivial . . .

11. *She day-dreams: "One day I will be living."* My portrayed person works so hard to improve herself but each time she seems to get somewhere, her achievements seem to be sabotaged and she has to start from scratch. She knows she has great potential; she is smart and talented and she does have skills. It's just that somehow she seems to get in her own way of being successful. She has no idea how other people do it. How can they be so happy and lighthearted? How can they have so much fun? Life is a drag and hers is a struggle. When she will have reached her Hidden Goal it'll be so much better and she will be able to really start living.

12. As time goes by, the Hidden Goal is never reached but she just cannot give it up. So she grows old while still working hard to get the fictional goal fulfilled. She spends her time working, and she is not interested in small talk or in what happens around her. She is not aware that she is and has been skipping her life.

I encourage you to write up your very own points and issues in this synthesis of how your life used to be AND could go on, if you didn't undertake something to make that shift toward a better life. Again, this list applied to me. If you have a hard time getting started with your own list you could start out with this one and modify it as you go.

The next activity is to reduce this portrait to its key elements. So going over numbers 1 through 12, you draw out of each section the main thought in such a way that you actually get a very short outline of the portrait. In this case that would look like this:

1. Body-less floating brain
2. Indirect Relationship with Self (Castle of Enmeshment)
3. On automatic pilot
4. Living "in a trance"; living in the past
5. People not actively seen for who *they* are
6. Conversations for the FgaS state
7. Work for the FgaS state
8. Living in the red circle of compulsion and addiction on the Map of Healing the SoS

   9. Senses dead or dying; being self-absorbed

  10. Mistaken state of being: from "everything is fine" to grandiosity

  11. One day I will be living—receding horizon

  12. Alone and missed out on life

Your personal, unhealthy opposites of the 12 healing statements mentioned in the beginning of this chapter are easy to remember, because you encounter them all the time in yourself. I have found that comparing the old ways to the new has several advantages:

- You take a good look at yourself, which helps in gaining self-knowledge.
- You get a sense of what patterns of behavior play an important role in your life.
- Your negative characteristics can function as a stepping-stone to get insight in why and how you do what you do (motivation).
- They can serve as a red threat to start structuring your plan of change.

  As an example: I always come late—Why does that bother me so much? What is at stake for me? I feel guilty and selfish—Is it about missing an appointment and cause an inconvenience to somebody else?—No, it makes me feel bad and I need to "Feel-good-about-Myself"—Why is that so important to me? Because it makes me feel like I deserve *to be*—Well, who says so? I think I have been brought up with that idea, etc.

Now that we have distilled what we would like to work on while changing from the dependency on a SSoS to being the master of our lives we are going to look into what the change in each of the steps would result in. In other words, what is the desired outcome to help us change to a healthy Restored Sense of Self? Note that sometimes we do not even have to work on these steps because they change automatically. When we become more tuned in to who we are, all the coping mechanisms of the SSoS-oriented System become obsolete, and that brings about a great shift in our behavior and in our emotions. So the process of change is not necessarily linear but as one thing changes many, if not all of them, change.

The opposite is true, too: When relapse occurs, the behavior related to each one of the steps turns to red, like synchronized traffic lights.

Here is the list as it served my own purposes. In the pre-healed state the key characteristics are experienced as the opposite of what is desired, and described in the twelve steps of awareness needed for implementing a healthy Sense of Self. They are in italic. If you relate to other images or if your symptoms of your dependency on a SSoS are different, then, by all means, replace this list with the images you relate to.

1. Being *a body-less floating brain* attached to a Vehicle **as opposed to** having a felt *body awareness* that reinforces a sense of me-ness.

2. Sensing the Self through the filter of parental (or virtual parental-) approval and thus in *an indirect way* **as opposed to** *experiencing the Self, things, people, and events in a direct way.*

3. Experiencing my Self as an extension of my primary caregiver, my Virtual, Internalized Parental Voice (VIPV), or my needy child brain of the past has become *my automatic pilot* **as opposed to** *I think with my own mind and I feel with my own heart.*

4. *Being, in trance, living in the past* (who is on the screen of my mind?) **as opposed to** *being in the Here and Now.* In this state we live "in trance." We are being continuously focused on repairing damage done in the past. You cannot easily spot the difference from looking at a person although a trained person starts to discern such symptoms as a less clear gaze in the eyes (a stare) or an overall lack of concentration.

5. *Not really seeing* other people for who they really are. Often a person is related to as if he or she were a key person in my past, who that person happened to have some similarities with. It can be the same complexion, sound of voice, stature, and one or all of these things trigger in me a person of my past that I have so-called "unfinished business" with, making me relate to the person as if he or she was that person of my past.

   Coming from a SSoS-oriented life style I assume that *that person's* entire life is (also) about me (and not about them) and that I am the center of the Universe and that everybody is there to serve my goals. I see people *only insofar as they have a function in my SSoS-oriented mind* **as opposed to** *I see people for who they are*: as individuals who are the center of their own Universes, with their own reasons, their own history and future, their own specific circumstances and possibilities.

6. *Using conversations* to facilitate *my need to get a "Feel-good-about-Self-"* as a SSoS. This type of conversation has nothing to do with the exchange of opinions or information **as opposed to** *conversations being there to transfer information or for the heck of it.*

7. Work functions *as a Vehicle* to ultimately provide a chance for me *to "Feel-good-about-Myself-"* as a SSoS, **as opposed to** *work being there as a tool to get things done*, to get from A to B or to Z. Work is the way the world gets things done. When not in pursuit of a SSoS I am focused on the content of the work, not on any Hidden Agenda. (Note: Quality-of-Life level of feeling content or satisfied is perfectly OK.)

8. Being a pawn in my caregiver's game and *the slave* of my (self-imposed) conditions **as opposed to** *I acknowledge myself* as a unique, independent, and autonomous human being with the right to my own tastes, preferences, opinions, values, and feelings, and the *choice* to express them.

9. Being *focused single-mindedly* on how to get my Ego-References done and (mis-)use and abuse my senses by overloading them with tasks they are not made to do, such as continuously scanning for opportunities to score, **as opposed to** being present to my senses and sensing myself. "I see and am present to my seeing and to what I see; I am present to hearing, and to what I hear: I am able to listen."

10. Living my life wishing and pretending *everything is fine,* so I can continue to work on my Ego-References and feed my *sense of grandiosity* that compensates my denied sense of inferiority. This **as opposed to** being aware that *relapse* into old habits of working my way up to a FgaS state as my only goal, is always lurking. And, as unreal as it sounds, I celebrate the relapse as an opportunity to become aware of how I have returned to the red path of addiction so I can get back on the green path (compare Map for Healing the Sense of Self in Chapter 9, page 130).

11. Being needy, controlling, and demanding or subdued, codependent, and unreliable, and skipping my own life in the process, **as opposed to** *celebrating existence.* I am now a whole person and live life based on my own criteria so that I am ready to meet, and healthily relate to, others.

12. Being only about myself and about compensating for my unmet needs in which I drag those living in my direct environment as well **as opposed to** I am ready to contribute to the world with my best Self, which leads to healthy *interdependence, which in its turn leads to effective community building and peace.*

Now that we have built a bridge between the two ways of being, our old one and the desired new one, we can single out the (positive) phrases that describe the change we want to make and detach them from our old patterns. That more detailed version can look like this:

1. I am going to be about *me*. I will work on having full access to my own life and I soon will be fully living *my own life*. I am my body.

2. I will experience things, people, and events in a direct way, not via something else (FgaS).

3. I will think for myself. "What do I really think of it myself?" is the question I will pose to myself continuously. I will work toward basing my decisions and motivation on my very own values and criteria.

4. I will check in with being in the Here and Now with my mind, on a regular basis, to truly live my own life.

5. I will work on seeing others for who they are. I will become fully aware that they live in their own bubble, with their own goals, their own demons, and their own past and future separate from mine.

6. My conversations will serve to transfer information, as entertainment, or for the heck of it. I will work on eliminating any Hidden Agenda (except for political ones of course).

7. My work/doing will be there for the sake of itself. It is to move from A to B or Z. That is how the world works. It no longer is to make me "Feel-good-about-Myself-" as a SSoS.

8. I will be truly living my own life. My life now will be based on my own needs and wants. I will have full access to my own preferences, opinions, and feelings, and have the choice to express them.

9. I will be fully aware that my five/six senses are a precious gift and I will be present to them. I will be in focus mode and directly motivated.

10. I am not so "fine" but recovering. I will stay aware that relapse is always lurking, especially in the beginning, or after sickness or jetlag, and I am prepared to start from scratch with my reconditioning process. I know a new pathway in my brain has to be created and that it gets better every day.

11. I will be ready to share my life with others, to receive from and give to others and be of service. I have no longer a Hidden Agenda of gaining a SSoS with that.

12. I will be independent, not needy or enmeshed with other people or with things such as work. I am ready for interdependency, the only way to create a healthy and flourishing community.

THE 12 HEALING STATEMENTS

Let us now reduce this list to its basic elements. That is what our personal 12-step program is going to look like. We now have distilled your concept of life and living. Here are your 12 Healing Statements:

1. My life and my body are mine.
2. I experience my Self directly.
3. I think for myself.
4. I am in the Here and Now.
5. I see other people for who they are.
6. My conversations occur to transfer information or for the heck of it.
7. My work/doing is to get from A-B or Z.
8. I have access to my own preferences, opinions, and feelings.
9. I am consciously aware of my five/six senses.
10. Relapse is always lurking.
11. I am ready to share my life with others.
12. I am ready to be part of a healthy community.

Please note that this is the same list I showed you at the beginning of the chapter. It will be interesting for you to compare this list with your personalized one.

Now let us go into more detail of each of the items on this most important list.

1. Being Aware of Your Body

The following exercise and its variants will help you restore your SoS through gaining awareness of your (own) body. In order to be able to access your "real" life, you need to be aware of and own your body. It is a funny thing, realizing that you really *have* and *are* your body at the same time. So this exercise is to gain understanding—by means of sensing—what it means to be *in* and *with* your mind and your body while being your body at the same time. After many repetitions of this exercise, you learn to truly own your body.

As you repeat this exercise and become aware of all the different areas of your body, you may come across certain questions about what the ultimate entity of your life and living is about. You might want to pause and consider what more there is to *you* as a person. Here we enter the realm of spirituality or religion, and it is not within the scope, nor the intention of this book to address these questions. With the quest of gaining a healthy Sense of Self we mean to provide a tool that can serve you to feel and function better on this planet. And one thing is clear: You *are* (the owner of) your body so you'd better focus on it to fully become aware of it.

The (Three) MMM's

You are the Master of this body and the life granted to you. You are not only the master; you are also the Manager of the energy that comes with the life that has been given to you, and you are also the Maintenance person who needs to take care of the Vehicles allowing this living to happen: your body, first and foremost, but also your mental and emotional well-being. You have the obligation, and the duty, to keep your body in good health.

This is an exercise to recognize, oppose, and dismantle *the Fear of Annihilation.* **If, thus far, we have perceived our right to exist as depending on the real (or virtual) approval of our parents, we need to become aware that our being and having the right to live is different from** what we feel we have to achieve to get other people's approval. Strictly speaking, it is a comparison that doesn't make sense: It is like comparing apples with elephants or oranges with polar bears. But it made sense to us as young children.

Find a quiet place where you will not be interrupted, and work through the following steps:

- Look at your body with an inner eye as if you see it for the first time in your life.

- Like a surprised toddler, discover all the areas of your body.

- Stand up straight and sense how your feet touch the ground and how your legs are supporting your whole body—"you." Now reach down to touch your toes with your hands and tell yourself aloud what you are doing. It is important that you also explicitly direct your mind to those areas you mention.

- Have your mind occupy and own the places of your body your hands are touching and have your body occupy your mind. In sum, experience your Self as a closely knit unit:

Exercise I

  - I am touching my toes with my hands and I feel my nails, the soles of my feet on the floor—I am touching the top of my feet, my ankles, my shins, my calves, the backs of my knees, my knees.

My hands rest on my knees for a while. They feel nice and warm. Now I feel my thighs, my hips, my belly, my stomach, my chest, and my shoulders. I feel my arms, my hands with my fingers. I feel my legs with my feet, my limbs. I feel my neck and my head with my hair.

- I feel my eyes, my ears, my nose, my mouth, and my skin.

- This is all me; this is all mine. This is my Self.

- I feel my heart beating, sending my blood traveling through my veins. I feel my lungs expanding and contracting, taking care of my breathing. I imagine and feel my liver; I imagine and feel my kidneys, spleen, and gall bladder. I imagine all my inner organs.

- I imagine my nervous system, starting in my brain and extending into even the remotest areas of my body.

- I imagine my hormone system, the biochemical messengers in my body.

- I imagine my reproductive system.

- I imagine my lymphatic system, part of my immune system, the soldiers of my body.

- I imagine my digestive system, spreading the nutrients to keep the fire going.

- It is mine. It is *me*. I am granted the use of this wonderful machine called my body, my Self.

Variation 1

Focus your awareness on an area of your body, for example, your knees. As you touch the skin of your knees, concentrate on that action: I am sensing my knees. You bring your awareness to your knees from the outside through your hands, but at the same time, you approach and occupy your knees with your mind from the inside. It is as if your heart travels through your body to your knees, explores them from within your body, and stays within them for a short while before traveling on to the next area you mention aloud and touch with your hands.

Variation 2

The following variation is a way to practice this sort of awareness even more. You can move your attention in order up from your toes to your feet, to your ankles to your shins, and so on, gradually climbing up your body.

You also can move your awareness and your hands from one random place to another that you decide on while still being in that first place. As you do this, it becomes clearer how you hop from one place to the other or rather what it is that does the hopping, or should I say who it is who does the hopping. For example, you are in your toes and you decide to hop to your right elbow, you stay there and give it your full attention—then you move on to your left ear until that is totally present for you, and then you skip to your stomach.

Variation 3

Another way to do this is not to hop from one place to the other but to travel there. Let us say you are with your attention in your knees and the warmth of your hands penetrates the area of your knees while your heart (attention) is also in your knees. Now you decide to go to your right elbow. But instead of hopping there, you follow a road as if your heart had legs and feet to walk up to that place, slowly. In your imagination, think of your body as a road map and your awareness as a little white light that travels along the highways, intermittently lighting up to show you where it is. Your hands travel with the light as well.

2. Experiencing Your Self Directly

When we have an indirect relationship with ourselves we are not fully aware of ourselves. ***We get the notion of being OK when we do something right and that gives us a sort of green light for being.*** So far that may have been the only moment we allowed ourselves to take a breather; the whole of the other time we are working on fulfilling the conditions that lead to that moment.

That moment we took that breather has been the only moment in which we had a sort of awareness of "being." So far that might have been the only moment of sensing something like "a Self," but we now know that it was a substitute for the real SoS. It didn't mean that the rest of the time we "*were not,*" but we were not aware of it at all. We were what I call "a floating brain"—a sort of mental process that makes sure we kept our plates in the air and did what we perceived needed to be done to get our SSoS prolonged, as said before: a matter of life and death. It is as if we were a head without a body; others might say we live from the head up and we are unaware of our body.

In this case we are in a direct relationship with the project we are working on, with the errand we need to bring to a good ending, with the job that needs to be done, but not with ourselves as a person—not with our body, not with our potential of independent thinking. We are not in the present as we are busy compensating for the past. We are not real. We are living in a fictional world of repairing the damage done in the past that we perceive to be our fault.

When we get rid of this wrong way of being in touch with what we thought was ourselves we experience ourselves by sensing all the aspects that form the self in an immediate way. There is no bridge in between who we are and what we sense: we are a whole body because we are aware of it; we are present to ourselves. We "see" ourselves and with that we "see" others as well.

In a direct relationship with yourself, your point of departure shifts from being your activity to your own person, to your own life and well-being. You become the determinant factor in your evaluations.

Here is what you can do to reinforce this direct relationship with yourself:

1. Complete frequent Motivation Checks.

2. Engage in physical activities while in the awareness of your body.

3. Touch and feel things so you experience your body as an intrinsic part of yourself.

4. Practice saying out loud "I" and feel it through and through.

5. Explore your emotions and notice how they feel and where they are felt.

6. Explore feeling pain and pleasure and notice how they feel and where they are felt. That is all you!

3. Think for Your Self

It might seem strange that we have to draw attention to this aspect, as many people might even feel insulted by the suggestion that they need to learn to think with their own mind. We were supposed to have learned that from those who raised us, we presumed.

Well, some of us think independently while others still use the criteria of their caregivers and take those for their own. But in this exercise we realize that we no longer need to live up to the conditions that were based on our caregiver's values. We need to learn to exercise and therefore form our own judgment, based on our own values that we have to develop. But first and foremost we need to wake up and be present to ourselves to even envision that possibility:

• Imagine your body and mind, "your system."

• Then imagine the two opposing forces—one, your true Self (say, green) and the other, the SSoS (say, red), as clouds that are continuously in motion throughout your system, exchanging places, colliding softly or violently and separating again. It is much like a bad weather condition in the sky, only you are containing the weather.

- Now imagine you have a magic wand, and with a light touch and a clear intent you touch these entangled red and green clouds, and immediately, *poof,* on your command, a shift takes place.

- The red clouds separate from the green ones. Now two groups form: the green group, our natural healthy and joyfully productive Self; and the red group, the elements tied to our SSoS–oriented System.

- Quietly and gently (remember, this element was, at one time, part of you) start to make sure the green clouds, your healthy part, grow and become stronger until there is no more room for the red clouds, which shrink and shrink and shrink until they are gone.

Once you have achieved banishing the red clouds (your old, addictive way of thinking), you are the true ruler of your system. Now you are the master of your thinking!

4. Being Present to the Here and Now

All behavior for people with a SSoS is rooted in the past. It is as if we have no connection to the present because, using the present as a Vehicle, we are single-mindedly focused on repairing the damage that occurred during our upbringing and was reinforced as we aged. Where we are seems to be of lesser or no importance because we are living in our head, in the past. If we do not do anything about it we are doomed to pull this cart on which we drag our Hidden Agenda with us throughout life. It makes our existence heavy, slow, and oftentimes unbearable. We need to leave that burden be and relieve ourselves of this dead weight, and become lighter.

The following exercise can help us to get in touch with the present time and location:

- Walk around and sense your legs. (That helps you to become aware of your body so it gives you the first indication that *you are.*) Actively observe, and note the following, saying each aloud:
  - I am [name location].
  - It is [morning, afternoon, evening, night].
  - My name is . . .
  - I am [a woman/a man].

Figure 12.6: The burden of our SSoS-oriented goal

- I am single/married.
- I have a [partner, sister, brother, husband/wife] named . . .
- I have children named . . .
- So I am a [mother/father, friend to, relative to].
- I touch the walls of [location]; they are real.
- On the screen of my mind are [name the people you are/have been thinking of].
- Life is about *my* experience of it, so I am now eliminating these people from my thoughts.
- I now am all by myself and owe responsibility only to myself.
- I now am all by myself on [date].
- I live life following the needs and wants of the present.
- I touch and feel with my hands certain objects that are [name locations around you/the area you are in] around me. They include [list objects as you touch them]. They are my reality now.

As always, you can add your own elements to this to customize it. The purpose of this exercise is that everything you become aware of that does not fit the present time and location needs to be examined in detail and recognized as alien to the present. Over time, this exercise helps you to become aware enough to give all things/people the place they deserve.

5. Seeing Other People for Who They Are

Due to my recovery from being addicted to a SSoS the role of other people in my life has shifted completely. In this Enmeshment with my caregiver most everything ultimately was aimed at giving to her, her fix of the FgaS state. I inherited this way of looking at the world, both by example and by my need, at some point, to get things my way.

It is narcissism: You have no doubt that you are the center of the Universe and the rest of the world turns around you. You think everything and everybody is there to co-operate and facilitate your needs and wants. Let us be clear, though, that we are not talking now about the needs and wants of the authentic self that we get in touch with when we have a healthy Sense of Self. Narcissistic people are a classic example of those not present to their Self. They are dependent on a SSoS. So we need to view that mind-set as described earlier in that perspective (see page 176).

People Living in Their Own Bubble

The truth is: Every single person has a right to be him- or herself. He or she is the king or queen of his or her own Universe in which everything turns around him or her. If you are lucky there are a few other people (or one) in your life in whose life you play an important role or any role at all. If this is a new look on your reality it may help you to visualize each one of us as living in a big bubble. Each of us is the center of his or her own bubble. Sometimes our bubbles touch and bounce away—sometimes we are allowed to occupy a little space in the bubble of someone else (your spouse, best friend. parent). But the main concept is that it is not natural or normal to invade a person's bubble all the time, nor is it healthy to live in the same bubble as somebody else (Enmeshment).

Being Ego-centric Is OK

So people are about themselves; they are not your pawns nor are they there to mirror back to you that deadly desired FgaS state. Becoming fully aware of this reality shifts your perspective of living. If you see that others are about themselves you may feel better that you, in your bubble, are about you. The mistaken belief that we are a better person when we are not ego-centric has made us believe that we need to make room for others all the time, give priority to others, give to others, and so on.

Figure 12.7: Each one of us is living in his or her own bubble

Healing Your Needs Creates a Better World

Here we need to make an important distinction between giving to receive (Indirect Motivation) and giving for the sake of giving (Direct Motivation). If giving comes from the place of Direct Motivation, it is great. But many of us are still very needy and if all of us were focused on working out our own issues and becoming less dependent on others or on what others possess, we would expect and allow others to do the same. Wouldn't that make the world a better place? It is therefore important to be aware of the fact that ultimately our life is our very own personal experience. Spending time and energy on our search for what is missing in our lives, to heal what is wounded, to patch what is leaking (Black Hole) is the best thing we can do both for ourselves and for the world. It is part of managing our system. We can only live the life of a (directly motivated) giving person when we are not needy ourselves.

So the next time you look at your spouse, be aware of the fact that that person is not only there for you. He or she is in your world but ultimately lives to fulfill his or her own dreams and goals. Your spouse is a different person than you are, or perhaps I should say a separate person from you. Stop expecting that you have the exact same ideas and intentions. We are born with equal rights to be ourselves and that means that nobody has to be like anybody else. If you are eager to do what you want to do, so is your spouse, your son, your daughter. Look in the eyes of your friends and gauge the depth of their being. It is funny how that dimension does not show on the outside. You just see a body that is tangible. But behind those eyes and in that body is a whole world: a past, a present, and a future. And you are just a small part of it.

Actively undertaking the effort to think this while being with somebody gives you the right perspective on your own position among others and it will teach you to see others as just as real as you experience yourself to be. At least that is how it was for me.

1. Just look at people and observe how they are about themselves.

2. Imagine them living in their own bubble and you in yours.

3. Open up your own bubble, and knock on the door of theirs and ask them to let you in for a while.

4. Back out of their bubble and go back into your own—then close the door.

5. Now turn the activity around: Someone knocks on the door of your bubble.

6. You decide whether you will let that person in.

7. You allow the person to be with you for a while and while doing that you are fully there for him or her.

8. At some point, when a natural impulse arises, you each go your own way.

6. Conversations for Transferring Information or for the Heck of It

The purpose of conversation is to transfer information or to enjoy talking with somebody. Conversations are not meant to provide us with the FgaS state as a SSoS. If you are one of us people, who perceives that everything and everyone in this world is there to facilitate your needs and wants, it is natural that you expect that others are there to give you that FgaS state because it is the only thing you crave.

Can you see how what others want to discuss does not really interest you? Can you see how what other people are busy with is not at all within the scope of people who are dependent on a SSoS? This exercise is to make a change in that perspective and therefore in this attitude.

Let me give you an example. I am at a party where I don't know many people. So I need to make an effort to meet new people. I have the feeling that nobody really is interested in talking to me even though I am being so nice and doing everything I can to make them feel good. Digging deeper into myself I find that all I want from them is a pleasant chat and then I can part from them with a FgaS state.

But the truth is that, if all I want is that FgaS state, I have a (subconsciously) premeditated goal and I am not really listening to the subject of our conversation. I am not open-minded! I am just trying to be pleasant and say the right thing at the right time so in the end I can go home with a FgaS state.

Usually that happens through making others feel good about *them*selves. What is the result? You might be surprised: People with a healthy Sense of Self sense that something funny is going on. They sense that they do not hit the bottom in you and they turn away from you, not interested. People with a healthy Sense of Self are interested in "the real thing"—the real confrontation or interaction. They do not want to waste their time on playing the game of lies. People with a lack of SoS might hang around you because you are one of a kind, understanding the need to play the game for your SSoS.

Awareness of Our Problem

When we accept that conversations are either about transferring information or for fun it rules out what we used them for: Vehicles to get a FgaS state.

Do you remember conversations that left you utterly frustrated when people just left you there, dangling with no closure, no FgaS state? By internalizing this concept, we gradually become consciously aware of what we are doing when talking to/with people. Our goal in recovery is having conversations with people for the sake of the conversation, to get to know a person, or to have a pleasant or useful time exchanging information. To be effective in getting there we need to analyze what has happened so far. We need to fully own the idea that what we are doing right now is rooted in the fear of not getting to our SSoS.

I Am Already

In order to be able to make that shift we need to become aware that *we already are* as the person we are. We already have what it takes to be ourselves. We do not need this SSoS, this FgaS state, provided by anybody.

We need to become fully aware that we are a closed living circuit for as long as we exist and that we have the ability to interact with other closed living circuits. This doesn't mean we cannot influence each other, but not at the level we have been looking for: depending on others to provide us material to "Feel-good-about-ourSelves," which then serves as our SSoS. Can you sense by now how stressful it is to get that outcome at all cost, and how forced it feels for others as well?

We can practice this new mind-set and attitude in life by staying utterly aware of what we want from the person we are conversing with. We need to learn to remember that there is nothing at stake for us in the way a conversation ends, for example. It does not matter whether it ends on a pleasant note or has a neutral ending. Even disagreeing is OK. We do not need a FgaS state as a result of it. All that matters is whether the message was delivered or received or whether or not we had a good time (on a Quality-of-Life level, that is).

Need (Compulsion) to Endlessly Prolong Phone Calls

If you want to prolong the conversation until that moment you feel safe to leave because you have what you came for, you are trying for a FgaS state. The moment you are able to get over that compulsion you will be better able to "see" and "meet" the other person. Here is a shortened version of the awareness you have to cultivate while speaking to somebody.

1. We need to ask ourselves, "What are my expectations and what is my (Hidden) Agenda?"
2. I *am* already.
3. I already have what it takes to be myself.
4. No SSoS (FgaS state) is at stake.
5. Practice with a friend or spouse.
6. Try it out in a conversation that you purposely set up with a person, who does not need to know you are doing this. It may not be totally fair (Hidden Agenda ☺), but if you do it to create a better world you'll be fine.

7. Work for the Sake of the Work

Work is there to get from A to B or Z because that is how the world works. The work is there for the sake of itself, and never to provide us with a

Substitute Sense of Self. ***We have to learn to distinguish our Selves from the work we are doing, as that is, I believe, the nature of the mental deviation that takes place in people who are workaholics (body-less floating brains).***

The problem is that, while at work, we are unable to take a break other than for the absolute necessity of having to eat. We are hardly aware that we are eating as our minds are busy with the next phase of our work. Having to go to the bathroom is a nuisance that can even make us angry.

Stress and frenzy, fear of not being able to function, fear of "screwing it up," fear of not getting the craved outcome of the Ego-Reference cause us to live under a continuous burden of anxiety. We have to monitor ourselves and everybody else in the environment and control the circumstances, protecting the possibility of a good outcome.

Our dependency on a SSoS for experiencing our Self means that we cannot go home earlier than the point at which we actually have reached the relatively relaxed state of "Feeling-good-about-Ourselves." We are bound to go on with our work until the result gives reason to "Feel-good-about-ourSelves". After all, that is the moment we work for in the first place. With that FgaS we have learned to fill in the void in us where there ought to be a Natural SoS. The moment that FgaS state is reached we feel we have the artificial placeholder of a Natural Sense of Self, and which functions as the backbone of our SSoS-oriented psyche. It leads to agony every time you have to abort your work.

By repeating the words of the steps over and over you will find that they end up making you aware of its content. You will wake up to see that you had built a wall of denial around the issue. By repeating the words, at some point they will start to resonate with the truth inside yourself. "Fake it until you make it" is valid here as well as for the other steps.

Here are some more suggestions as to what you can do to implement this new way of looking at work:

1. Learn by heart and repeat over and over: The work is there to get from A to B or Z; never to give me a FgaS state as a SSoS.

2. Do a sincere Motivation Check: Take what you are doing at work and find out if it functions as a Vehicle to get to a Hidden Agenda and through that to a Hidden Goal. Remind yourself of what they are.

3. Choose two days of the week in which you block time to assess one element that you truly enjoyed completing at work and why you enjoyed it. Were you able to score with it?

4. Then, turning it around, assess one element that you truly despised at work and why you despised it. Did it not serve your SSoS-oriented efficiency?

5. Pick up an activity that has no score potential but that you always wanted to do. Find out what *you* really like and do it.

6. Help somebody else out with a job that has no score potential and make sure he or she does not notice you were the one who did it; stay anonymous.

8. Accessing Your Preferences, Opinions, and Feelings

First you have to be able to see that you are not really present to your own needs and wants. You are obsessed with making things work the way you perceive life to be. What you think are your tastes, opinions, and even feelings are opportunistic choices rooted in the need to score. How would I look best to get a good mirror back? What would be the best thing to do so I get a FgaS state? Let me stay vague in my opinion so I can avoid being confronted and left without an approval.

But what about you? What do *you* really like that is *not* aimed at scoring but that is just for the heck of it? What do you like to do that is purely for your own enjoyment? What are you really interested in for the sake of experiencing it? This is the part of the lives of people who are SSoS-oriented, that ties into what I have said earlier: You are skipping your own life altogether.

If everything you do, want, need, think, invent is of service to the SSoS-oriented goal there is no juicy connection to your own inclinations, talents, or aversions. In this state, a person is intrinsically unable to experience any true feelings of joy or even sadness. Every norm that is applied is based on the efficiency for the SSoS-oriented System and has nothing to do with the human aspects of living: randomness of feelings and inclinations, passion and compassion.

What do you have to do to wake up your very own emotions? How do you get access to your true likes and dislikes, your fun and your true grief?

1. Remove the SSoS-oriented goal from its throne and take that seat yourself.

2. Explore what lightens you up, what makes you happy.

3. Undertake new activities and make sure they are not score oriented.

4. Spend time on doing seemingly useless things but that make you feel relaxed.

5. Make a list of hot topics, things you know you should have an opinion about and read about them, formulate your opinion, and express it out loud.

6. Find out what styles of fashion you like, what type of food, what type of music and explore further; in short, start to have a life.

9. Being Consciously Aware of Your Senses

Maybe you find yourself noticing that your eyesight worsens. You wonder if it is due to your age, and yes, you do not hear so well anymore, either. Are your taste buds affected? What used to taste so good has lost its appeal. When you flatten your hand to straighten the sheets of your bed, the sheets feel odd. In the shower, there are weird areas on your back that seem insensitive to the water temperature.

The problem is that you have lived from the head up, focused on getting your Ego-References achieved or perfected. After many years of this detrimental habit, your body seems to have slowly shut down. That is a very alarming situation, and when your senses dull, it is a warning sign: You have identified yourself with your Vehicle most of the time and everything you do or think has to do with surviving within the SSoS-oriented System. Your stress levels and degree of exhaustion are high.

Becoming actively aware of your five senses after having barely used them and taken them for granted for so many years will bring you to use them with focus and intent. They no longer are means to get to your SSoS but little miracles that have been given to us. How wonderful is it to be able to see the face of your children or a beautiful landscape, the sheet music on your piano, or the flowers in the vase on your desk. Once we become aware of that, we realize we need to be utterly grateful for our senses and actively enjoy them by using them with intent.

Once we can let go of all our heavy (SSoS-oriented) tasks and unrealistically high goals in favor of just living and being, it absolutely does not mean that we cannot do anything anymore. If anything, it means we can actually do *more* because we are present to it and have the right (Direct) Motivation.

The following are a number of suggestions you can work on in order to become more present to your five senses. Some of these you can do at home, at work, or even virtually, in your mind; others require you to go out for the specific mission of becoming (more) aware of your senses.

1. Here are a few statements related to each of the five senses that we can repeat and make conscious to ourselves:

I watch and see. I am fully present to the process and sensation of seeing and to what I am seeing.

I hear and listen. I am fully present to the process and sensation of listening and to what I am hearing.

I use my nose to smell and I register the fragrance. I am fully present to the sensation of smelling and to what I smell.

I taste and register the various sensations. I am fully present to the process of tasting and to what I am tasting.

I touch and feel/sense. I am fully present to the process of feeling/sensing and to what I am feeling/sensing.

I Sense my Self. I am fully present to what I am Sensing.

2. Take an afternoon walk at a park, work in a garden, enjoy a five-minute break on your porch at night to stand in the light of a brilliant full moon.

3. You can visualize scenes you would like to see in your life, things you think are beautiful or that are moving you, and exercise all your senses one by one:

I stand in front of a huge castle and I touch the marble stones with my hands—I look up in the crisp blue sky while I sense the fresh, green grass under my feet—I listen to the song of the birds—the garden of the castle is full of colorful flowers that spread a heavenly scent—soon I will be tasting the nectar that a hummingbird drops on my tongue.

10. Remember That Relapse Is Always Lurking

The moment your Restored SoS is settling down somewhat you need more than ever to remind yourself that the Black Hole is always lurking. Anything that used to function for you as an Ego-Reference and that goes well now, because it was initiated as a Quality-of-Life level action or experience can nonetheless be co-opted and pulled into the Black Hole, which sucks up everything that goes well and that in the past could have been used by the SSoS-oriented System to score.

When you are using the 12 Healing Statements in your recovery process, make sure that the Black Hole is patched and covered with the first step: body awareness (see the story of the old man and the canes); otherwise, "it goes well" becomes a trigger for the SSoS-oriented System to kick back in. After all, it was your life's purpose to have certain things go well and now that they do, the temptation is too big (for the old Survival System) to not use it to score.

So there needs to be awareness not to fall back into that old system at all times. That is quite difficult as the pull to forget about it is big. ***Remember though, that pull is coming from the SSoS-oriented System.*** Your Restored Self benefits greatly from the awareness that triggers to score can arise at any time.

So I need to keep my motivation direct and my eye on the ball (my real goal). The moment I sense jitters, frenzy, anxious sweating, or heartbeats I need to interpret this as warning signs: I might have shifted from the green path onto the red one (see Figure 9.1). Not to mention if I get frustrated beyond reason, do not sleep, or show other signs of depression. Those are symptoms of the SSoS-oriented System being active.

Now you need to STOP what you are doing and do the 12 steps very consciously. That'll help to bring you back into your real Self.

Here are a few examples on how I managed to overcome the danger of the lurking Black Hole. You are invited to use your own imagination and creativity:

1. I envisioned the Black Hole as a hole in the floor I was walking on. That hole was a hole that went all the way to the other side of the earth. I taught myself that I needed to be careful not to step in it.

2. To help myself make the situation less dangerous at some point I decided to create a bottom for that hole by taking a piece of wood and shoving it underneath it.

3. Later I came up with the idea of putting dirt on top of the wood that now was the bottom of the hole and sow grass seeds in it. As the grass was growing I put a little fence around it so I would not inadvertently step on it.

4. At other times I envisioned or almost felt the Black Hole being located somewhere above my left hip: for a few days in a row I imagined it growing a scab.

5. I made a drawing of the Black Hole to create more conscious awareness.

6. Go over the Magic Formula (see Chapter 13).

7. You might want to keep a special journal as a place in which you detail your struggles. You can record your good or bad days, congratulate yourself for good days, and possibly even give yourself a proverbial "star" rating—"Today was a gold-star day. Each time I found myself slipping into . . ." Or, "Today was a bronze-star day. I know I did not do as well as yesterday, but that's okay. At least I am able to recognize that I slipped. Tomorrow, I know I will do better."

11. Sharing Your Life with Others

Celebrate your life and share yourself and your life with others! But this time around share your life with others as a non-needy person. This time around, you are not dependent on the outcome of your achievements or on what other people think of you. You are becoming more and more skillful in shutting up that Virtual, Internalized Parental Voice.

It is necessary to first have your act together before undertaking socializing with hopes of a healthy positive outcome. If you present yourself in your former needy state to other people you will encounter what that situation attracts: negativity, rejection, dependency. If you wait until you truly sense yourself and experience yourself as your home and anchor, you are a valuable party for a person to interact with. If you bring in independency, you attract others who have that same ability. Together we can be, work, or have fun while not being a heavy burden on others—and people sense that independency very distinctly.

Warning

It is so much easier to stay grounded when you are by yourself. You will find that the moment you are with other people, even with people who are close to you, you relapse. It is quite a challenge to keep your new ways going when among other people. You likely will have to experience that a few times to learn that you have to be extra alert to not become SSoS-oriented and make a FgaS state your ultimate goal.

Interaction with others, especially intimate interaction, tends to pull you toward this old desire of getting the keys to the Castle of Enmeshment. It feels like you want to share your bubble with the other person at all cost—keep in mind that we are separate people at all times. This can be a bit of a problem after having been with someone, making love, as by the nature of lovemaking, it is a moment in which you are together with another person in one bubble. Just be alert of the danger of wanting to stay there, wanting to prolong that moment, feeling misunderstood afterward, or having problems sleeping. With awareness this too shall pass.

I would like to refer to being independent from someone's opinion or emotional reaction to you for your sense of who you are. We can certainly help each other out and be of service to each other. The reason relationships so often crash is because of this hidden dependency of one or even both of the parties and the perceived importance of the fiction that is at stake. If we are self-sufficient for our SoS we can healthily function as interdependent teammates, community members, fellow citizens, or even as members of different religions and races. A healthy Sense of Self is a prerequisite for being able to be who you are. If we make sure we have one ourselves, teach it to our kids, and allow others to do the same, it will definitely make the world a better and more peaceful place.

Here is what you could work on every day, or apply when in need, to center yourself:

1. If all is well by now you have at least memorized and are reasonably able to stick to the 10 statements that precede this one. Now get to the crown of the reconditioning program, which is only doable when all the other statements are in reasonable shape. So if not, keep working on the 10 preceding steps.

2. Think about what kind of role you have in a particular group; it helps to become aware when you slip into living for your SSoS.

3. Envision yourself in a specific setting that appeals to you and that you would like to see happen. For example, I see myself giving a party for my numerous friends and family. I see big dining tables with healthy food and wine. I see music and dance. I see happy people of all ages all around me and I am poised and balanced, yet thoroughly enjoying the feast and the company.

4. Actively undertake steps to find groups you feel comfortable with or organize a night out or a coffee break with a friend, no matter how busy you think you are.

5. Take the initiative to set up a party or celebration for somebody you value or actively listen to what they are willing to share.

6. Give a number of hours of your time to volunteer in an environment you like.

12. Being Grateful for All You Have and Receive

Now that we are developing our Restored SoS our criteria change. The values we apply to judge things and ourselves as well are shifting greatly. *We* come from a situation in which everything turned around getting a SSoS: what we did, what we planned to do, what we achieved, what we thought was important, and what we avoided and rejected. We used to evaluate all of these aspects of life on the scale of what their importance could be for our strategy to satisfy our Ego-Reference, to reach a Hidden Agenda, and finally get to our Hidden Goal.

Now we have become the most important person in our lives. Our lives turn around ourselves and we are no longer limited or constrained to spend our time "hunting butterflies." We have discovered the freedom to be ourselves, and the joy of living our own lives. We get to pick and choose our preferences based on who we really are. We are learning to discover what we really like and developing our own opinions on this.

An abundance of life comes our way and it is all for us for as long as we live. We have no Hidden Agenda anymore and can apply all that richness to our own satisfaction. If we are healthy we will automatically be grateful for that. If we are not yet healthy we hope that our lives will improve now that we have restored our Sense of Self. Many processes become natural for our body as well. It is my expectation that we can take care of many ailments by becoming who we are. Not being a doctor, I am not in the position to make any predictions but it makes sense—if our system functions naturally then there is no reason for disease.

When we have realized this step, life has become about living it. We know ourselves now; we have become real. That means we have a better sense of what our potential is and where our boundaries and limitations lie. We are aware of our body and nothing is needed as a bridge to experience ourselves; we think for ourselves and are present to what takes place in our daily lives. We really "see" other people, are able to hear what they have to say. We work for the sake of getting something done. We have developed a personal preference and we know we can act on it when we chose to do so. We also are ready to share what we think about things. We find satisfaction in "playing" with what has been given to us in our lives and are aware that triggers that lead to our past need to be scrutinized.

Here are a few suggestions of how to implement this:

1. Enjoy the fact that you have a body—you can move it to the music.

2. You can develop skills that strengthen and help in the maintenance of your body and keep it in shape: go to the gym or take up yoga. You can choose to do a sport.

3. You can make love.

4. Practice feeling less victimized by your personal circumstances; now that you have a Restored SoS you can spend 100 percent of your creativity and energy on improving your situation.

5. You can decide to actively share your experience of the SoS Method to help others gain a better life.

13 | More Affirmations and The Magic Formula

In this chapter you will find recapitulations of former findings but in a shortened version so they are easier to remember. A number of these statements need to be learned by heart and be processed repeatedly. After numerous times it is to be expected that you suddenly "get it."

Your recovery will go faster as you soak in these truths:

Learn just to "be"!
My life is first about "being." Not until I sense that "I already am," can I consider thinking about "doing."

To whatever extent you can, and as often as you can, actively put aside your work, or whatever "doing" provides you with a sense of identity, and for a time, experience "nothing." That might involve being physically still, breathing slowly, and allowing your mind to slow down or at least shifting into observing it rather than being trapped in it *as* it. In other words practice being more than your mind. Incorporate all other aspects of your self, that you have a notion of by now.

For those of us who are spiritually inclined the following awareness extension might prove helpful: Right in the middle of that nothing, sense how it is *you* who experiences it. Who is the *you* experiencing it? What "place" is it which you are calling "You?" Those two questions are a fruitful, beneficial, healing, ongoing inquiry.

Learn to accept that others create and "have a life" as well as you do.

Affirmation: I accept that others "are" as well as "I am." I admire and appreciate what they do, who they are. In other words, I do not have to have what they have. I do not have to have the same skills as they have. I do not have to have the same circumstances as they have. I am myself and they are themselves!

As often as you can, simply choose to feel good about yourself *no matter what*! As often as you can, choose to *play* your role in life, while not taking yourself and your importance among others so seriously. Begin to notice that "I" is a different "place" from the places of your roles in life.

MORE AFFIRMATIONS WHILE EXERCISING BODY AWARENESS

The following exercise will help you reduce anxiety and reclaim authority over yourself, your opinions, your goals, and your desires. While you are repeating these affirmations for yourself you need to work on constant body-awareness as it was shown to you in Exercise 1 in Chapter 12. This will remind you primarily of the fact that *you* already *are* and that you are not in need of a FgaS state as a SSoS. Being imbibed with that knowledge will help you to reduce anxiety and step out of the cycle of addiction to a SSoS, as shown in the Map of Healing Your SoS, in Chapter 9.

What also helps is to keep reasoning, out loud, the way a SSoS-oriented person reasons, on purpose now, to learn the relationship between the various concepts thoroughly. You will poke through the logic of it. Fully understand that the FgaS state was a result of the need for approval that was mistaken for acknowledgment. That acknowledgment was not withheld from you because you were not good enough; it was a problem the parent had. By living up to the Ego-References you tried but will never get what you are actually ultimately after: acknowledgment as a separate and real respected human being, preferably by that crucial person who didn't give it to you in the first place.

My achievements are being sucked into the Black Hole.

Here is what I told myself: I am making it hard on myself by trying to live up to the conditions, and when things go well they are sucked into the Black Hole. That is all based on my need for approval, which isn't even acknowledgment. So isn't it about time I grow up, uncover the buried adult in me, and start acknowledging myself as an autonomous person? Isn't it about time I leave those (maybe even deceased) parents be and live based on my own criteria?

No More Fear of Screwing "It" Up

Because I know that I already am a body and a mind of which I am the Master, the Manager, and the Maintenance person, now I really should not have to worry about screwing "it" up anymore and bodily symptoms, such as (eye-)migraines, insomnia, etc., are of the past. "It" is a fiction anyway; I am safe in myself so *I do not care anymore.* Note: read for "it" the "Feel-good" state that functions as a SSoS.

Insight into the Reality of My Struggle

The irony is that only when I stated this did I become painfully aware that the only person whom my physical symptoms of stress and anxiety have an impact on is *myself,* but now I mean the real *me.* I am the only one who is suffering the pain of the migraines, the lousy feeling of not having slept well. Normally that awareness wouldn't even be within my scope because I was so busy conforming to my Ego-References.

You need to repeat these awareness exercises many times so that at some point you have moments in which you realize "this is too silly to be true—to be so terrified of something that isn't even real." And those moments do come.

INCORPORATING THE USE OF NLP AND THE LAW OF ATTRACTION

From my own process of recovery, I have concluded that if my *perception* is "that I am not being seen and heard, that I have no voice or face," then I will continue to create that *reality*! It is only at this very moment that I am discovering this new problem-solving approach, which includes Neuro-Linguistic Programming, visualization techniques, various techniques applying the Law of Attraction, techniques that aim at emotional freedom, and many others. There is a wide array of possibilities when it comes to solving emotion-based issues. How well they work, I am not yet in a good position to say.

I have noticed that the influence of positive thoughts is empowering to us physically as well as psycho-emotionally. It could very well be true that our external circumstances do nothing more than reflect our inner world and that our belief systems ultimately can be held accountable for what happens or not to us in life. I decided not to run the risk that this is just a fable and so I have started to focus on becoming the master of my mind instead of its victim.

Within the context of this work, it is not appropriate to elaborate on those topics just mentioned, but I did want to mention them as a next step on the stairs of self-improvement/healing. There are many books written on these subjects and they are intriguing at the least. What I want to say here is that it seems crucial to change your belief systems in positive ways so that you can create a reality that fits your needs and desires much better.

A good way to get started on this new path is by positive affirmations that you repeat to yourself on a daily, even hourly basis. I see all the above as new territories to explore while working toward a healthy SoS.

The following list of affirmations is only an indication of what I worked with. It includes statements that, at some point in my process, I was constantly reaffirming to myself, but the list is by no means complete.

- I am being seen and heard. I do have a voice; I do have a face.
- I *am* already, and others are all ready to give me what I need!
- My perception of myself is positive.
- I do have a place/family/friends, and I belong.
- I feel safe.
- I am free to be myself!

Note that when creating your own affirmations, it is important not to use negatives! For great affirmations, you need to find a way to express things in positive language.

In 2011 I wrote,

I do admit that occasionally relapse still happens to me, because the Substitute Sense of Self–oriented System is a survival system and thus is hard to eradicate. I am a whole lot less worried (or panicked) when symptoms of stress show up, though, as I now recognize where they come from. I know how my growing thorough awareness that "I am an independent and autonomous person, I don't depend on the outcome of my actions or on what others think of me, I do not have to satisfy the judgment of my VIPV" can help decrease their frequency even more.

Now, in 2013, I write,

It rarely happens to me that I fall back. Specific situations still trigger my old ways, for example, after having gone through the process of being sick, with fever, using drugs, and returning back to normal. Let it not come as a surprise that you might have completely fallen back into your old SSoS-oriented ways and not even be aware of it. It requires reading of Chapter 12 to become aware of it and brush up your newly gained neural pathways. It is a bad surprise but rest assured, if you take it seriously, you regain your lost territory within a few days to a week. Another trigger for relapse is traveling and jetlag. Travel is very disruptive to the healing process but it also forces you to review and recondition yourself once more. You then come out stronger. It is quite a path, but if I have followed it, so others may as well. I need to mention that the earlier in the process the more disruptive triggers you can encounter: intense movies, a great night sleep, sexual activity in which you abandon yourself totally and lose your sense of reality, are a few of them.

HOLDING ON TO YOUR NEWLY RESTORED SOS

Make staying in touch with your Real Self the most important task of the day, the week, and the month. This seems logical in hindsight, but when you are right in the middle of trying to "sober up" from your addiction to "earning" the SSoS, nothing seems more important than getting your Ego-References taken care of. You are used to spending your time and effort to getting things (circumstances, people) lined up and smoothed out so you can score credit points on the virtual chart of the SSoS-oriented goal.

If there were a chart for measuring your SSoS-oriented activity and achievements, you could fill in how high your score was on a particular day. To restore and maintain your SoS, you need great mental discipline. You have to be creative in this reconditioning process: create *visual aids* for yourself. Here are a couple of ways you can do that.

Look at Figure 13.1, which we saw in a previous chapter. Imagine that the healthy (green) path is the path you have to travel instead of the unhealthy (red) path. You can make a drawing/painting of it. That is what I did and it helped my imagination.

Use Figure 13.1 and visualize where you would be at any given moment in time.

1. Learn your list of *Ego-References* using the Motivation Checklist in Figure 12.4 (page 185). Learn them thoroughly, by heart, so you know them inside and out, upside and down, even in the middle of the night.

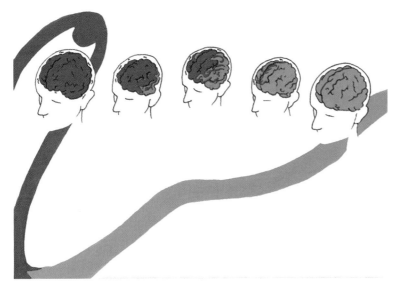

Figure 13.1: Switching from the addiction to a SSoS to a HySoS

2. Check out the symbols in the Glossary; they all helped me deal with the issues. You can order a set of those illustrations so you can play with them while learning about yourself and the HySoS Method in a fun way, at http://bit.ly/SoSVocabulary.

3. Know what you are all about. Do you still believe that *your Hidden Agendas* are going to repair what went wrong in your past and serve your life in a healthy way?

4. Write down on a big piece of paper what the one thing is you were all about, your Hidden Goal. Does it still mean as much to you? What does it stand for? What are synonyms for it? For example, if you feel you are all about being accepted by others, perhaps for you, being accepted may be synonymous with

the (internalized/virtual) approval and acceptance of the parent,

a sense of belonging,

a feeling of being part of something,

a feeling of being safe,

a feeling of being allowed to be,

a feeling of being alive,

being taken into account,

not being an embodied ghost,

not experiencing humiliation,

not being ridiculed,

plainly existing, and/or

a Substitute Sense of Self.

A PLACE TO CALL ME: A SELF-CONTENTMENT EXERCISE

The more relaxed your body and mind are while doing these exercises, the deeper and more lasting the effect they will have on you each time you do them.

First, empty your mind. Then, imagine your chest has a large, spacious area around your heart and lungs. Take a deep, slow breath, expanding the lower part of this area first, then your ribcage, to let a lot of air into your lungs until you feel as though you will burst. Then exhale. As you do this, your heart grabs the opportunity to pump fresh blood throughout your body. That feels good! Do that one more time and notice how good it feels. This sensation is self-contentment: to be happy for no reason.

Do this exercise a few times throughout the day, whenever you remember to or whenever you finish dealing with a stressful situation. By emptying your mind first and then focusing on your physical structures, you are forcing yourself to be in touch with yourself (see Statement 1 of the 12 Healing Statements in the preceding chapter).

NEW FREEDOM, NEW NOW

As your (former) self, defined by and dependent on all your Ego-References, fades from your awareness, out of your life, and as your recovery process dismantles your SSoS-oriented System, which had so much power over you and kept you compulsive, addicted, and enslaved to your Fear of Annihilation, you finally can be free!

Remember that those conditions you were addicted and enslaved to fulfilling were adopted in the past and, even though they were useful to you at the time, in the Now they are neither relevant nor useful. They are detrimental and limiting; they have been preventing you from reaching your potential. Stay at the steering wheel of your own ship (read: body, mind, activities, goals) by doing a Motivation Check every so often. It is a tool to manage your mind. Pretend you mind is a (computer) system and you are its manager. Pretend your mind is a room: if your mind were a room, you would not allow it to collect clutter. You would clean your room on a regular basis. A Motivation Check cleans your mind, so ask yourself questions such as "Do I have a Hidden Agenda with this or that? Am I still caught up in the cycle of Vehicles–Ego-References–Hidden Goals–Substitute Sense of Self?"

Scrutinize your emotions, your experiences. As often as you can, ask yourself, "How is my level of irritation and anger?" "What is my quality of life? Am I irritated, angry, or is there a boiling volcano underneath [from Hindrances leading to rage] that I have difficulty managing?" The latter is indicative of SSoS-oriented activity. Review your motives and manage your Self!

Analyze these examples and create some of your own!

LISTENING TO YOUR BODY

I urge you never to give up. Have compassion for yourself. In my case, my situation of seeking approval still sometimes ends up with my getting an ocular migraine from the stress and tensions I deal with when I sense potential Hindrances/obstacles to my almost-achieved Substitute Sense of Self. Even when I consciously aim at steering away from it the tension causes a physiological overload.

For me, an ocular migraine is a signal that I have relapsed. Dr. Joe Dispenza would explain this as the memories and emotions of the past manifesting themselves. I then need to direct my attention to my body with an exercise like the one discussed earlier in the preceding chapter and become aware that I already AM through sensing my body. That way we learn no longer to identify with the emotions/memories that are causing the stress and tension. Instead, I *consciously* answer to the situation with a different emotion, that is, I change my pattern of behavior.[14]

When I get an ocular migraine, I now realize that means I have "fallen off the wagon," to use a phrase from addiction recovery. The migraine to me is a signal I have to get out of the mode of sensing myself through the criteria of the SSoS-oriented System and get into sensing myself in the right way and

---

[14] Joe Dispenza, *The Reinvention of Self*, vol. 2 [audio CD]. Produced by Armenus Productions LLC, 2011.

become aware that I AM already, so nothing is at stake. Then I follow my own life's path again, as opposed to being the slave of my Substitute Sense of Self–oriented System. Now when I sometimes feel anger, sadness, and hopelessness, the anger is mostly oriented toward obtaining the Substitute Sense of Self. Deep down there sometimes is still a reluctance to give up my Substitute Sense of Self because I was about to score (addiction and denial). I then feel sadness because I am creating trouble for myself, and not creating trouble was one of my Ego-References. Then I feel hopelessness because I realize I will once more have to stop whatever I am doing and spend considerable time on managing myself in order to get back on the right track.

Despite these unpleasant symptoms, at least I know what is going on. Being honest to myself and being clear in my motivations are tools that I feel empowered by! I just need stamina and to kick myself in the butt (compassionately!) and try again. My true life's path is the one I am treading and I am able to walk it, every time, a little longer.

I feel the urge to mention the therapy called Quantum Leap[3]. In the latest phase of my own healing this work has greatly helped me to reduce any symptoms that were still lingering. This therapy, developed in the United States by Dr. Sherry Buffington, provides insight into who you authentically are at the core of your being, helps you discover and release old patterns that linger from your childhood experiences, and eliminates the blocks that you have developed over your lifetime that have prevented you from living fully and successfully. In just hours you are able to establish beneficial conscious and subconscious patterns that free you from the past and propel you to the life and outcomes you long to experience faster than you might now imagine possible.

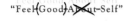

Magic Formula

A way of remembering the gist of the SoS Method, whereby you move away from the addiction to "Feeling-good-about-yourself" by crossing out the judgmental word about *and placing* good *in parenthesis, leaving "Feel Self" or "Sense Your Self."*

THE MAGIC FORMULA

As a bonus here is the **Magic Formula**! It will help you to remember the gist of the SoS Method. It came to me when I was finishing writing up all the elements and explanations of this work and made total sense. We started out with the concept of "Feeling-good-about-Self" and how that is the most important drive in the life of a SSoS-oriented person.

Well, after all is said and done, here is a unique way of remembering what to do, when you feel challenged by the side effects of being addicted to a SSoS for your Self-experience. The change in the direction of our awareness we have to make at that moment is comprised in the Magic Formula:

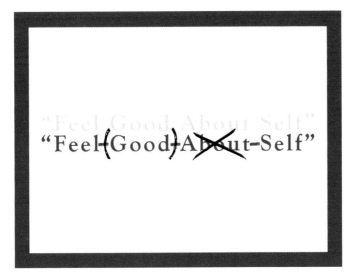

Figure 13.2: The Magic Formula

Move away from the addiction to "Feeling-good-about-Yourself."

Cross out the judgmental word *about* and put the word *good* in parentheses.

What remains is "Feel Self," or in other words, Sense Your Self!

That is all you have to do!

Appendix I
The Comparison Chart

HOW TO USE THE COMPARISON CHART

If you begin to suspect your life is more about compulsively fulfilling conditions instead of actively choosing your do's and don'ts, this chart will help you to identify in which category (A or B) you fit. Here is a short reminder: Group A consists of people with a Natural Sense of Self; Group B refers to those of us who lack a Sense of Self, and hence depend on a Substitute Sense of Self. Then there is group C that we use to label the people who have gone through the motions of the HySoS Method and end up with a Restored SoS™.

Read through the statements that describe the symptoms that belong in each of the categories and select which ones most appropriately apply to you. Then determine which column most of your answers are in. That is your group. Knowing your group puts your reality in perspective and gives you a starting point in your quest to improve your life.[15]

---

[15] These statements are based solely on my observations and self-experience and are not scientifically-confirmed. This self-test is for your own informal use. By using it in any way you agree to indemnify and hold harmless, Healthy Sense of Self, LLC, and everyone associated with it for any consequences of your engagement in this HySoS Method.

Figure A.1: Characteristics of having a Natural Sense of Self, a Substitute Sense of Self, and a Restored Sense of Self		
Group A Having a Natural Sense of Self	Group B Lacking a Sense of Self and therefore having a Substitute Sense of Self	Group C Having a Restored Sense of Self
1. GENETIC FACTORS		
Possibly stronger genetic predisposition with regard to whatever factors are related to development of Sense of Self.	Possibly weaker genetic predisposition with regard to those factors (this is a question rather than a statement).	No change in original genetic predisposition.
2. PARENTING		
Received adequate, supportive parenting as a building block for the development of an independent Natural Sense of Self.	Had a parent/caregiver who was excessively focused on own self (self-absorbed) and unable to adequately mirror a healthy Self to the child.	For optimal healing and sustained health purposes I suggest limited or no contact with original parent/caregiver.
3. MOTIVATION		
You have the ability to focus on the content of the action or goal "The thing is done for the sake of itself." There is no "Hidden Goal." Your Motivation is Direct.	You are dependent on the outcome of your actions, achievements, and events and on other people's opinions. Your focus is on your "Hidden Goal" which results in "Indirect Motivation."	You have gained more ability to focus on things for what they are. Increasing "content-oriented" focus and therefore much better results. Gradually more "Direct Motivation." Alert: occasional relapse.
4. "FEELING-GOOD-ABOUT-SELF"		
Feeling good about yourself is a Quality-of-Life matter for you. Everyday life has its ups and downs and that is all there is to it.	Excessive/obsessive need for reaching the state of "Feeling-good-about-Self" because it is experienced as a Substitute Sense of Self and a matter of life or death.	Ever-decreasing anxiety due to ever lessening need for "Feeling-good-about-Self" state because a Restored Sense of Self is created. Feeling good about myself becomes a Quality-of-Life thing and nothing existential is perceived to be at stake anymore.
5. EMOTIONAL LIFE		
Mild emotional peaks and valleys; overall not easily hurt or excited. Emotions are integrated and rooted in Self. Energy available for happiness and joy.	Emotional roller coaster: deep valleys and depression. Need for rewards and "highs." Emotions are created by the SSoS System and are not in any direct relationship with the person's well-being.	The emotions related to Substitute Sense of Self gradually even out; emotions become Quality of Life–emotions; you experience milder and much more balanced moods.

6. ALONE/BELONGING		
Comfortable being by themselves depending on their authentic nature; potential leaders.	Excessive need of others for feelings of belonging or group-identity and for being mirrored to ensure getting feedback on how to feel about yourself.	In touch with true, natural, personal inclinations about balance of aloneness and need for belonging (different for each individual).
7. RELATION TO REALITY		
Realist. Living in the "Real Reality" and being able to focus on the things in it. Very much "present."	Idealist, Utopian, not in touch with Reality. Not present but living in a "trance." Comes up with non-reality-based solutions to world problems and is angered when nobody wants to listen to them.	"Realist apprentice"; aware of own situation and willing to work on it. Aware of tendencies to come up with "theoretical dream solutions" and starting to understand why they are not relevant in "Real Reality." Growing awareness of what the world/life is really like.
8. INNER ENERGY—PRESENCE IN WORLD		
Inner sensations of clarity and balance; steady sensed presence of life-energy flow. Potentially "charismatic" because of "being present" in world. Generous energy.	Inner sensations are chaotic and confused; continuous collision and competition of energy molecules upon closing eyes (can be experienced in ears as tinnitus). "Presence" to the outside world is low. Needy energy.	Inner sensations of energy clear up and become quieter (behind the eyes, in the head when sensed in meditation or upon going to sleep at night). Overall increasingly more "connected" and, as such, learning to be "present" in the world and to others.
9. FOCUSED ATTENTION VERSUS SCANNING ATTENTION MODE		
Living in **Focus Mode**: Present with attention in the frontal lobes through which there is the ability to focus on "actual real life" and freedom to attend to anything relevant to the moment and to genuine personal well-being and authentic goals.	Continuously in **Scanning Mode**: Attention is in the back of the head (the past). Not in touch with self or actual real life.	Leaving Scanning Mode behind and replacing it with Focus mode. Increasing ability to focus on actual real life; developing ability to focus on genuine personal well-being and authentic goals.

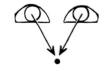

Focus Mode

Relaxed movements of the eyes, with the ability to have eyes rest in the same place for extended periods of time.

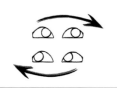

Scanning Mode

Eyes constantly moving.

10. MASTER OF YOUR LIFE		
You are the Master of your life; you are able to live in your own bubble, independently and potentially interdependently.	SLAVE OF FULFILLING CONDITIONS Slave of Early Childhood Survival Strategy★; dependency-oriented, SSoS-oriented. Self-centered.	Becoming Master of your life and thus ready for teamwork and cooperative activity.
11. SEE AND ACCEPT OTHERS		
Others are acknowledged as well as the Self is. You are able to actually look at others and see them for who they are. Ability to listen to others and actually hear them.	NOT SEEING OTHERS Others and Self are being seen and heard only when considered useful for Self-serving (usually Hidden) Goals; others are considered as pawns, Vehicles or Hindrances to fulfilling Ego-Reference conditions. Transference onto others of key figures from the past.	Others are being seen and heard for who they really are. Acceptance of Self leads to acceptance of others, which opens many possibilities of interactivity.
12. DEDICATION AND WELL-BEING		
You are doing what needs to be done or is desired, taking into realistic account one's own well-being and one's possibilities and/or limitations. Healthy sense of boundaries.	COMPULSIVENESS AND LACK OF SELF-CARE Compulsive and obsessive behavior; no room for failure; dependency on the outcome. Doing what serves the needs of the SSoS, regardless of one's well-being or limitations.	Letting go of controlling behavior. Learning to distinguish dedication from compulsion and act on it; experiencing more and more dedication and less compulsion.
13. SLEEP		
You normally sleep well.	INSOMNIA You are lying awake at night, subconsciously obsessing about being able to function and find Vehicles for preserving the state of "Feel-good-about-Self-" as a Substitute Sense of Self.	Sleeping much better, knowing that you ARE already and don't depend on living up to specific conditions. No Fear of Annihilation; peace of mind and a connection to one's own being.

14. HEALTH and EMOTIONS		
You experience normal health; a normal level of emotions.	Panic attacks, eye migraines, regular migraines, anxiety, depression, suicide.	Elimination of excessive fear, anxiety, panic attacks, awareness of value of one's (own) life.
15. ANGER		
You allow yourself to be upset, but it's on a healthy Quality-of-Life level.	RAGE and VIOLENT BEHAVIOR, CURSING Issues with excessive unreasonable anger, rage, violence.	Feelings of desperation dissolve; frustration on healthy Quality-of-Life level.
16. STRESS MANAGEMENT		
Healthy stress levels, generally managed well.	CONTINUOUS HIGH STRESS-LEVELS Your QoL-level is increased by SSoS or stress, which leads to chronic high- and unmanageable stress.	Healthy stress generally managed well.
17. SUCCESS/FAILURE IN LIFE		
High likelihood of success in endeavors, in life.	WRONG FOCUS Prone to chronic and widespread failure in life endeavors (because of focus on Hidden Goal instead of on the endeavor as itself).	Focus on the "real thing" instead of Hidden Goal; absence of self-sabotage, being visible to others because of being present energetically creates greater openings to success.
18. FLOWING		
Going with the flow of life; able to "improvise."	SUPER-CONTROLLING Controlling self, others, and circumstances; inflexible, no improvisational skills; no flow. Thrown and angered by unanticipated turns of events.	Trusting the process of life; not having attachment to outcomes brings back the flow and drops need for control.
19. DECISIONS AND COMMITMENT		
You are generally at ease with decision making and commitment. Comfortable making choices.	INDECISIVE You're often in flight-or-fight mode, which makes for erratic behavior and bad decision-making skills. Uncomfortable in making choices and committing.	There's no reason for flight or fight anymore. Growing ability to decide, choose, and commit. You are getting to know your own preferences and opinions and stand up for them.

20. AWARE OF OWN VALUES		
You generally know what you want, care about, and value, as being aspects of your Self.	FULLY SSoS-oriented Unable to make up mind as there is no "real" person present in you. What counts is how things serve your Hidden Goal.	Now you are discovering what you truly care about, want, and value. Able to set priorities and boundaries and gauge your own potential.

21. AUTHENTIC TASTES AND PREFERENCES		
Your personal preferences and tastes are well-developed and felt as aspects of Self.	NO PREFERENCES Tastes and preferences are not personally authentic; they are used to "score" for Substitute Sense of Self.	Now you are developing authentic personal tastes and preferences, sensed as aspects of Self.

22. EATING PROBLEMS		
Less prone to eating problems; any problems could be due to indulging oneself or issues with moderation.	Prone to eating problems such as anorexia or bulimia if eating is used as a Vehicle to Sense the Self. Eating helps to feel grounded.	You don't need food to help you in grounding or experiencing your (Sense of) Self.

23. SENSE OF TIME		
"Tomorrow is another day! What doesn't work today I can do tomorrow!" Healthy ability to let go.	NEVER ENOUGH TIME Perceives achievements to be of highest importance; no relaxed perspective on time, because achieving Ego-References is always highest priority at any given moment.	Achievements, actions, and events become Quality-of-Life things and there is increasingly more ability to let go and "bide your time."

24. USE OF EYES		
Use of eyes as what they are meant for: safety and observing environment.	EYE-STRAIN/FATIGUE Your eyes are always on hyper-alert, used for scanning opportunities to get a SSoS.	Less attachment to the outcome of things so less stress on eyes. Eyes can relax, be off-duty.

25. TEMPERAMENT, MOOD		
Evenly-tempered, and emotionally balanced.	You are never in an "average mood." Often over-excited, driven but for the wrong motivation, frenzied, anxious, sensitive, high-strung. Or feeling non-existent, wretched, flat, depressed.	Much calmer, more in touch with authentic temperament.

26. THE BODY'S CENTER OF GRAVITY		
You experience your body's center of gravity in your lower belly (called Tan-tien or Dahn Jon depending on discipline and culture). The traditional Abdominal Power House. Life energy is spread evenly throughout the body.	Felt center of gravity as if outside of body (compare: Enmeshment). During activities you are mostly "in your head"; tension in neck and shoulders blocks energy from going into the head (reduced oxygen in head)—all kinds of brain problems (vision, hearing, head colds, congestion).	Felt sense of location of self is more in the body (heart/abdominal area)—strain taken away from the brain—less tension in nervous system and muscles—healthier breathing (more oxygen in the head).
27. MOTION SICKNESS		
No car/motion sickness.	Prone to car/motion sickness nausea and dizziness. Lack of balance.	Reduced car/motion sickness due to "grounding yourself."
28. FEAR OF CROWDS		
Normal relationship to crowds.	Fear of crowds due to experiencing a lack of Self. Feeling lost and not present among all others in a crowd.	Normal response to being in crowds.
29. EMOTIONAL BALANCE, STABILITY		
Stays balanced, because things don't affect the "core" of oneself.	Easily aggravated, nervous, upset, and offended because everything is perceived as a threat to maintaining the fragile and fleeting SSoS.	Increasingly and more often better balanced.
30. SENSITIVITY TO LIFE		
Normal sensitivity to all the aspects of life.	Possibly a Highly Sensitive Person (HSP).	Less sensitive. Less frequent experiencing of things or people as Hindrances in daily life.
31. ENERGY IN STOMACH		
Stomach energy normal; emotions experienced as related to one's actual own personhood.	"Butterflies" in the stomach on perceived (SSoS-oriented) success.	A calm stomach; no overexcitement.
32. ATTAINMENT OF LOVE AND HAPPINESS		
Normal sense of ability to attain and experience love and happiness.	NOT WITHIN REACH Your heart is squashed under the stress of the perceived immediate necessity of achieving the Hidden Agendas through the Vehicles for the Ego-References.	Love and happiness are felt to be within reach, possible.

33. TENSION VERSUS RELAXATION		
Normal body posture and muscle tones. The heart leads!	FREQUENT INJURIES Cramped muscles that lead to knots and pain in neck, back, and shoulders (dislocated vertebras). The head leads!	Much more relaxation, which is improving all the time. Learns to balance the head and the heart and to let the heart lead!
34. PRONENESS TO ACCIDENTS		
Accidents happen and are experienced on a QoL- level.★	PRONE TO ACCIDENTS Due to erratic and ill-managed behavior more accident-prone.	Behavior becomes more responsible to the degree of decrease of proneness to accidents.

Appendix II
Considering War and a
Healthy Sense of Self

I<small>F WE COULD GET PEOPLE TO DO THE WORK NECESSARY TO DEVELOP AND MAINTAIN</small> a Healthy Sense of Self (SoS), we would increase our potential to solve conflicts in a nonviolent way both in our personal lives as well as on a global scale.

It is crucial that people such as you and local leaders, as well as those in the federal government, recognize the importance of a healthy SoS as a prerequisite for conflict management and resolution. Next, we want to ensure that ways are found for clearly instructing those in the new generation on how to rely on sensing themselves for experiencing the Self instead of being dependent on the outcome of their activities or on what other people think of them.

To that purpose, we need two things: We need parents to be willing to assess their own SoS, work on it if that turns out to be necessary, and we need the support of the school system. We are talking about a shift in perspective that may lead to happier, healthier, and more productive lives for the next generation. Involving the school systems would greatly help in implementing this new SoS perspective among the general population. Considering the skill to sense one's Self an important part of the various school's curriculum, equal to, reading, writing, and math, would be a great step in the right direction.

Imagine the differences that could be made, if we agreed, not only, that all people are born equal, but also that we all have the right and the duty to fully be ourselves. If only we would acknowledge the differences that exist between individuals and encourage the exploration and expression of these differences, without having to fear judgment by others. The students' ability to manage conflicts among each other would be greatly enhanced and possibly reduce bullying, because we all would learn to speak from a place of our own truth. The "person" who the student is in the first place would no longer be overlooked and would become an important "body" behind the good grades. It would enhance students' self-confidence and development of their own tastes and opinions that would help them make healthier choices in life.

This is an ambitious project perhaps, with a most desirable outcome. For who, other than the war industry, of course, would not want war to be on its way to extinction and have people living in contentment?

Here are some reflections on the role that a healthy SoS could play in smoother conflict resolution in the world.

First we need to ask ourselves what draws people to join the military in the first place. When saying "the military," I mean the military in any nation, and more specifically the U.S. military. Here are four motives for joining the military:

- The need to belong to a group
- The historical model of looking up to, or being perceived as, a hero
- The need for education and opportunities
- Commitment to the actual cause of the war

Let us take a closer look at each of these potential reasons and study how a healthy SoS could cause people to have different needs and therefore react differently to life situations.

1. The Need to Belong to a Group

Many people feel a need to belong to a group. This need can be experienced at various degrees of urgency ranging from healthy to excessive and unhealthy.

History justifies the need to belong to a group. Life has always been uncertain and temporary; therefore, it makes sense to team up and tackle the problems of surviving together. By belonging to a larger group (e.g., a gang, a town, a country, a race, or a religious group), we feel less vulnerable to life's inevitable threats to our own health, happiness, and well-being and that of our children. Belonging to a group, no matter what kind of group it is, makes us feel stronger. Membership of a group can function as a space in which people can feel safe because, alone, we are scared. It can give us a sense of identity that makes us feel like being bigger than ourselves.

The problem is that identifying with groups comes with a price. A group can give us a reason for behaving a certain way or can make us feel useful. We can be of service to the group or feel proud to be a member. The truth is though, that group identity can extend and take over what ought to be our own personal identity. As the author of the SoS theory I say that the group identity functions as a Substitute Sense of Self (SSoS).

If our society would encourage us to focus on becoming a whole person by gaining a Healthy SoS in the first place, we would be less compelled to join a group to fill in the emptiness that a lack of SoS has left in us. The SoS Theory points out how desperately we need to fill that emptiness. It does not take much imagination to see how membership in a group can function as a way of fulfilling a SSoS for a person dependent on a SSoS. The dangerous result is that the person becomes completely dependent on the outcome of what happens in and with the group.

Chances are that people develop a need to control what happens in and with the group in order to ensure that things work "just so," which can easily culminate in conflicts with other groups. When these conflicts are rooted in emotional needs, such as maintaining your SSoS, they can reach a high degree of intensity, which can lead to unfair behavior or leadership. For an individual, it means identification with the values of a group can generate thoughts such as "If my group is attacked, I feel threatened in my SSoS. I am ready to kill to maintain my SSoS. I am even ready to blow myself up or to let my children be used for that to keep my group safe."

A nation can be considered a group as well; so, too, can the military. Being committed to one or more of these groups is not a problem if we stay present to ourselves and to reality at all times, when it comes to decision making. When we have that emptiness inside, however—and unfortunately, in most cases, we are not aware of it—then we may find a way to obtain a SSoS by being a member of such a group, and by identifying with performing certain tasks or aiming for a certain position within the group. It is good to be aware that a group offers a great number of hiding places, that can function as an easy placeholder for the need every single human being has to identify with "who we are as a person," and the gratifying identification of ourselves with being a member of that group. In other words, being a member of a group is an effective way to fill that inner emptiness and to provide opportunities to "score" as well!

Fanatics

However, the nature of being dependent on a SSoS is that we are extremely scared to lose our Vehicle for experiencing our SSoS. The fear of not being considered a "real" person (Annihilation), together with not being in touch with one's (Indirect) Motivation for being a member of the group, could lie at the root of fanatical behavior. In an attempt to ensure the group's survival, which is needed to safeguard its members' SSoS, people proclaim the group's rules as their ultimate truth and use these rules as a Vehicle to safeguard their group identity (as a SSoS). This provides a deeper understanding as to why, then, they are willing to kill or die for the group's preservation.

To this subject there is another aspect to consider: A person has lost the connection with his or her Self, in a way, already does not exist, meaning that he or she has nothing to lose with dying for the group. Nobody, who consciously owns his body and his life, nobody in his or her right mind (i.e., with a Healthy or a Restored SoS) would go this route. Being truly in touch with who and that you are is a counter indication to killing in general.

If only we were able and willing to take into account that people in other groups (e.g., nations, armies) are doing the exact same thing (fighting), out of the exact same fear. Both of us are prepared to defend our group at the costs of our lives or the lives of those we have learned to call our enemy. Both of us are just people who find ourselves in the exact same situation: being scared perceiving that we have found a crutch to walk through life with, by belonging to their group. Isn't it so sad? Imagine if we would rely on ourselves for our own identity; would we still be inclined to fall victim to being forced to kill for the group or being killed?

2. The Need to Look Up To or Be Perceived as a Hero

Needing to be a hero is a historically sanctioned and inherited perspective. At one time, people couldn't have had a more honorable job than serving their country—being ready and available to go to war and fighting for the values of the group they felt a part of. Back then we didn't have a large-scale overview of what happens in the world as we have these days. There was no radio, television, or Internet. There were no cellphones. People didn't make friends with people on other continents. There were few international and interracial marriages. Values, religions, and political convictions motivated people to unite. They would draw people to stand up to those who threatened the group because they had different values or because the one group had attacked the other. All this was done with the admiration and respect of family and friends who stayed at home.

In terms of civilization and society, we have changed quite a bit. We are now aware that all people have the same needs and wants. We now understand that most people try their very best to make things work. We still do have a problem, however, with having insight in what motivates different ethnic groups, individuals who embrace specific religions, or subcultures such as "bikers," "punks," or "chavs." In spite of knowing that we are all equal, we feel threatened by those who believe different things because we do not know enough about other cultures, religions, or groups.

But, when we take a good look at it, aren't we in a similar situation with our friends, our relatives, or even our spouses and children? Do we fully understand what their goals are in life and what ultimately motivates them? How about ourselves? Do we have enough self-knowledge to be able to say what we are all about?

Yet, in spite of these similarities in our reality on a small scale, our choice to turn to war for conflict resolution has not changed at all. Instead, people from all levels of society still take pride in becoming more cunning in conducting war by developing more sophisticated ways to destroy the enemy instead of using their time and efforts to find ways to meet each other on a basis of equality. As in the microcosm, so it is in the macro. By applying the SoS Method, which explains how many of us work and what oftentimes our ulterior motives are, I see a great potential to reduce conflict and war.

3. The Need for Education and Career Opportunities

There are other, practical reasons for joining a group such as the military, including college tuition assistance and broader career opportunities. These reasons may appeal to some people, but it could very well be that, had these same people not been pawns in *their* parents' lives, but had been taught to be themselves instead, they would not need the military as a surrogate family. If these men and women had experienced the necessary stimuli and space to explore and become themselves, they would have been more connected to their own needs and wants all along, and not so desperate to use a group such as the military to provide them with meaning and opportunities. They would have a clear sense of who they are and what their lives are worth to them, and think twice before selling themselves to a war machine.

4. Commitment to the Actual Cause of the War

As a child, I often wondered how people reached the point at which they could make lampshades from the skin of women's breasts or how soldiers could come into your house and throw little babies up in the air to catch them with their pointed bayonets, right in front of their horrified parents. I asked myself, who, in his or her right mind, would have the need to make other people so scared that when they had to hide in closets from the Gestapo (the secret state police in Nazi Germany), their heartbeats could be heard in the adjacent room . . . and why was this necessary?

What moves people, specifically young men, to opt to go to war, has been a theme in the life's work of war photographer Tim Hetherington. In his book *Here I Am*,[16] Alan Huffman describes Tim's life and work. It is as if by visiting the locations where war took place and by taking photographs of what the gruesome effects of war were, Tim Hetherington tried to force himself to find an answer to the big questions of "Who commits these atrocities?" and "Why?"

Tim came to the interesting conclusion that the reason young men get involved in combat seldom has anything to do with the core reason of the war itself. He concluded that there was, quite often, a relationship to a form of heroism that they had picked up on in photos, movies and on television—an association game, that is not at all based on reality. It would be interesting to do some research to find out if it was maybe a lack of SoS that led these young people to give their very lives to the military.

I highly recommend watching the movie *Restrepo*[17] and taking a good look at the faces of the young men and women who have been tricked into going to war by the offer of having their college tuition paid. They have just barely grown out of childhood and have no idea what they are getting into. En route to the fight, they are like children going on an outing, and only when they find one of their mates dead on the field of combat, or see him or her crippled for life, does reality hit and a real fear sink in. They ask themselves, "What the heck am I doing in this foreign country, where I do not know the way nor the language to ask for what I need? Where I have no idea of what keeps the minds of the local people busy?" In addition, neither they, nor their loved ones, anticipate the psychological and emotional damage they return home with, if they return at all.

Isn't it a cruel deed to enroll and deploy these youngsters who, it is clear to me, may not even have had the fortunate setup in their earliest years to develop a Healthy SoS. War is a way of problem solving that is archaic! It may have worked in the past! In this day and age, however, our leaders should know better, and rather than relying on violence to solve issues, they should be moved to function as teachers in nonviolent problem solving to those of us who are still ignorant!

---

[16] Alan Huffman (New York: Grove Press, 2013).
[17] Information on *Restrepo* is available from Wikipedia, http://en.wikipedia.org/wiki/Restrepo_(film) (accessed April 29, 2013).

HOW CAN A HEALTHY SOS MAKE A DIFFERENCE?

How does a dependency on a SSoS—or better said, a lack of SoS—relate to the people who are perpetrating acts of violence in times of war?

People with a healthy Sense of themselves know what they want in life; they also know their boundaries. That enables them to come up with a plan for their living and their lives, and they are unlikely to feel the need to turn to higher authorities to do that for them. They certainly would not consider giving their lives to people who then use them for their own purposes, just as their self-absorbed, abusive parent used to do. They are able to manage themselves and let their lives be an expression of their own opinion and preferences. They do not need to be rewarded for good behavior by a person who is higher in rank for they intrinsically and sincerely know their own value.

People who lack a SoS, however, do not have a clue what to do with themselves because deep down inside, all they are working for is to satisfy their need for a SSoS. And if there were any deeper cause that governs their lives, it would be to search and find themselves, more than anything else in the world. But most often, people are only concerned with living up to their Ego-References and experiencing the "Feel-good-about-Self" (FgaS) state through actions they have developed over their lifetime and that are based on their Early Childhood Survival Strategy (ECSS). When these people are placed outside of their comfort zone into a totally unfamiliar situation, where there is no social control and no familiar milestones, they lose what meaning they thought they had in life. They become depressed, because the situation doesn't allow them to work on their SsoS, which generates anxiety and anger. Rage and violence seep into their behavior and become hard to manage. It can be expected that these people are prone to losing all sense of reality. When something triggers it, they might snap!

Now I understand that when such an angry person fights in the war, away from social convention, and when he or she is not in touch with him- or herself, it seems likely that the buried anger can turn into heartless revenge. Because these people already experienced not being seen and not being accepted for who they really are (themselves), there is no room for empathy in their hearts as their anger finds a way to be released, and atrocities may be performed on harmless people. I refer here to the Zimbardo prison experiment mentioned previously (see page 111).

What war does is awaken in every fighter his or her suppressed anger, turning it into violence. Nobody in his or her right mind would ever consider killing another person. Only people without a healthy SoS, those who "are not home" in their own being and have no sense of the value of a life, not even, and especially, not their own, can be recruited for this job. And in the process they involuntarily express their own (suppressed) anger.

The military, as it functions right now, does want people with a lack of SoS. If a soldier does have a SoS, the military makes sure to beat it out of them (e.g., see the movie *Full Metal Jacket*[18]). With a healthy SoS, you are in your right mind and are not inclined to function as an orders-obeying robot. People in their right minds would not give their lives away because others tell them to do so.

Now let us go back to the SoS Theory and Method to see how it relates to what can happen in times of war, and study how having a healthy SoS could make a difference.

Similarities in the Dynamics between Individuals and between Groups

I see similarities between the micro and macro levels of the patterns in us, human beings, ways of living. Understanding deeply what happens between parents and children can give us insight on what happens on the global stage. The dynamics that occur between family members are the same that take place between members of gangs, groups, and nations in conflict.

Why is it is that children do as their parents do and not as their parents "say?"

Children of parents who are dependent on a SsoS, have developed a great need to be acknowledged and cannot do anything other than attempt to fill in that need, just as their parents did. It is not a choice; it is a need or much rather even a drive and life or death is perceived to be at stake (Fear of Annihilation). Parents may have the best of intentions and try to overcome their own flaws, but their SSoS-oriented nature relentlessly chooses for them, giving priority to getting away from those perceived life/death threats so that, in spite of people's best intentions, little progress is made from one generation to the next.

When parents use their children as pawns in their own emotional games that they call their lives, children end up feeling unacknowledged as a potentially independent and autonomous human being. These children will

---

[18] Information on *Full Metal Jacket* is available at the Internet Movie Data Base, http://www.imdb.com/title/tt0093058/ (accessed April 29, 2013).

become dependent on a SSoS with all the drama, upheaval, and negative impacts on their lives that the SoS Method describes and will help overcome. Once the behaviors associated with a SSoS are learned, they don't suddenly change when one is outside the confines of the family; in fact, people tend to look for situations that mimic these childhood experiences. An authoritarian institution is a great substitute for an unreasonable and abusive parent.

When leaders do not acknowledge their subordinates as independent and real people but as pawns in their games, an escalating power play can be set in motion. If, for example, a country does not want to lose face, things have to be "just so," and if these actions are being thwarted, the country can impose a similar control mechanism to try to force things in its favor, which can generate a process that is humiliating for the other party. This process isn't so much geared toward solving the issue as it is toward saving one's face.

The moment our parents acknowledge us as equal to themselves, the moment that they really "see" us, we lose the acute need to work our way up to "being seen and heard." Instead, we can pay attention to learning how to become the Master, the Manager, and the Maintenance person of our own life and body.

This all ties into how a group functions internally as well as how groups interact with each other. When there is a need or much rather even, a drive, and life or death is perceived to be at stake (Fear of Annihilation), the nature of the interaction is most likely to be more violent in its character than when every group respects itself and feels respected and acknowledged by the others.

It can happen that the ways family members deal with each other, or entire families relate to each other, are based solely on the SSoS-oriented needs of its members. Imagine a well-known scenario, in which a mother rules the family shown from behind the scenes—she dominates her husband and uses guilt trips with her children. Everyone in the family wants to "Feel-good-about-him- or herself," the elephant in the room that nobody is aware of, and that influences the subconsciously chosen behaviors of each family member. Add to this the absolute need to get the desired outcome from those behaviors for all parties, due to the dependency on the outcome for their SSoSes, and we have the perfect setup for drama. Prolonged and intense arguing, rage, violence, desperation, and codependency are the immediate results.

When an organization is run by one or more people with a Healthy SoS, there is real Self-based reasoning for the group's actions. People know their talents and their boundaries, and communication can and must be the tool used to help solve issues. However, when the reasoning is SsoS-oriented, and there is a perceived dependency on having things "just so," flexibility is gone and the road to power struggles lies wide open.

This scenario is possible even in groups that have the intention of serving a "good cause." There can be so much struggle among the volunteers to get the job that potentially gives the most credit that the cause gets lost and out of sight. The powerful PTA parent or the driven organizer of school sports events may do well by doing a Motivation Check every so often. This person may realize that much of what he or she is doing serves his or her own SSoS-oriented goal.

It isn't too big of a step to compare what happens on the micro level to what happens on the macro level of politics and governmental mediation and intervention. When people live together, differences in points of view will exist, but when emotions are dependent on the outcome, differences in opinion are pulled to a more intense level with the risk of escalation.

U.S. military interventions in countries such as Vietnam, Afghanistan, or Iraq, for example, are comparable to the job of the missionaries who went to expand the one and only religion *they* thought was the truth. How soothing it is (for your FgaS as part of the SSoS, even as a nation) to perceive that your opinion is the right one and that the others are all wrong. "The poor people, we have to save them from themselves because they do not even know they are wrong."

Even though the motives for these type of enterprises may be more complex there is a certain audacity in thinking that older cultures, such as those found in Asian countries, would be better off to organize themselves based on Western principles. Why not focus on our own story, solve our own issues, clean up our own unfinished business with our own family members and relatives, and work on becoming a whole person, one who is capable of effectively communicating with others and team up to make our world a better place?

I would not go so far as to say that *all* war can be avoided or be eliminated. The occurrence of war could be reduced, however, because people with a Healthy SoS are not belligerent or inclined to go to war any longer, and are better able and willing to solve conflicts that arise, in a peaceful way. This alone is reason enough to start educating people on how to strengthen or regain a Healthy SoS.

Self-knowledge as a Tool Against War

I offer this plea for the pursuit of self-knowledge as a tool against war and as a general global guideline for humanity, not as a tool that will immediately solve particular current situations in the world. However, I offer it with the conviction that, if each one of us would work on ourselves, we would eliminate a lot of fear and anger in ourselves, which would reduce many factors that contribute to war. This book is not the place for further elaboration on this subject but would have been incomplete were it not mentioned.

A Healthy SoS as a Condition That Reduces War

I strongly believe that a healthy SoS leads people to experience less rage and violence. People, who have a strong Sense of who and what they are, have a reduced need to fight or to engage in quarrels. If we all would work on our SoS and help our children get a healthy SoS, the futility of war would become more obvious. The need and the passion for war would die out because people would become self-reliant and content.

WITH A HEALTHY SoS, we can no longer justify war or, therefore, going to war! Here is the reasoning for that: If I consider it my highest goal to be myself, then I will want the same for others. Consequently, I will never try to enslave others or have them live according to my rules. I also would never take from them what they legitimately own, nor will I feel the need to copy them. There would be no reason to find fault in other people or to put them down to justify our own desperate need for acknowledgment. We would simply live and let others live as well.

THE DIFFERENCE A HEALTHY SOS MAKES

By actively taking care of instilling a SoS in children and by acknowledging them as independent people with a free will, we do more than help them live the lives that they are entitled to. We also prevent anger from building up in them, anger that can seep out at unexpected moments. Let it be clear to your children that they are not an extension of yourself but that they are their very own persons.

What I hope to achieve with the SoS Method includes awakening in everybody the firm decision to stop killing each other and to take personal responsibility for our living together on this planet based on independent thinking. This is only possible when you have a strong Natural or healthy Restored SoS so that you respect your own and (with that) other people's lives and opt to use your life in a positive, compassionate manner in service to yourself and of others.

THE SOLUTION LIES in personal growth! For your identity, you need to actively make yourself independent from belonging to a group. You need to gain enough self-knowledge to recognize when you are dependent on the outcome of achievements or on what other people think and say of you. You need to learn how to successfully eliminate that dependency by restoring your SoS. If we all do that we will be able to coexist in peace as independent, yet interdependent, human beings. Many disagreements would then disappear, and the ones that do not would be solved in a different way.

Only with a healthy SoS can you be free from being dependent on others. Only when you are independent and self-sufficient, living as a whole person, can you be in an interdependent relationship with others and form a healthy community. Healthy communities are what the world needs because people in healthy communities are prone to live in peace and to truly contribute to a better world.

The opportunity to be your own person makes you feel at home in your own skin. You would not want to risk your body, your life, for anything in the world because you know it is your only way into the world. You would have full respect for the gift of life and the opportunity of living, and you would not dream of throwing that away because a government deems it necessary for its citizens to fight in a faraway country.

SUMMARY

As you can see, there are seeds in the SoS Method that can potentially help reduce war and change the nature of conflict resolution. We are referring here to an ideal situation, and we know too that the world doesn't seem to lend itself to the implementation of such a theory. However, every decision about how to react to a specific challenge or conflict that an individual makes counts. These decisions add up affecting not only one's personal living environment but also the world at large.

To change the foundation of society, we need to start with child rearing and parenting. We need to inspire our young parents to work out their own unfinished business with their caregivers so they can be fully present for their offspring and treat them with the respect they wanted for themselves. By doing so, we could create a ripple effect among the world's population of a growing effort for every individual to gain a Healthy and/or Restored Sense of Self™. This way, we can make a huge impact on the world and turn potential warzones into collaborating communities, because people who know their SoS do not depend on a military intervention to whatever conflict is playing out. We *are* already, and thus, we are meant to live—all of us!

Glossary

Annihilation

A strong perception of being overlooked, not being seen and heard, not being taken into account, not having any impact in one's environment, which is experienced as non-existing.

Black Hole

A felt sense of emptiness of not finding within you a permanent presence "you, already existing and being-as-you," that causes anxiety, and an urge to fill itself with feeling good about yourself.

Direct Motivation

Motivation that is ordinary, simple, and based in the present, with no agenda of filling a subconscious need based in the past.

Direct Relationship with Self

A healthy sense of "being your own purpose," which includes experiencing your Self in a healthy, basic way rather than from filtering your evaluations of your achievements through other people's criteria.

Distorted Mirror

The process by which the primary caregiver is unable to effectively acknowledge their child or children as he or she is too wrapped up in his/her own problems and emotional neediness, and the child inevitably and naturally concludes that it *IS* the way it sees itself reflected by the caregiver.

Early Childhood Survival Strategy (ECSS)

Conclusions, drawn subconsciously by infants/toddlers about how to get their needs met when they do not feel acknowledged as separate (unique) beings by their caregivers. This process becomes the foundation for an unhealthy way of experiencing the self.

Ego-References (ER)

Subconsciously accepted requirements to feel and behave in certain ways, and achieve certain results, in order to feel approved, as a substitute for feeling like a "real person."

Enmeshment

An unhealthy relationship between child and primary caregiver. The child's identity and motives are merged with the adult's, which leads to extreme dependence on approval.

Fear of Annihilation

Terror in anticipation of the experience of being unheard by, and invisible to, others.

"Feeling-good-about-Self" (FgaS)

The temporary state of "I am okay now," which results from getting approval and which the person perceives to be necessary in order to have the right to exist.

Focus Mode

Relaxed movements of the eyes, with the ability to stay fixed in the same place for extended periods of time, and which indicates a grounded mood or person who does not have a Substitute Sense of Self.

Hidden Agenda

A subconscious purpose that drives single instances of behavior or action, which is not the obvious, ordinary, expected purpose. This purpose is, instead, geared toward fulfilling the conditions that a person perceives as necessary to fulfill in order to feel safe and on her way to the ultimate objective as described under "Hidden Goal."

Hidden Goal

A person's subconscious, ultimate objective of getting the approval of his or her caregiver, approval which functions as an unhealthy substitute for feeling valued and related to (acknowledged) as a "real" person.

Hindrance

Any obstacle that can lead to anger or rage, which can be a gateway to violence or its counterpart, depression.

Indirect Motivation

The motive for doing something is not what it appears to be; instead, the real motive is to get the temporary emotional state that substitutes for a lasting sense of being a "real" person.

Indirect Relationship with Self

In an Indirect Relationship with Self a person experiences that he or she is existing through achievements and/or the responses of others. It gives the person a positive, but temporary sense of "being," instead of a healthy lasting sense of existing as the person he or she is.

Inner Conflict

Two or more competing incompatible inner "mandates" for behavior aimed at achieving approval, by someone using approval to feel alive.

Lack of (Natural) Sense of Self

The person never developed a natural, ongoing, inner knowing that he or she is a "real," independent human being.

Magic Formula

A way of remembering the gist of the SoS Method, whereby you move away from the addiction to "Feeling-good-about-yourself" by crossing out the judgmental word *about* and placing *good* in parenthesis, leaving "Feel Self" or "Sense Your Self."

Mirroring

The subtle, mutually subconscious process by which the primary caregiver conveys to his or her child a sense of either being a means to fulfill the caregiver's emotional needs or being a "real" and unique person—a sense that the infant accepts as the truth of who he or she is.

Motivation

In general, what creates an incentive or urge to do or avoid something. Motivation is the drive that determines behavior.

Motivation Check

A crucial tool in getting clear about the crooked nature of our (Indirect) Motivation, which serves to (a) detect Indirect Motivations and Hidden Agendas in your Self and (b) to record and become familiar with what your Ego-References, Hidden Agendas, and Hidden Goal are.

Natural Sense of Self (NatSoS)

The subconscious sense—developed normally in childhood—of being a "real," definite person, who has an unconditional right to exist as he or she is, regardless of what others think, feel, or say about you.

Quality-of-Life level (QoL level)

A level of experiencing life events that are responded to in proportion to the actual effect they have on one's life, as distinguished from the level on which one's sense of existing is perceived to be at stake.

Real Self/Authentic Self

The always-existing, purest core of a person's physical and non-physical identity as Being You.

Restored Sense of Self™ (RestSoS)

The result of a healing process that develops a steady awareness of being an entity not dependent on the outcome of fulfilling conditions, and which fills a previous inner emptiness.

Scanning Mode

A person's eyes moving around restlessly searching for opportunities to "score" (see below), which would fill the need for approval and feeling good about themselves. Scanning Mode use of the eyes indicates activity aimed at achieving an unhealthy way to experience one's Self.

Scoring

Being successful in using a Vehicle to improve on an Ego-Reference; a success that feels like gaining "points" toward the goal of getting parental approval, which results in a "Feel-good-about-Self" as a Substitute Sense of Self.

Sense of Self (SoS)

A conscious or subconscious awareness of existing independently as a unique and potentially autonomous human being and of what intrinsically comes with it in your daily living.

Substitute Sense of Self (SSoS)

The lack of a sense of autonomous existence experienced by children whose caregivers relate to them as an extension of themselves, and that creates a compulsive drive for approval.

Substitute Sense of Self–oriented Goal (SSoS-or. Goal)

A person's subconscious, ultimate goal of convincing the parent to change his or her negative opinion about "me" into a positive one, which then gives "me" a feeling of being a "real," normal person.

Substitute Sense of Self–oriented System (SSoS-orSys)

The entire subconscious complex of needs, behaviors, motives, habits, beliefs, goals, and fears that generates achievement-based approval, as a base for a sense of being.

Vehicle

An activity or behavior used to display the performance of specific skills or character traits rather than being used for the obvious, ordinary goal of the action or behavior. The performance is ultimately aimed at getting approval.

Virtual, Internalized Parental Voice (VIPV)

The often-repeated verbal and non-verbal messages through which parents talk to their children becomes (almost) hardwired in the child's mind so that it is perceived as an unquestionable truth (about and) by the child.

Epilogue

Reflections on the degree of difficulty of healing from an addiction to a SSoS . . . and why it is worthwhile anyway!

EVERY DAY, MORE OF "ME" THAN JUST MY *MIND* GETS TO KNOW THAT I REALLY can completely let go of my need for a Substitute Sense of Self—that this need is a fiction I have used as a crutch for over 60 years as I didn't have anything *else* to hold onto—because I had a lack of Sense of Self. I held this belief for such a long time, it was tough to let it go. Persistence and the appropriate tools (like the exercises offered in this Method, guided imagery) assisted me greatly to continue on the chosen road.

I hope these final thoughts inspire you to never give up working on overcoming what went wrong in your (early) childhood and adolescence. I say "went wrong," but who am I to wonder if things really went wrong; maybe it is just a part of our journey to figure these things out. Whether there is, or ever will be, a "happily living after" is questionable. My hunch is, that by the time we know the end of the story, the book of life is finished. It is a bit cruel in a way but, here again, who am I to say that? I do not know the Alpha of life; how can I expect to know the Omega?

For me, it all started when, as a very young child, I felt I had to convince my mother that I was worth being taken into account, being considered a "real" person with a real presence of my own, instead of a pawn in her life and doings. In order to get my needs met, I engaged in fulfilling "conditions" to get her approval, which developed into an Early Childhood Survival Strategy, on which I then became dependent.

When I started on the process of healing myself from this dependency, I did not imagine that it was all about freeing myself from an addiction to parental approval (in real life or internalized). The thing that has surprised me most is the lack of immediate co-operation of my own body. I would encounter such tenacious resistance from my own body. Nothing fell in place, just like that. One by one, the building blocks of my survival strategy needed to be removed from the wall that separated my real self from living my (real) own life.

During the years of implementing my Restored Sense of Self™, the pull of the Black Hole has been astonishingly strong and has taken me by surprise at moments in which I was caught off-guard while (finally) just having fun. Anything "good" on a Quality-of-Life level that happened to me was drawn into that void and was used and co-opted by it in the attempt to fill itself up with a Substitute Sense of Self. And this always immediately triggered great anxiety and insomnia. And finally, when I was able to stay on track during the day, a relatively good night sleep would erase the gained re-conditioning of my restored Sense of Self that I had worked so hard for, and physical symptoms (eye-migraine) or plain anxiety would kick in upon awakening. I had to be utterly cunning to stay at the steering wheel of my own life and body during those moments, but I managed! And it still gets better every day.

Hannibal took his elephants over the mountains in the year 218 BC; in all modesty, I do not believe that my efforts to heal myself were anywhere less in caliber. (Note: I don't compare myself to this great Carthaginian military commander but merely use this comparison to indicate how much effort it took me to get this reconditioning done.)

Here is a relevant quote from Kevin Toohey,[19] which is based on one of C.G. Jung's insights in *The Autonomy of the Psyche*:

"Psychologically, sometimes a destructive complex or affect is so destructive that it requires a heroic effort to turn away or escape. The magic carpet is the means by which this is affected. The carpet is a product of spinning. We can say it represents the story of individuation. At any one point in life, we often cannot see how the experience or threads of our lives form a tapestry that tells the story of Self. The escape from the destructive tendencies in the unconscious is made by comprehending thread by thread, the meaning of one's life experiences, and one's fate."

[19] As described in an article from Kevin Toohey's "The Frog Princess" as it appears in the book *Jung Talks, 50 Years of the C.G. Jung Society of Melbourne*, edited by Annette Lowe. Kevin Toohey is a Melbourne, Australia, Jungian analyst and a past-president of the Melbourne Jung Society.

My hope in presenting my work to the world is that people of all walks of life might be impacted and become aware that many of us need to examine our own presence in the world, so that we can be of most benefit to our children. We need to (learn to) live in such a way that we have gotten what we need from life, *before* our offspring demand our attention, so we do not need to prove ourselves through them.

We have to become fully aware of the responsibility we take on when we decide to raise a next generation. Parenthood used to be a thing we "did" because we could and everyone did it; I wonder if humanity can sustain that approach. It might be better if we all took steps to own such a great responsibility—each of us for ourselves—and work our way toward a healthy (Restored) Sense of Self for ourselves.

A healthy Sense of Self is what it takes to be yourself. Being yourself then makes a healthy Natural Sense of Self within reach for our children. Once we have these two generations set up with a healthy Sense of Self, the world will be a better place. It won't be easy, as I previously described, but little by little . . . goes a long way!

Acknowledgments

To Rev. Alia Aurami, Ph.D., my collaborator

A deep and heartfelt "thank you" to you, Alia, for helping me through times of doubt and hardship by listening to what I had to say and believing in it. Your elevated and non-judgmental approach was as water to the seed of my thoughts and thinking—and you know that a seed can be a seed for a long time but eventually it needs water to grow and flourish.

Thank you for your stress-free approach, your "living and working while going with the flow"—which was the only approach that would work for me, and one that is such a rare quality in people these days. Only this viewpoint on things opens doors to synchronicity and "what is meant to be" confidence, which is the route to go with a work of this caliber.

Thank you for giving the work priority when needed and letting it sit when it had to mature. Your deep understanding of the issues at hand, and of the human psyche and soul, has been an angelic contribution, without which this work would not exist in the shape and form it now has. The clarity in such a complex subject did not come from an "English-as-a-second-language" person like myself, but from your erudition and your steady dedication. Your having the benefit of the greater good in mind when giving your time to this Method is a great gift to humanity, and I am sure many people will owe you for that.

I feel honored to have had the opportunity of getting to know you better. I really enjoyed the process of building this work with you as a team whenever the process allowed that. I have learned through working closely together with you, Alia, that people have a right to stay their own persons even when that means not agreeing. I also have learned that "not agreeing" doesn't mean the end of a friendship, but rather a beginning.

I want to state that the words above are to be multiplied an infinite number of times as an almost cosmic quantity of thanks to you, Alia. It is hard to express what I owe you for organizing the material of the website and first draft of the Method into the first edition of this work of reference of the Sense of Self Method. You have given it not only your time and utmost focus and dedication, but you offered everything a person can possibly bring to a project for the sake of a better world!

It was a great process with a great outcome!

To Lily Burns, Executive Assistant

A deeply felt "thank you" to you, Lily, for the way you have performed what I asked you to do. Not only were you punctual and neat with what came out of your hands—or should I say out of your computer?—but you were dedicated and available. You always were prompt in doing what needed to be done and your dedication clearly showed each time you offered your suggestions, for example, for the procedures of editing a file, that made my life so much easier.

Your heartwarming presence as a person, as well as your family members who have been so supportive and productive, is a true asset to HealthySenseofSelf and to my personal life. I am truly in awe of the way you deal with personal challenges, and never let them interfere with the work you are asked to do.

I consider myself lucky to have run into you at the appropriate time, because without you (and your family) this project would have a lot fewer visual aids and promotional material than it proudly has at this moment. Thanks for offering your good and creative energy!

To my daughter, Laura Vogels

To you Laura, a loving "thank you" for your artful drawings and their high-quality execution. Thanks to the fact that I was your first boss, I have been able to benefit from your drawing and designing skills.

As my daughter, you were living the preceding and resulting effects of the SoS Method. I feel lucky to have discovered and encouraged your fine drawing hand and delicate interpretation of the concepts discussed in this work. I am extremely grateful that you decided to make room in your busy life as an actor to work out the illustrations and the book cover. No one but you could have done that with such graceful simplicity. I always had great fun communicating with you about making our projects come to life, knowing you would pick it up so effortlessly. I still think you should do a course in faux-finish, but I am well aware that you have so many talents that choices need to be made.

Having been your "boss" on this project, I know you will have great success with whatever is going to be your way of making money.

To my daughter, Kim Vogels

Kim, I am so very grateful for your ongoing support of the ideas of my work. You have effectively and beautifully created the videos on the layers: (http://healthysenseofself.com/store/members/members-area/holispsych-archive/Method/sense-of-self/defining-self-related-concepts/visual-aid-video-lego/).

It was good to share with you the explanation of the layers of Self, where you helped me to get the right wording so that young people would also be interested and able to read it. A fresh approach to a difficult subject is what you brought to the visual aids as well as in your suggested strategy for working with social media. I am truly happy that you have survived so well, being (one of the) guinea pig(s) of the SoS Method. By participating you helped my project unite our family in a combined support of it. Your positive feedback on what the SoS Method means to you as a successful actor has made me very happy.

To my in-house editor and C.O.O. Deborah Drake

Deborah, I highly value you for your ongoing general support, your availability as an editor and writing coach, and for the brain-storming sessions you facilitated to "find my voice" as an author. You encourage me to render my thoughts in an authentic, maybe at times somewhat unconventional way, all the while prioritizing understandability. You have been instrumental in drawing out and preserving the much-valued authenticity in my writing-voice. You have come to understand what the SoS Method could do for people and you love evangelizing it. You always come in with fresh comments on what others have to say about subjects that are related to the SoS Method, which has helped us find our rank and place in this complex (writers and bloggers) Universe. I may hope for a long-lasting and fruitful collaboration for the sake of spreading the word and for the sake of our friendship.

To my husband, Werner Vogels

A heartfelt thank you to you, Werner! Through thick and thin you have believed in me, and it has taken about 25 years, if not a little bit more, to see the fruits of that investment. I sincerely hope that the various "returns on investment" will lighten somewhat the burden of your providing for a family with a cross-continental lifestyle.

The digital age has, like all other things under the sun, an upside and a lesser side to it. However, I am very grateful for your expertise in "all things digital" as it has been a secure base with which to start this project and as a continuous force of support it has been of crucial importance to make it a success.

In addition I wish to acknowledge the contribution, in the final phase, to the various editors and staff of Bookmasters: Sharon Anderson, Tim Snider, Wendy Jo Dymond, and Nancy Ahr. If the book is getting the message across, it is greatly thanks to your hard work on it!

~ Antoinetta Vogels

Index

Testimonials for Antoinetta Vogels and HealthySenseOfSelf

"Working with Antoinetta Vogels has provided me powerful insight into my own physical and psychological ailments. Through frequent discussions with her, I am learning to find and restore my Sense of Self. Antoinetta is extremely passionate about her work in helping others, and she frequently takes time out to check in with how I am doing, truly doing, on all levels, and will give helpful advice when appropriate. I'm grateful that our paths have met in this journey to find one's true Self."

—*L.B., Executive Assistant to Antoinetta Vogels, HealthySenseOfSelf*

"There is hardly anything more basic about us than whether our sense of being a 'self' is dependent on others' approval, or is healthy and solid within us. Through the courage of investigating her own Sense of Self so deeply, and developing ways to make it more healthy, Antoinetta Vogels' highly original work has the potential to profoundly improve not just individual lives, but our whole human ways of relating."

—*Rev. Alia Zara Aurami, Ph.D., Minister*

"I am somewhat of a skeptical person but my wife pointed out to me that Antoinetta Vogels' Sense of Self Approach really creates unexpected openings in solving quite a number of child-rearing questions. By becoming aware of our own Hidden Agenda we are able to make different decisions that greatly benefit our children's and our family's well-being. More recently, the Sense of Self Approach to aging has helped me personally cope with the unexpectedly rapid terminal diagnosis of an elderly relative who is very important to me. Rather than labor under the distraction of the false expectation of what 'a good son should do,' I've been able to help where help was needed without ignoring my very real sadness."

—*D.I., Entrepreneur*

"Being exposed to Antoinetta Vogels' Sense of Self Method helped me understand better a few of my clients as a business coach and also some friends who I suspect suffer from depression. I also gained another, much more understanding way to look at people who make bad choices. I suspect that when I have to deal with difficult personal issues in the future, which are unfortunately inevitable for anyone, the awareness of my Sense of Self will be very helpful."

—*P.H., COO, Pro/Vision Coaching, Inc.*

"Antoinetta Vogels creates a safe place for exploration of the Self based on her Method on the Healthy Sense of Self. Her empathic approach to helping a person solve his or her issues was soothing to me. It was revealing to me to learn that your Sense of Self is something that is either present or absent. When absent, its substitute is an imposter and trusting it leads to trouble. Her work resonated with my journey of healing from past hurts and habits nudging me to go deeper. After attending only one lecture, I have identified a new hang-up and I feel I can truly overcome my hurts and experience peace in my nature. I am so excited about her upcoming book. It will restore the peace that many are searching for in their lives."

—*Aliceann Christy, R.N., Seattle, WA*